KNOWLEDGE BY AGREEM

KNOWLEDGE
BY
AGREEMENT

The Programme of Communitarian Epistemology

Martin Kusch

CLARENDON PRESS · OXFORD

OXFORD
UNIVERSITY PRESS

Great Clarendon Street, Oxford OX2 6DP

Oxford University Press is a department of the University of Oxford.
It furthers the University's objective of excellence in research, scholarship,
and education by publishing worldwide in

Oxford New York

Auckland Bangkok Buenos Aires Cape Town Chennai
Dar es Salaam Delhi Hong Kong Istanbul Karachi Kolkata
Kuala Lumpur Madrid Melbourne Mexico City Mumbai Nairobi
São Paulo Shanghai Taipei Tokyo Toronto

Oxford is a registered trade mark of Oxford University Press
in the UK and in certain other countries

Published in the United States
By Oxford University Press Inc., New York

© Martin Kusch 2002

The moral rights of the author have been asserted

Database right Oxford University Press (maker)

First published 2002
First published in paperback 2004

British Library Cataloguing in Publication Data

Data available

Library of Congress Cataloging in Publication Data

Kusch, Martin.
   Knowledge by agreement : the programme of communitarian epistemology / Martin Kusch.
      p. cm.
   Includes bibliographical references and index.
   1. Knowledge, Sociology of. I. Title.
   BD175 .K875 2002   121—dc21   2001054551
ISBN 0–19–925122–3
ISBN 0–19–925137–1 (pbk.)

10 9 8 7 6 5 4 3 2 1

Typeset in Spectrum MT
by Kolam Information Services Pvt. Ltd, Pondicherry, India
Printed in Great Britain by Biddles Ltd, King's Lynn, Norfolk

For Sarah

Preface

Contemporary philosophers can be classified in terms of the other—non-philosophical—fields of inquiry that most impact on their respective philosophical work. For present-day epistemologists and philosophers of science the most influential fields are cognitive science, evolutionary biology, neuroscience, and physics. I belong to the small minority that believes that some of the most important challenges to philosophy today come from the sociology of knowledge. In this programmatic essay I sketch how epistemology must change if it wishes to do justice to what is valuable and lasting in the sociologists' insistence that knowledge is a social institution. This essay is not, however, an introduction to the sociology of knowledge. I seek to bring out the fundamentally social nature of knowledge through a discussion of philosophical theories. My aim is to arrive at, or recapture, some of the sociologists' insights by discussing philosophical texts and arguments.

I am grateful to the University of Cambridge for a sabbatical term in the autumn of 1999, and to the British Academy for a Matching Term Award in the spring of 2000. Most of the book was written during this period of eight months. I spent the autumn of 1999 at my old alma mater, the University of Edinburgh. Special thanks are due, as always, to Carole Tansley for her friendship and for her help with a thousand practicalities. Celia and David Bloor entrusted their exquisitely furnished New Town flat into my clumsy hands. (No wonder that David's influence can be felt throughout the pages that follow: most of these pages were written in his study.) For this many thanks.

As far as commentators are concerned, I am most grateful to David Bloor (again), David Chart, Harry Collins, Michael Esfeld, Sarah Gore Cortes, Jeremy Gray, Matthew Ratcliffe, Simon Schaffer, and two anonymous referees for Oxford University Press. All of them read the whole manuscript and made numerous critical and constructive comments. Anjan

Chakravartty, Anandi Hattiangadi, Jonas Larsson, Peter Lipton, Donald MacKenzie, and Paul Teller read versions of various chapters and prevented me from many mistakes. Anjan's and Anandi's very detailed comments on Parts I and II, respectively, were especially valuable.

Central chapters of the book were presented to audiences of philosophers, sociologists, and psychologists in Bath, Cambridge, Cork, Edinburgh, San Sebastian, Sheffield, and Toronto. Particularly memorable was a presentation of 'truth finitism' to the Moral Sciences Club in Cambridge in 1998: questions by Michael Esfeld, Jane Heal, Susan James, Tim Lewens, and Hugh Mellor forced me to rethink a number of issues.

I also owe a very substantial debt to two reading–discussion groups in the Department of History and Philosophy of Science in Cambridge. The Epistemology Reading Group discussed relativism and feminist epistemology for two terms in 1998, and I learned much from these meetings. The Sociology of Knowledge/Social Epistemology Group met regularly during the academic year 1998/9. Although I benefited from the input of all participants and speakers, as far as this book is concerned I feel especially indebted to a talk by Miranda Fricker and to various comments by Katherine Hawley.

It was my good fortune that I was able to present central themes of this essay in two undergraduate lecture courses (in the autumn of 1998 and the spring of 2001). Students' comments and questions more than once helped me to see where my arguments needed improving.

Many of the ideas expounded in this book were first tested in informal conversations with friends, students, and colleagues. I must begin by thanking three colleagues: Nick Jardine, Peter Lipton, and Simon Schaffer. Nick prevented me from adopting the group mind hypothesis; Peter set the standard for clarity and rigour; and Simon told me where my work belonged. I could not have written this book without them. Encouragement and/or critical questions also came from Louis Campos, Hsing-Zen Chen, David Gooding, Mia Gray, Matthias Hild, John Holmwood, Susan James, Dominick Jenkins, Bernard Katz, Ki-Heung Kim, Matthias Klaes, Marja-Liisa Kakkuri-Knuuttila, Jeff Kochan, Erna Kusch (who, yet again, kept me up to date on the German intellectual scene), Sanjoy Mahajan, Massimo Mazzotti, Yuvel Millo, Ilkka Niiniluoto, Maureen O'Malley, Pauline Padfield, Catherine Pickstock, Irene Rafanell, Mike Rich, Ulinka

Rublack, Steve Shapin, Norman Sieroka, Patricia Soley Beltran, Mark Sprevak, and Steve Sturdy.

Last, but not least, I am grateful to Peter Momtchiloff for accepting this book for publication, Charlotte Jenkins for seeing the book through to publication, and Laurien Berkeley for her help with the copy-editing process.

I dedicate this book to Sarah Gore Cortes for her support—intellectual, emotional, culinary, and much else besides. I started thinking about this book shortly before we had our first coffee together. Serious writing began the same week we bought communal tablecloths and clothes racks. And one week after a first draft was completed, friends and family showered us with rice—at last a philosophy book with a happy ending.

M.K.

Contents

PART I *TESTIMONY*

PART II *EMPIRICAL BELIEF*

PART III *OBJECTIVITY*

Figures

INTRODUCTION

The subtitle of this book combines two concepts that, until now, have led separate lives in philosophy. 'Epistemology' is the better known of the two. It refers to one of the core disciplines of philosophy. Epistemology studies questions like 'What is knowledge?', 'How is knowledge acquired?', or 'What can we know?' 'Communitarianism' refers to a position in political philosophy.[1] Communitarians insist that the community is, in the order of explanation, prior to the individual. Moral individuals do not precede moral communities; moral individuals can be understood only through their membership in moral communities.

This book proposes 'communitarian epistemology' as a label for a specific position in epistemology. An epistemology qualifies as communitarian if it makes two claims. The first claim is that the term 'knowledge' and its cognates, like 'know' and 'knower', mark a *social status*—like 'head of department'. It follows from this idea that the existence of knowledge is dependent upon the existence of communities. Social statuses exist only in so far as there are communities that constitute, impose, or grant these statuses. The second key claim of communitarian epistemology is that the social status 'knowledge' is typically granted to, or imposed on, *groups* of people. The second claim formulates a second and additional sense in which knowledge is social. Knowledge is not just social in that it is a social status; it is also social in that it is typically attributed to groups rather than to individuals. But note the 'typically' in the second claim. While the first claim is without exception—knowledge is always and everywhere a social status—the second claim speaks only to typical and central cases of knowledge. In other

---

[1] Key communitarian texts are Sandel (1982), MacIntyre (1988), and Taylor (1989).

words, it allows that there are exceptional cases where knowledge is attributed to individuals outside communities.

Communitarian epistemology contrasts with most traditional and contemporary positions in epistemology. Its competitors conceptualize knowledge as analogous to natural kinds, like aluminium, or as similar to artefacts, like works of art or spiders' webs. Since these alternatives to communitarianism fail to recognize knowledge as a social status, they happily think of knowledge as the primary possession of individuals rather than groups. For such individualistic forms of epistemology knowledge is social only in so far as it is transmitted from one individual to another.

Communitarian epistemology differs from social epistemology. 'Social epistemology' has come to refer to two rather different programmes. I shall call them the 'science policy programme' and the 'complementary programme'. The science policy programme seeks to determine ways of making science more democratic and accountable to the public. It also hopes to increase our ability to choose between the development of different kinds of knowledge. This hope is based on the assumption that one can influence the collective production of scientific knowledge by manipulating the social organization of scientific communities. Changing social organization leads to a different type of knowledge.[2] Communitarian epistemology is not a form of science policy. Its goal is to understand, rather than change, epistemic communities. Nevertheless, communitarian epistemology agrees with the science policy programme on one important point: epistemology and politics are more closely connected than tradition would have it. To understand knowledge is to understand epistemic communities; and to understand epistemic communities is to understand their social and political structures.

The complementary programme in social epistemology tries to remedy the shortcomings of traditional individualistic epistemology.[3] Advocates of the complementary programme distinguish between individual and social aspects of knowledge. They believe that traditional individualistic epistemology was on the right track as far as the individual knower is concerned. But they criticize the tradition for its alleged blindness regarding social

---

[2] See Fuller (1988) for a defence of this view of social epistemology.

[3] The chief advocate is Goldman (1999).

aspects of knowledge—regarding how much we learn from others, for example. Social epistemology is the required additional field needed to remedy this blindness. Communitarian epistemology is more radical than the complementary programme. It not only maintains that the tradition is negligent of social aspects of knowledge; it also insists that the tradition is also wrong regarding the category of the individual isolated knower itself. Put in a nutshell, for the communitarian usually there is no such knower.

One can introduce a position either monologically or dialogically. In the first case the author develops her stance without much regard for earlier and contemporaneous work. The monological method has the advantage of clarity and simplicity. Readers need not constantly change gear between exposition of the new and criticism of the old. But this obvious advantage of monologue often is more than offset by several disadvantages. Readers may not be convinced that the allegedly novel view really is as new as its author proclaims. And readers may not appreciate the need for a departure from the received alternatives. This essay therefore relies on the dialogical method. I shall develop communitarian epistemology in continuous discussion with other philosophers. I shall undertake to show that communitarian epistemology gives superior answers to their very own questions.

This essay is 'an invitation to', rather than 'a system of', communitarian epistemology. It does not offer communitarian proposals concerning all traditional epistemological problems. Instead it focuses on just two important such issues: the nature of testimony and the rationality of empirical beliefs. I believe that the strengths (and possible weaknesses) of communitarian epistemology come out clearly with respect to these central topics. I intend to address other central epistemological questions (such as the nature of a priori knowledge) elsewhere. At the same time I hope that at least some readers will accept the 'communitarian-epistemological' invitation extended to them here.

Undoubtedly, more than one obstacle stands between the guiding ideas of this essay and their appreciation by most of its readers. Most of these hindrances, I suspect, have to do with certain 'realist' or 'absolutist' intuitions about language, truth, reality, and objectivity. Anyone who gives free rein to these intuitions is bound to find communitarian epistemology intolerably relativistic. These intuitions therefore need to be addressed, despite the fact that many of them have their proper place not in epistemology but in other fields of philosophy. I do so in Part III.

The communitarian epistemology developed here is not free of intellectual debts. The most immediate debt is owed to the four leading sociologists of scientific knowledge: Barry Barnes, David Bloor, Harry Collins, and Steven Shapin. Indeed, the starting point of this book was the attempt to translate some of their central insights into the language of epistemology, and to work through the tensions that result from such translation. However, this book does not aim for a faithful translation. One important respect in which this book is unfaithful to the above-mentioned authors is that is does not focus specifically on *scientific* knowledge. This is based on the belief that, at least as far as their basic 'socialness' is concerned, scientific and ordinary forms of knowledge do not differ from one another. Moreover, my attempt to bring together sociology of knowledge and epistemology does not leave either side unchanged. In other words, I go beyond the sociologists in a number of respects. I also differ from the sociologists in that I do not rest my argument on the presentation and discussion of case-studies (in the history of science).[4] Instead, I rely on a bundle of time-honoured philosophical ways of arguing: I seek to show that individualistic (and otherwise 'anti-communitarian') views are incoherent and fail by their own standards; that they have unwanted consequences; that they contradict our everyday experience; or that they cannot be made out to cohere with other well-entrenched views. I hope I have done better than simply pit intuition against intuition, or claim against counter-claim.

My debt to the sociologists of knowledge is the most immediate, but it is not the only one. Barnes, Bloor, Collins, and Shapin have not developed their ideas in a vacuum, and they have not just drawn on traditions of sociological theorizing. Most of their insights have emerged through a careful and critical reflection on the philosophical writings of Mary Hesse, David Hume, Peter Winch, and Ludwig Wittgenstein. I cannot imagine what contemporary sociology of knowledge would be without this philosophical background. I emphasize it here in order to downplay the distance that exists—in the

---

[4] This should not be misunderstood as a lack of respect for such studies. I have written two book-length case-studies in the sociology of knowledge myself. See Kusch (1995, 1999).

mind of many epistemologists—between the sociology of knowledge and the philosophical study of knowledge.

This distance can also be reduced by pointing to a further important philosophical body of work that—like this book—builds upon both sociology and philosophy: feminist epistemology.[5] Feminist epistemologists have investigated communitarian-epistemological themes for the past fifteen to twenty years, and I have greatly profited from their insights. If I do not discuss feminist epistemology in any detail here, it is only because our respective viewpoints are too close for such discussion to be helpful in clarifying and defending the distinctness of the communitarian position.[6]

I have written this book for both epistemologists and sociologists. In my attempt to be accessible at least to advanced undergraduates in both fields, I have sought to explain even widely used concepts. And yet it must be acknowledged that this is not an altogether easy book to read. Any project that runs counter to widely held intuitions and the mainstream of the discipline is bound to appear difficult and demanding. This study, I fear, is no exception to this rule.

[5] I have particularly profited from studying Alcoff and Potter (1993), Antony and Witt (1993), Code (1991), Hankinson Nelson (1990), Harding (1991), Lennon and Whitford (1994), Longino (1990), and Tanenisi (1999).

[6] Similar considerations have persuaded me not to engage here with writers in the so-called Continental tradition. Critical theory and philosophical hermeneutics have influenced my thinking since my undergraduate days in the 1980s, and I can see their influences everywhere in this book (especially Gadamer 1960 and Habermas 1981). At one stage I even considered using the label 'hermeneutic epistemology' for the position I am defending here. I gave up on this idea when I recalled that for many Anglo-American epistemologists 'hermeneutics' is synonymous with obscurity and sloppy thinking.

Part I

Testimony

Chapter 1

QUESTIONS AND POSITIONS

Any communitarian rewriting of epistemology had better start by considering testimony. This is because old and new forms of epistemology typically use 'testimony' as a covering term for all social aspects of knowledge.

Traditional epistemology thought of testimony as a mechanism for the transmission of knowledge from one individual to another. You know on the basis of testimony that Cambridge is cold in the winter if you hear about the cold winters in Cambridge from an honest reporter. Alas, the tradition paid only scant attention to this type of knowledge. It distinguished testimony from other 'sources of knowledge' only in order to set it aside and to concentrate on other problems. Fortunately, things have started to change. Since the early 1980s interest in testimony has grown rapidly. Perhaps this growth was stimulated by the sociology of knowledge and the feminist critique of philosophy and science. These days testimony is almost a fashionable topic among epistemologists; and it is becoming difficult to keep abreast of all of the new developments. Perhaps it will be useful then to have a short taxonomy of the main questions currently pursued:

Questions concerning linguistic usage and intuitions. How do we talk about the knowledge that we receive from others, and what common-sense 'theory' of testimony can we reconstruct on the basis of our talk?

Questions concerning cognitive and social psychology. What are the psychological mechanisms by means of which we (as individuals) adopt or reject what others tell us? How do these mechanisms compare with, or relate to, mechanisms involved in perception, memory, or inference?

Questions concerning social life. Does the rigour with which testimony is assessed vary with social context? What role does testimony play in social life in general? What social norms or conventions govern the social institution of language in general, and 'telling how things are' in particular?

Questions concerning testimony and trust in the sciences. What is the role of testimony in the natural and social sciences? How critical or gullible are scientists when it comes to assessing the work of their colleagues? How do scientists go about making their testimony acceptable to others? Which social and political influences play a role in the acceptance or rejection of testimony?

Normative questions. How narrowly or how widely should we define testimony? Is our general reliance upon testimony justifiable? And if so, what kind of justification do we want? How much should we trust others in questions of knowledge? How should we assess others' competence and honesty? Do some of the answers given to these questions provide reason to change our philosophical views of knowledge? How central should testimony be in our overall view of knowledge?

Epistemologists' discussions of testimony usually do not separate out these various questions. And often there is good reason for them not to do so. To mention just one example, questions concerning social life might overlap with questions concerning the role of trust and testimony in science. After all, science is itself a form of social life. And thus we can ask, in the context of science, whether the rigour with which testimony is assessed varies with social and scientific context.

My aim is to introduce communitarianism into epistemology. To do this is to explain why individuals can know only in so far as they are members of epistemic communities. This endeavour involves identifying and exorcizing epistemological individualism. As concerns testimony, we find two main expressions of such individualism. The first is the long-standing neglect of testimony. As I have already mentioned, traditional epistemology has little time for testimony. And when the tradition does pause momentarily to talk about testimony, it does so in a disparaging manner—thus in turn justifying the neglect. The second expression of individualism in the epistemology of testimony is the way in which testimony is delimited and defined. First, the scope of phenomena investigated under this title has been disappointingly slender. There is more to the social dimensions of knowledge than the reporting of past, or timeless, facts. There is also the creation of new knowledge in the very act of speaking. Think of utterances like 'I hereby declare you husband and wife'. Second, even within this narrow range of phenomena, epistemologists have missed important communitarian insights. The reporting of past facts is a much more complex social practice than epistemologists have allowed for. It is more than the mere transmission of knowledge from one individual to another. And third, the manner in which testimony is compared to other sources of knowledge often reveals a reluctance, or even an outright refusal, to engage with the facts of our epistemic interdependence on each other. That, in any case, is what I hope to show in what follows. It is sometimes said that the current interest in testimony signals the end of epistemological individualism. It should now be clear why I disagree with this assessment.

I will not be concerned with documenting the neglect of testimony. The target of my criticism will be the second symptom of individualism distinguished in the last paragraph: individualistic theories of testimony. I shall have to cover a fair bit of ground. Lest the fundamental divide be lost in the details of the discussion, it is perhaps best to start with a fairly abstract formulation of the contrast between individualistic and communitarian views of testimony.

The individualistic view of testimony. Testimony exhausts the realm of social aspects of knowledge. Testimony is not a generative source of knowledge: it does not constitute communities and statuses. Testimony is nothing but the transmission of a complete (pre-existing) item of knowledge from one individual to another. The items in question are deliveries of the testifier's perception, reason, or memory. Testifier and recipient need not belong to the same group. Social phenomena, like belonging to the same group, are not relevant parameters for understanding testimony. Testifier and recipient possess only minimal social knowledge. In the case of the testifier social knowledge consists of knowledge of who is able to understand the testimony. In the case of the recipient social knowledge amounts to some capacity for cheater-detection, and some information about the reliability of different types of people. The recipient's (conscious or unconscious) calculation of the testifier's trustworthiness is done according to standards that are assumed to be universal.

The communitarian view of testimony. Testimony is one of several social aspects of knowledge. Testimony is not just a means of transmission of complete items of knowledge from and to an individual. Testimony is almost always generative of knowledge: it constitutes epistemic communities and epistemic agents, social statuses and institutions, taxonomies (including taxonomies of the natural world), and the category of knowledge itself. Testifier and recipient can be singular or plural. In the normal case both are members of the same community, and they share common goals and interests. Their membership in the same group matters to their interaction. Being members of the same group inclines them to have normative expectations concerning each other's honesty, competence, and gullibility. Moreover, to be a competent recipient of testimony amounts to being able to justify publicly one's assessment of the reliability of a given testifier. Finally, standards of evaluation are always local.

I shall discuss testimony in four steps. In Chapter 2 I shall focus on philosophers' attempts to define the *scope* of testimony. I shall suggest that this scope is much too narrow to meet the goal of capturing 'our epistemic interdependence'. In Chapter 3 I shall turn to one of the most controversial issues in the epistemology of testimony. Suppose I tell you that I have blue eyes. What is it like for you to come to believe, on the basis of my telling, that I do indeed have blue eyes? And what should it be like? Some philosophers think that the process by means of which you come to believe that I have blue eyes does, or should, involve assumptions about my honesty and competence. Other epistemologists disagree and maintain instead that testimonial knowledge can be acquired without any such assumptions being in play. I shall reject the central assumptions of both camps and argue that both camps remain tied to the individualistic view of testimony. Chapter 4 is about another central debate in the epistemology of testimony: Can we give a general argument for why it is rational to have trust in the words of others? And what kind of argument is adequate? Reductionists maintain that in order to justify testimony we need to show that its deliveries coincide with those of other sources of knowledge. Fundamentalists propose that testimony can be vindicated in some other, non-reductive, way. I shall refuse to choose between these two positions. Instead, I shall opt for quietism and contextualism. To believe that testimony needs a general vindication is itself an expression of individualism. All we can (and occasionally need to) justify is our reliance on specific informants in particular circumstances. Hence individualists are in error when they conflate an instance of testimony with the very idea of testimony. Finally, Chapter 5 is more directly concerned with motivating and defending a communitarian theory of testimony and knowledge. I shall discuss the work of two other epistemologists (who have anticipated central aspects of my own view) before moving on to laying out my own position in more detail. I shall argue that my two allies move from individualism to communitarianism in a somewhat half-hearted fashion. In developing my own fully communitarian stance, I shall draw on work in the sociology of knowledge.

Chapter 2

THE LIMITS OF TESTIMONY

There is no widespread agreement among epistemologists on how best to delimit the category of testimony. Understood most narrowly, testimony has its place in legal contexts; testimony is given from the witness stand. Taken in its widest sense testimony stands for our 'epistemic interdependence', that is, for the fact that, as knowers, we are dependent upon others in a plethora of ways. In between these two extremes we find a position that equates knowledge by testimony with knowledge gained from others' present- or past-tense indicative say-so.[1]

As if this were not complicated enough, the above three positions can overlap in two distinct ways. The obvious way is that a broader conception of testimony includes the narrower one; for example, testimony as indicative say-so obviously includes legal testimony. The less obvious way runs in the opposite direction: some philosophers assume that a theory of testimony as indicative say-so is tantamount to a theory of our epistemic interdependence.

Unsurprisingly, philosophers whose understanding of testimony varies in these dimensions think differently about how testimony functions, or of how gullible we ought to be in accepting it. Your assessing the trustworthiness of a witness in the courtroom is (it is hoped!) very far from your estimating my honesty and competence when I tell you that I have blue

---

[1] A good although traditional discussion of the limits of testimony is part 1 of Coady (1992). The inflation of the term is lamented in Quinton (1982).

eyes. And whatever our theories about cases such as these, they might well not add up to a general theory of our epistemic interdependence.

Why has the term 'testimony' experienced such inflation? The answer must be sought within the philosophical tradition. Traditional epistemology refers to four so-called sources of knowledge: perception, memory, reason, and testimony. Perception covers both outer perception of the physical world, and inner perception, or introspection, of one's own mental states. Reason includes intuition as well as deductive and inductive inference. Perception, memory, and reason are taken to be faculties of the individual mind. They are, as it were, 'onboard resources' (Craig 1990). Testimony on the other hand is the social side of knowledge. And when traditional philosophy speaks of testimony it means knowledge gained from others' indicative say-so.

No doubt philosophers have always been aware that there are other kinds of learning from others, kinds that do not fit neatly under learning from indicative say-so. Such 'misfits' include learning by imitation, knowledge due to conversation, or knowledge on the basis of collective stipulation (as when parents say 'Let us call our newborn Maria'). Perhaps philosophers have hoped that such cases would reduce straightforwardly to one of their four traditional sources, or that the category of testimony might be expanded a bit to accommodate these cases. Be that as it may, the philosophical tradition has usually avoided these thorny issues by declining to consider testimony in the first place. While philosophers have written extensively about perception and reason, they have only rarely discussed testimony, and when they have done so, they have commented on it only briefly and in a dismissive manner. The following passage from John Locke is an especially notorious and often cited example:

For, I think, we may as rationally hope to see with other Mens Eyes, as to know by other Mens Understandings. So much as we our selves consider and comprehend of Truth and Reason, so much we possess of real and true Knowledge. The floating of other Mens Opinions in our brains makes us not one jot the more knowing, though they happen to be true. What in them was Science, is in us but Opiniatrety . . . (Locke 1975, I. iv. 23)

And such sentiment is not a thing of the past. It can still be found in eminent contemporary philosophers. Jonathan Barnes is a case in point:

No doubt, we all do pick up beliefs in that second-hand fashion, and I fear that we often suppose such scavengings yield knowledge. But that is only a sign of our colossal credulity: [it is] a rotten way of acquiring beliefs and it is no way at all of acquiring knowledge. (Barnes 1980: 200)

One can advance two (compatible) explanations as to why many epistemologists have come to equate testimony and epistemic interdependence. According to the first explanation, philosophers' conceptual conservatism, their reluctance to add new sources of knowledge to the traditional four, has inclined them to inflate the category of testimony beyond its original everyday meaning. Evidence for this hypothesis comes from the fact that cases of learning by imitation have been assimilated under the category 'gestural testimony', and cases of language learning as 'ostensive testimony' (Audi 1997: 415). According to the second explanation, it is philosophers' intellectual conservatism that has disposed them to equate epistemic interdependence and knowledge by indicative say-so. Philosophers have found it difficult to imagine that epistemic interdependence could run any deeper than what is suggested by the scenario of one individual reporting facts to another individual.

Philosophers' attempts to widen the category 'testimony' notwithstanding, the original legal meaning of the term is still dominant. It always lurks in the background as the central 'intuition-pump' behind theories of testimony. Put differently, the intuitions that epistemologists try to accommodate in their theories of testimony are tacitly based on the legal case. Take for instance the core individualistic idea that testimony is not a *generative source* of knowledge, but at best a *mechanism for the transmission* of knowledge. One meets this claim in many philosophers writing on testimony. Among them are such well-known figures as Robert Audi, Michael Dummett, Elizabeth Fricker, and Alvin Plantinga.[2] Audi writes: 'Testimony is not (except incidentally) a generative source of knowledge; it does not produce new knowledge independently of building on knowledge someone already has' (1997: 418). Dummett draws the natural consequence from this by denying that testimony deserves to be called a *source* of knowledge at all: 'Testimony should not be regarded as a *source*, and still less as a *ground*, of knowledge: it is the transmission from one individual to another of knowledge acquired by whatever means' (1994: 264). As these authors see

---

[2] Audi (1997, 1998); Dummett (1994); E. Fricker (1987); Plantinga (1993*b*).

it, mere say-so cannot generate new knowledge; at best it can pass on the speaker's knowledge to the listener.[3] This claim fits our intuitions about legal testimony perfectly. We want the witness to pass her knowledge on to us. And we want her knowledge to be based on her perceptions and her memory; not on hearsay. We do not want the witness's say-so to produce new items of knowledge. All we want is that her knowledge of past items becomes our knowledge too. The focus on the legal case is thus one of the pillars that supports the individualistic view of testimony.

Naturally, even within the courtroom, the intuition in question (i.e. testimony *qua* say-so is not a generative source of knowledge) accords only with the witness's say-so to the jury. It does not suit the judge's verdict 'I hereby convict you of murder'. Or, to choose a less gruesome example, it does not apply to the registrar's statement 'I hereby declare you husband and wife'. Philosophers of language speak of the registrar's speech-act as an instance of a 'performative', and they distinguish performatives from so-called 'constatives' (Austin 1962). A constative speech-act like 'The cat is on the mat' has been carried out successfully if it 'fits' an event or state of affairs in the world—for example, the event of the cat sitting on the mat at the time of the utterance. A performative speech-act on the other hand has been successfully executed if the world 'fits' the content of the utterance. And enacting the performative speech-act usually ensures that the world does indeed fit the utterance: in many cases it is enough that the utterance is heard by witnesses for this to be the case. The world fits the registrar's utterance in so far as the couple and the witnesses hear her make the utterance. Their knowledge of the utterance creates, or is, a new social fact, the fact of the couple possessing the social status of being legally recognized as a married couple.[4]

As even this brief analysis makes clear, 'performative testimony' is an important generative source of knowledge: the say-so constitutes a social fact, and it does so by creating a new item of knowledge for the couple, the witnesses, and the registrar herself.[5] Given the ubiquity of performative

---

[3] Here and elsewhere I speak of 'speaker' and 'listener'. That should always be glossed as 'speaker or writer' and 'listener or reader'.

[4] See Ch. 5, 'Performatives and the Communitarian Epistemology of Testimony', for references and details.

[5] It is also a new item of potential knowledge for anyone who participates in the institution of marriage.

speech-acts in everyday life, it is prima facie surprising that epistemologists of testimony have not considered them. And yet it is only prima facie surprising. It is exactly what one would suspect given the influence upon philosophers' thinking of the original meaning of the word 'testimony'. To avoid further damage, philosophers would probably do well to give up the term 'testimony' altogether, or else confine it to its original meaning. 'Epistemic interdependence' is well suited to take charge of the currently broadest meaning of testimony; and perhaps 'communication' could act as the term for the transmission and creation of knowledge in linguistic contexts. In this book I shall not follow my own advice, however. I want to make sure that epistemologists see the relevance of my suggestions and criticisms for their work on testimony. I fear that my reform of the vocabulary would reduce that probability; my changing of words might be misunderstood as my changing the subject. Unless otherwise indicated, 'testimony' for me will be roughly synonymous with '(learning from) communication'.

My insistence on 'performatives' as a form of testimony is not just motivated by a desire for a more complete coverage of different forms of speech. It is central to my thinking about testimony as a whole. To anticipate ideas to be developed later in Chapter 5, in my communitarian epistemology performative testimony is involved in all forms of testimony. It is through performative testimony that we impose social statuses. There are more social statuses, however, than just the familiar statuses of 'husband', 'wife', or 'registrar'. One of my central claims will be that 'knowledge', 'knower', and 'rule' fall in the same category. The imposition of the latter statuses is dependent upon 'communal performatives' like 'We hereby declare that there is a unique commendable way of possessing the truth, and we hereby call this way "knowledge" '. We never hear such communal performatives since in reality they occur only in a fragmented and widely distributed form. They occur as aspects or moments of all forms of testimony or communication, performative and constative.[6]

---

[6] Of course, performatives and constatives do not exhaust even our linguistic means for transmitting and generating knowledge. Imperatives, questions, and expressive utterances ('Oh what fun it is to write about epistemology!') will deserve their own analysis. But this is not a task that I shall set myself here.

Up to this point I have followed epistemological tradition in confining 'our' in the phrase 'our epistemic interdependence' to adult humans. And yet, judging by how we use phrases like 'I learned from so-and-so that such-and-such', or 'I taught so-and-so that such-and-such', we are very tolerant as to who are possible 'so-and-so'. We allow that knowledge can be gained from the 'say-so' of babies, parrots, books, papers, instruments, and record-ing devices. We can gain knowledge from a child or parrot even though the child or the parrot cannot be said to have knowledge themselves. If I know that my eyes are blue, and I tell as much to my parrot, then you can learn about my blue eyes from listening to my parrot's imitation of my voice. The case of the parrot can perhaps be accommodated by the traditional view of testimony as a transmission of knowledge; it just so happens that the transmitter lacks understanding. The case of measuring instruments like speedometers or thermostats fits less well; and yet a number of epistemolo-gists wish to include our learning from instruments under the category of 'knowledge by testimony'.[7] I shall have little to say about instruments here. I shall simply assume that instrument-reading is best dealt with as a problem in the epistemology of perception.

Above I have been critical of philosophers' ways of delimiting the category of testimony. But I wish to end on a more positive note. I therefore hasten to emphasize that adults' indicative say-so (i.e. the core area of most epistemo-logical work on testimony) is indeed a very important source of knowledge. A very considerable proportion of the things that we claim to know we have learned from others' say-so. We know from the reports of others when and where we were born; who our parents are; which name we were given at birth; or what we were like as young children. A good part of language-learning consists of being told how words and grammatical constructions are used correctly. Our teachers, parents, and friends, as well as the media of mass communication, teach us close to everything we know about history, and much about the social and natural worlds we live in. Try stripping away from your stock of knowledge everything that you have acquired in this way from others. Chances are you will come to the conclusion that not much of substance remains.

---

[7] Burge (1998) is a fascinating discussion of the relation between testimony and computer proof.

Chapter 3

INFERENTIALISM —PRO AND CONTRA

One of the most central contemporary debates in the epistemology of testimony concerns the question whether our adoption of beliefs based on testimony is, or should be, 'direct' or 'inferential'. Does our adoption of beliefs based on testimony involve inferences containing premises about the testifiers' competence and honesty? Or is testimonial belief-adoption direct; that is, does it happen without any such premises and inferences? Can I acquire testimonial knowledge by perceiving what I am told?

It is not easy to summarize this debate. What makes it difficult is that the participants usually run together four different levels or questions:

Phenomenology.[1] What is our inner, introspective experience of how we adopt testimonial beliefs (i.e. of beliefs based on testimony)?

Cognitive psychology. What conscious or unconscious psychological mechanisms are involved in our adoption of testimonial beliefs?

Normative epistemology. How would an ideal (fully rational) knower adopt testimonial beliefs? and

Pragmatics. How do we talk about, and justify, the adoption of testimonial beliefs?

I have earlier granted that epistemological theories of testimony must often mix issues of different kinds (e.g. sociological questions and questions

---

[1] By 'phenomenology' I here simply mean introspective experience.

concerning linguistic usage). In the debate over inferentialism, however, this practice has been a source of confusion.

I have two further criticisms relating to this debate, and both are really diagnoses of epistemological individualism. The participants in the debate over inferentialism regularly commit the sins of 'psychologistic reification' and 'social dilution'. Philosophers are guilty of a psychologistic reification when they turn a salient pattern of outward (i.e. usually linguistic) behaviour into an alleged pattern of inner experience. Epistemologists of testimony commit this sin when they invoke a so-called 'phenomenology' or 'inner experience' of testimony. They fail to see that the latter is misbegotten talking with others, at best (as I shall explain below). 'Social dilution' is an insufficient appreciation of the diversity of social life. In the case at hand it amounts to neglecting the diversity of conditions under which testimony is given and assessed.

For its participants, the debate over direct versus inferential belief-adoption is first and foremost a question of phenomenology.[2] Take a normal and straightforward case of perception; say, my perception of the blue sky outside my window. The phenomenology of that perceptual experience suggests that this perception is direct: I look out of the window and, next thing I know, I find myself believing that the sky is blue. What I certainly do *not* do in this case is draw any kind of inference of the form:

> I seem to be perceiving a blue sky.
> I have no reason to believe that my eyes are deceiving me.
> Ergo: I am perceiving a blue sky.

There are of course perceptual situations where inferences of this sort are involved. For example, I might have occasional attacks of colour-blindness, or some wretch might sometimes pin pictures of blue skies to the outside of my window. In such exceptional perceptual scenarios I might well (have to) reason my way to the belief that the sky is blue.

---

[2] I am here taking as my primary examples the two positions of Antony Coady and Elizabeth Fricker. See Fricker (1987, 1994, 1995) for inferentialism. Inferentialism is also advocated by Lipton (1998). Criticisms of Fricker can be found in Bhattacharyya (1994), Chakrabarti (1994), and Welbourne (1994). The anti-inferentialist position is advocated in Coady (1992, ch. 8), Austin (1979), Dummett (1994), McDowell (1998), and Strawson (1994). McDowell's treatment of the topic builds on some comments on testimony in Evans (1982).

Is ordinary knowledge by testimony like ordinary perception, or is all knowledge by testimony like the exceptional cases of perception? That is, is knowledge by testimony inferential? Do you—in normal circumstances—believe *directly* that the sky is blue when someone, say a colleague or friend, tells you so? Or do you run through an inferential process? Assume that I am telling you over the phone that my eyes are blue. Then, according to the 'inferentialist', the following process will take place in your mind. You perceive my speech-act of telling you that my eyes are blue, and thus you form the belief:

Belief$_1$: MK claims that his eyes are blue.

Belief$_1$ is a perceptual belief, not yet a testimonial belief. It is the belief that *I have claimed* that my eyes are blue. It is *not* the belief *that* my eyes are blue. Belief$_1$ is perceptual and direct, according to the inferentialist. This is because the recognition or identification of a speech-act is a matter of *direct* perception. We do not first hear sounds and words only then to *infer* that a certain speech-act has been performed; we hear the speech-act *directly* for what it is.[3] The candidate testimonial belief in our example is belief$_2$:

Belief$_2$: MK's eyes are blue.

How do we get from belief$_1$ to belief$_2$? The inferentialist claims that we get there by inference, and that we need the additional premisses of me being, at least on this occasion, both honest and a competent judge of colours. Elizabeth Fricker, the best-known advocate of inferentialism, even holds that the normal adult recipient of testimony forms a 'psychological theory' of the speaker (Fricker 1994: 155); and that judgements of trustworthiness regarding the speaker are part of such a theory.[4] Putting all this together, we get the following inferential picture of how you form your testimonial belief about my eye colour:

Belief$_1$: MK claims that his eyes are blue.

[3] Perhaps it would be more adequate to allow for various degrees of directness. There might be cases where the belief is neither (fully) direct nor (fully) inferential. I shall follow the tradition here in ignoring such intermediate cases.

[4] Alvin Goldman's version of inferentialism is based on Bayesianism. Because of its technical nature I shall discuss it only in an appendix (Appendix I.1).

Ancillary information (drawing on a psychological theory of MK): MK is, on this occasion, competent and honest.

Ergo: *Belief₂*: MK's eyes are blue.

Fricker also speculates on how we form our beliefs about speakers' trustworthiness. She assumes that we usually treat trustworthiness as the default position, but that we always 'monitor' speakers for tell-tale signs of dishonesty and incompetence (1995: 403). (I shall shortly consider the question of how conscious all this is supposed to be.)

We have now familiarized ourselves with the inferentialists' claims regarding the phenomenology of receiving testimony. We can now move on to their views on the cognitive psychology of testimony. Here by 'cognitive psychology' I refer to conscious and subconscious psychological mechanisms that do not feature in our phenomenology of testimony. To begin with, Fricker tells us that the monitoring for tell-tale signs of insincerity and incompetence usually takes place subconsciously (1994: 150). And, presumably, even the above-mentioned inferences are often subconscious. Indeed, I have gone well beyond Fricker's own words in constructing, on her behalf, a straightforward phenomenological reading of her 'inferentialist position'. And yet there are good reasons too for attributing the phenomenological reading to her. Indeed, as I shall argue further down, she needs that reading in order to be able to retain the contrast between testimony and perception.

As concerns normative epistemology and pragmatics, Fricker again refuses to draw a sharp boundary. This is unobjectionable given that she sees her normative epistemology arising out of a critical reflection on our epistemic practices. How does the distinction 'direct versus inferential' work in the normative realm? According to Fricker, to say that we are entitled to adopt a given type of belief directly (i.e. without monitoring the speaker) is tantamount to us having 'a presumptive right' to trust the *source* of beliefs of that type. If we do have this presumptive right with respect to a given source, then we are entitled to adopt beliefs directly; if we do not have this right, then we must arrive at our beliefs via an inferential process. Fricker formulates 'the presumptive right thesis' for testimony as follows:

PR thesis: On any occasion of testimony, the hearer has the epistemic right to assume, without evidence, that the speaker is trustworthy, i.e. that what she says will be true, unless there are special circumstances which defeat this presumption. (Thus she has the epistemic right to believe the speaker's assertion, unless such defeating conditions obtain.) (1994: 125)

Fricker insists that no rational person could possibly accept the PR thesis; it runs counter to what we know about language and human psychology:

Does not mere logic, plus our common-sense knowledge of what kind of act an assertion is, and what other people are like, entail that we should not just believe whatever we are told, without critically assessing the speaker for trustworthiness? We know too much about human nature to want to trust anyone, let alone everyone, uncritically. (1995: 401)

Fricker's alternative to the PR thesis is the tripartite policy of always monitoring the speaker for tell-tale signs of insincerity and incompetence, relying on generalizations about whom to trust (philosophers have a better track record than car salesmen), and treating trustworthiness as the default position. The last-mentioned part of the policy comes down to this: if none of the typical incriminating tell-tale signs have been found, then we are entitled to treat the speaker as sincere; a positive proof of her sincerity is not needed.

I have given a lot of space to the exposition of Fricker's ideas. I have done so not only because she gives the clearest statement of the inferentialist position, but also because she provides us, via negationis, with an excellent characterization of the central ingredients of the 'direct' view of testimony. The latter view is held by Anthony Coady, Michael Dummett, John McDowell, and Peter Strawson, among others.[5] The arguments for the 'direct' position also straddle the boundaries between the phenomeno-logical, the communicative, and the normative spheres. Coady, for instance, invokes phenomenology as an argument against the inferentialist norma-tive account:

[This is a] difficulty for the idea that testimonial knowledge could ever be direct. After all, it may well be urged, the rational person does not believe just any and every thing he is told. His assent must be mediated by a consideration of the veracity of the witness, his reliability . . . the probability of what he says, and so on. Thus mediated, our belief in what he says must count as inferentially based . . . Plausible as this argument seems, it would surely be fallacious. The first problem with it is that it

[5] See n. 2 above.

is at odds with the phenomenology of *learning*. In our ordinary dealings with others we gather information without this concern for inferring the acceptability of communications from premises about the honesty, reliability, probability, etc., of our communicants. I ring the telephone company on being unable to locate my bill and am told by an anonymous voice that it comes to $165 and is due on 15 June. No thought of determining the veracity and reliability of the witness occurs to me nor, given that the total is within tolerable limits, does the balancing of probabilities figure in my acceptance. (1992: 143)

Coady also allows that 'there are many cases in which answers of the form "Jones told me" ... are enough to support claims (directly) to know' (1992: 143). Coady's normative position is close to what Fricker calls the PR thesis. Although we are obliged to suspend belief when we have reason to distrust, there is no general duty to monitor the speaker for tell-tale signs of insincerity and incompetence.

Who is right: the inferentialist or her opponent? My answer will leave both camps dissatisfied: both are partially right and partially wrong. As concerns the phenomenology and psychology of adopting testimonial beliefs, I suspect that both sides of the dispute are guilty of a psychologistic reification of a social practice. No doubt, we all are able to recall and imagine all sorts of social settings in which we justify perceptual and testimonial beliefs. Sometimes our justifications consist of a simple and direct 'I saw it' or 'Jack told me so'. At other times our justifications have the structure of elaborate inferences, like 'I saw it, and the lighting was adequate, and I had taken off my sunglasses', or 'Jack told me so, and he is an expert in this matter, and I have yet to catch him telling a lie'. These cases are clear and distinct in their public and communicative form. I doubt, however, that in addition to such memories we have much of a phenomenology of such cases. At best, our phenomenology of perception and testimony consists of imagined public scenarios of justification—completely derived from, and secondary to, the real-life settings. There is no determinate phenomenology of testimony over and above imagined talk. And what little phenomenology there is fails to distinguish perception from testimony.

I take it as indirect evidence for this interpretation that inferentialists feel the need to go underground, that is, into the subconscious, in order to defend their views. If we cannot find the monitoring in our phenomenology, then surely it must happen subconsciously. And who knows what takes place down there; it might well be monitoring. The same immunizing move might also seem to rescue the inferences themselves. But not quite. For if the inferentialist escaped her opponents in this way, she would surely score a mere pyrrhic victory. The starting point of Fricker's argument is a contrast between perception and testimony: perception gives us direct knowledge, knowledge based on testimony gives us inferential knowledge (Fricker 1987). The contrast disappears, however, once we let subconscious processes figure in the story. If the inference involved in the assessment of testimony is subconscious, then testimony is back where perception has been all along. After all, ever since von Helmholtz psychologists and physiologists have assumed that perception involves unconscious inferences.

At first sight, the central bone of contention between Coady and Fricker seems to be the duty to monitor. According to Fricker, the hearer must monitor the speaker in order to be justified in adopting a belief based on the speaker's testimony. According to Coady, the hearer is not obliged to monitor at all; all that is needed for her to be justified is that she did not notice anything suspicious. As Fricker sees it, Coady's example of the telephone bill shows that in the end Coady admits that monitoring must always take place. Coady's phrase 'within tolerable limits' points, so Fricker claims, to precisely 'the active sub-personal monitoring of the speaker by the hearer for signs of lack of sincerity or competence' (1995: 405). I beg to differ. The last quotation suggests to me that what divides Coady and Fricker is not so much the difference between monitoring and not monitoring as the opposition between *active* and *passive* monitoring. Fricker seems to rely on the idea that one can only detect something if one has been actively monitoring for it. There are indeed events and states of affairs that we can only detect by actively monitoring for them: for instance, driving along the highway I can only detect that I'm going slightly faster than 70 miles per hour if I keep actively monitoring the speedometer. But there are plenty of other things that I can notice without any active monitoring. For instance, I do not need to actively monitor my chin in order for me to notice the fist that lands on it. I notice the punch because the monitor (in this case, nerve endings) is in constant passive monitoring mode. This monitor is 'on', and sensitive to the appropriate stimuli at any time, even without any 'action' on my part. Applied to the case of testimony: detecting or noticing that someone is probably lying to us does not presuppose that one has been actively monitoring for this possibility. It is enough that something we hear or read does not fit with our other beliefs about the matter, the situation, or the speaker. That is to say, our prior beliefs might have a filtering role for the things we are told. But filters are not active monitoring devices; filters are passive.

I have argued that Fricker and Coady are guilty of a psychologistic reification of talk about testimony. I now turn to my accusation of 'social dilution', that is, of neglecting social variation. I do not mean to deny that Coady and Fricker mention the fact that we treat different sorts of speakers differently. Indeed both epistemologists make this obvious point. And I applaud them for it. What I do fault them for is that they do not draw the correct conclusion from this observation. The correct conclusion would be to acknowledge that even their respective favourite models of testimony-assessment are only of local applicability.

To see this we need to adopt the attitude of anthropologists or sociologists, and treat Coady's and Fricker's normative pronouncements as data. We should then ask questions like the following: 'In what language games do the respective norms have their natural home?', 'Where and when do we expect recipients of testimony to monitor the testifiers explicitly and consciously?', 'Where and when do we expect a looser form of monitoring, that is, a form of monitoring that drifts in and out of awareness or consciousness?', 'Where and when are we happy to tolerate testimony-reception simply on the basis that nothing has struck the hearer as suspicious?', 'Where and when are we content to treat trustworthiness as the default position, and where and when do we think of insincerity and incompetence as the default position?', or, 'Where and when do we expect the recipient to be able to mount an inferential argument, and where and when are we satisfied with a direct answer?'

I shall not try to answer these questions here. It is not important for my argument that I do so; what *is* important is that they do have answers. In other words, the norms identified by Fricker and Coady, as well as some other bundles of norms for testimony-assessment, all do have their place in social life. And thus it is a futile exercise to attempt to determine which ones of these bundles of norms we *really do* follow. We follow all of them—*in their respective contexts*. Coady and Fricker each go wrong in trying to reduce the spectrum of modes of testimony-reception. They treat their favourite end of the spectrum as the basic case, and they generate other cases either by relaxing the conditions of the paradigmatic scenario (Fricker), or by tightening the demands of the prototypical case (Coady). To my mind, such philosophical clean-up operations do not enlighten.

It cannot hurt to conclude by stating the anti-individualistic moral of this chapter explicitly. An epistemology of testimony worth its salt had better avoid engaging in psychological speculations about subconscious processes; it had better stay clear of the misbegotten project of a phenomenology of testimony; and it had better give proper heed to the diversity of social practices surrounding the giving and receiving of testimony.

Chapter 4

THE GLOBAL JUSTIFICATION OF TESTIMONY

REDUCTIONISM

How can we provide a *general* justification for a given *type* of knowledge? The intuitively most plausible answer is 'reductionism'. The reductionist's answer is simple: justify the given knowledge in terms of another, more secure, and more fundamental form of knowledge. How can I justify my knowledge of the external world? 'Try to derive it from your knowledge of your own mental states', says the reductionist. How can I justify my trust in other people's words? 'Try to reduce testimony to more secure sources of knowledge, like perception, inference, and memory', says the reductionist.

Reductionism is usually a form of 'foundationalism'. Foundationalism is the view that justification comes to an end once we have reached a level of beliefs that needs no further justification. These bedrock beliefs are 'fundamental' or 'foundational'. Naturally, not all forms of reductionism need to be committed to foundationalism. For instance, a reductionist with respect to testimonial beliefs might insist that we need other forms of belief in order to justify our trust in testimony; but this same reductionist might deny that these other beliefs are all fundamental, or that these other beliefs divide into more or less fundamental ones. Nevertheless, as we shall see in a moment, it is helpful and illuminating to see reductionism concerning testimony as a form of foundationalism. Reductionists about testimony are foundational-ists at least by temperament.

Taken in its most radical form, the reductive project concerning testi-mony amounts to justifying our testimonial beliefs in terms of perceptions, memories, and inferences. First, the reductionist asks us to match (memories of) perceptions of others' reports with (memories of) perceptions of states of affairs; she invites us to check whether the contents of what we have *perceived* as others' reports have tended to match what we have *perceived* as events and states of affairs in the world. And second, we are meant to use 'ampliative in-ductive inference' in order to get from the past to the present and future.[1] That is, we are meant to notice the match between reports and facts in the past, and infer by enumerative induction that future reports and facts will coincide as well. This will then license our belief that *p* when told that *p* by others.

In the last paragraph I formulated the reductive project as one addressing itself to 'us'. The 'us' here is not to be taken as 'us as a group' however, but as 'us as individuals'. In order to be epistemologically responsible, each one of us must carry through the reductive justification for himself or herself. I cannot rely on you having established a general match of report and fact. After all, I could only know from you that you had done so if you *reported* your findings to me, and if I have not yet carried out the reductive project myself, then I am not yet entitled to trust you. The reductive project with respect to testimony is thus an *individualistic* endeavour: others must prove their epistemic mettle at the bar of my own perceptions and memories. This reductionism is a form of *foundationalism*: on the one hand, the reductive epistemologist partitions our beliefs into beliefs of two kinds, those that are epistemically safe and foundational (beliefs based on perception, memory, and inference), and those that are epistemically unsafe and unjustified (beliefs based on testimony).[2] On the other hand, the reductive epistemolo-gist assumes that the latter beliefs can be made safe by connecting them in the right way to the former beliefs. Beliefs based on the individual's percep-tion, memory, and inference thus function as the foundation for the individual's beliefs based upon testimony.

---

[1] In an ampliative induction we infer a generalization from evidence about its instances; for instance, having noticed that several New Yorkers have a great sense of humour, I conclude that *all* New Yorkers have a great sense of humour.

[2] Foundationalism will be discussed in greater detail in Part II.

The most notable proponent of the need for a reductive justification of testimony was David Hume, and current discussions of reductionism continue to centre on his ideas.[3] Here are the central passages from Hume's *Enquiry concerning Human Understanding*:

there is no species of reasoning more common, more useful, and even necessary to human life, than that which is derived from the testimony of men, and the reports of eye-witnesses and spectators. . . . It will be sufficient to observe that our assurance in any argument of this kind is derived from no other principle than our observation of the veracity of human testimony, and of the usual conformity of facts to the reports of witnesses. It being a general maxim, that no objects have any discoverable connexion together, and that all the inferences, which we can draw from one to another, are founded merely on our experience of their constant and regular conjunction; it is evident, that we ought not to make an exception to this maxim in favour of human testimony, whose connexion with any event seems, in itself, as little necessary as any other. . . . The reason why we place any credit in witnesses and historians, is not derived from any *connexion*, which we perceive *a priori*, between testimony and reality, but because we are accustomed to find a conformity between them. (Hume 1966: x. i)

Hume's reductionism can be challenged on a number of grounds. A first, obvious, strategy starts from reconstructing Hume's argument as follows. Think of all the bits of information that have been, are, and will be offered to you as knowledge by others. For some of these bits you will also have first-hand knowledge on the basis of your individual 'on-board' sources of knowledge, that is, perception, reasoning, and memory. You can then distinguish between three groups of testimonial reports: (*a*) reports confirmed by your first-hand knowledge; (*b*) reports in conflict with your first-hand knowledge; and (*c*) reports for which you have no first-hand check at all. Hume then reasons as follows: Reports confirmed by my first-hand knowledge (category (*a*)) vastly outnumber reports in conflict with my first-hand knowledge (category (*b*)). It is rational for me to assume that this ratio will also hold for reports of category (*c*), that is, reports for which I have no first-hand check at all. Hence it is prima facie rational to trust new reports. The objection to this line of reasoning is clear. Although reports confirmed by my on-board resources vastly outnumber reports in conflict

---

[3] There is some controversy over the question whether Hume is a reductionist at all. A negative answer has been returned by Faulkner (1998) and Welbourne (forthcoming).

with my first-hand knowledge, reports confirmed or refuted by first-hand knowledge are in turn vastly outnumbered by reports for which I have no first-hand check at all. And thus, to generalize from the former to the latter is a bad generalization; it is as if I were to infer from the fact that you (the reader) take an interest in this book that every human being does.

Another way to challenge the possibility of the proposed reduction (of testimony to perception) is to point out that perception is always already 'laden' with testimony. How can we hope to reduce testimony to perception if the way we perceive the world is to a considerable extent shaped by concepts and categories that we have learned from others? We perceive mountains, bridges, boats, wedding rings, or policemen; it surely does not make sense that we could do this without having learned the categories 'mountain', 'bridge', 'boat', etc. from others. This observation fatally weakens the appeal of the reductive project. It also throws doubt over the claim that perception is more fundamental than testimony. Peter Strawson formulates the point thus:

Consider the overwhelming extent to which *what* we in fact perceive, the very nature or character of our perceptual experience itself, is determined by the instruction, the information, we have already received from the word of others. To apply ... a phrase of Wittgenstein's, much, perhaps most, of what we see we could not see *as* what we do see it *as*, without the benefit of such instruction.... If we are to say, as we must, that the knowledge we derive from testimony depends on perception, must we not equally say that the knowledge we derive from perception depends generally on testimony ...? (Strawson 1994: 26)

The most influential interpretation and critique can be found in Anthony Coady's *Testimony: A Philosophical Study* (1992). Here we need not go into all aspects of Coady's discussion, but some of his arguments are well worth going over in detail. A first critical observation by Coady concerns an ambiguity in the way Hume formulates the reductive project. Hume writes throughout in the first-person plural; he writes as if determining the reliability of testimony was a collective project. But for reasons already mentioned above, this would be circular: an advocate of reductionism concerning testimony cannot possibly allow that testimonial beliefs are justified by *reports* of how perceptual reports fit with reality (1992: 80).

Several lines of attack in Coady concern the two elements we are meant to check for 'fit': reports and objects. Hume makes clear that the two relata are 'kinds of reports' and 'kinds of objects'. But how are we supposed to interpret 'kinds of reports'? Suppose we were to define different *kinds of reports* in terms of different *kinds of reporters*. Then our reductive justification would amount to something like this: 'We rely upon testimony because we have each personally observed a correlation between expert (or authoritative) reports and the kinds of situations reported in a large number of cases'. But how can we pick out the expert reports without already knowing who the experts are? We are not permitted to get information on the experts from others, or else we are back in a circular justification. Thus we can only determine the experts by checking how well their reports fit the facts. In this latter case, however, we again end up in a circle: we want to justify our reliance on testimony by checking whether experts' testimony fits the facts they report. Thus we need to find the experts. But in order to find the experts, we need to know whose reports fit the facts (1992: 83–4).[4]

Assume then that we try the second way of determining kinds of reports: kinds defined by the *content* of the reports. In this case I am supposed to check whether reports about the sun shining fit (in the relevant way) my perception that the sun shines; or whether reports about the Scots being heavy drinkers fit (in the right sort of way) my perception that the Scots drink a lot. Coady's central objection to this idea is this:

the whole enterprise . . . in its present form requires that we understand what testimony is independently of knowing that it is, in any degree, a reliable form of evidence about the way the world is. . . . It is a clear implication of this that we might have discovered (though in fact we did not) that there was no conformity at all between testimony and reality. Hume's position requires the possibility that we clearly isolate the reports people make about the world for comparison by personal observation with the actual state of the world and find a high, low, or no correlation between them. But it is by no means clear that we understand this suggestion. To take the most extreme discovery: imagine a world in which an extensive survey yields no correlation between reports and (individually observed) facts. In such a colossally topsy-turvy world what evidence could there possibly be for the existence of reports at all? (1992: 85)

---

[4] Coady's criticism works only if we equate 'reporters' and 'experts'. But this we need not do. Many other types of reporters might be distinguished: reporters that are sober, alert, in full possession of their senses, honest, etc. It is questionable, however, whether this would get Hume out of his difficulties. For in order to know whether someone is sober, alert, in full possession of their senses, honest, etc. we will usually (have to) rely on further testimony.

Taking this argument to its natural conclusion, Coady argues that if all testimony were false, then a shared language could not exist. If parents never report correctly on the meaning of words, then children cannot learn the language. And if all utterances of a speaker are false, then there is no way in which an interpreter can begin to establish hypothetical links between the speaker's sounds and features of the world. If a Finnish speaker repeatedly produces the sound 'koira' in the presence of a dog, then (assuming that her reports are true) you might venture the (correct) guess that the sound 'koira' carries the meaning 'dog'. But if her reports are always false, then 'koira' might refer to anything whatsoever: to ballet performances, to 25 August, or to knife-sharpeners. Put in a nutshell, Coady's overall argument comes down to the following three-liner:

> Global falsity of testimony is self-refuting.
> Hume's project presupposes the possibility of the global falsity of testimony.
> Ergo: Hume's reductionist endeavour is itself self-refuting.

Coady's analysis according to which Hume's reductionism implies the possibility of global falsity is controversial. As Peter Lipton (1998: 18–21) sees it, Humean reductionism is merely committed to the view:

> (*) Each and every report, *taken singly*, might turn out false.

It is not, however, committed to:

> (**) All reports might turn out false *together*.

Lipton is right to say that Hume's argument does not commit him to (**). But Coady's argument can be restated and saved in a weaker form. Imagine Coady asked Hume (or the Humean) whether all testimony could be false together. How could the Humean defend a negative answer to the effect that it could not? It would be very odd for him to justify a negative answer by saying things like the following: that language learning presupposes largely true testimony; that general dishonesty would destroy the very idea of testimony; or that there are conceptual reasons why most testimony must be true. It would be odd for him to give these justifications since— by Coady's standards—any one of them could also be used as a global justification of testimony. As Coady sees it, if any one of these can do the work of ruling out the possibility of global failure, then they can also do the job of providing a global justification of testimony. And then the inductive argument becomes superfluous. In other words, commitment to an inductive global argument in favour of testimony leaves one without resources to argue against the possibility of global failure. This is all Coady really needs.

Be this as it may, contemporary epistemologists all agree that our reliance on testimony cannot be globally justified in terms of exclusively individual on-board resources. Weaker, more minimal forms of reductionism are still advocated, however. Lipton (1998), for instance, urges the acceptance of so-called 'rule reductionism'. The idea is to find mechanisms of belief-formation that are common to the different 'modalities' (of perception, memory, or testimony). Lipton's favourite mechanism is 'hypothetical induction'.[5] This suggestion will surely be acceptable to all sides, though one might doubt that the label 'reductionism' is apt here.

Fricker's minimal reductionism is a more contentious idea.[6] She suggests that each of us should trust testimony as a source of knowledge since most testimonial reports we get fit, or 'cohere', with the system of beliefs we already have—never mind whether these older beliefs were themselves formed on the basis of testimony or on the basis of some other source of knowledge. Put differently, the idea is that the global justification of testimony should take the forms of an 'internal vindication' (Fricker 1995: 409).

I am not convinced that, even in this minimalist form, reductionism is a plausible position. The problem with the project of internal vindication is

---

[5] In hypothetical induction, or 'inference to the best explanation', one infers a hypothesis that would best explain the evidence. Seeing fresh graffiti on my office wall I infer that someone must recently have been in my office. This inference is inductive rather than demonstrative since it is merely 'reasonable' rather than logically compelling to draw this inference: in principle someone might have been spraying my office wall from behind the closed door, perhaps using keyhole surgery equipment.

[6] Fricker (1995: 409). Fricker speaks of 'local reductionism'. I avoid this term here in order to distinguish two views. The first view holds that all justification of testimony is local. We can justify our belief in this or that piece of testimony, but we cannot justify our reliance on testimony per se. This position I call 'contextualism', and a 'local form of justification'. Fricker's view is that we can produce more than just local justifications (in the sense just defined). But these further, more general justifications are not of the Humean reductive kind.

that it contains too much circularity. I am supposed to trust testimony in general because on many occasions testimonial beliefs have cohered with my prior testimonial and non-testimonial beliefs. Obviously, this is circular, but maybe we can live with this level of circularity. However, this is not all. We need to ask from where we get our standards and criteria for determining what constitutes a reasonable level of fit or coherence between beliefs. And how do we know that we have applied these criteria and standards correctly? Surely these standards and criteria are themselves learned from others, and thus due to testimony; and so are assurances concerning the correctness of our applications of these standards. Thus internal vindication amounts to testing testimony against testimony on the basis of standards provided by testimony. This is too much circularity for my taste. It is hard to see how anyone can increase their confidence in testimony on the basis of such an argument.

Fricker is still working under the shadow of the individualism of global reduction. Each one of us is supposed to establish with respect to his or her own system of beliefs that testimony is a reliable source of knowledge. The problem is thus still the traditional one: Why should I trust others in questions of knowledge? In my view, asking this question is itself a deep—perhaps even the deepest—expression of individualism in epistemology.

Fricker seems to me to draw the wrong conclusion from the failure of foundationalist global reductionism. The failure of foundationalist global reductionism gives her cause to adopt a more moderate form of reductionism, that is, the project of justifying the reliability of testimony in a circular fashion. But what is wrong with global reductionism is not that it seeks a foundationalist rather than a coherentist justification of testimony. What is wrong with reductionism is that it seeks a justification at all. There are cases where we can make sense of circular justifications, and where they are fruitful. A circular justification of our general reliance on testimony is not among such fruitful cases. The ways in which constative and performative testimony constitute us as knowers simply run too deep. Trying to get behind them, even in a circular fashion, amounts to 'digging below bedrock'. Put differently, testimony constitutes the shifting standards of justification. And for precisely this reason it cannot itself be globally justified.

FUNDAMENTALISM

I have not yet shown that testimony (*qua* communication) does indeed constitute the shifting standards of justification. That is to say, I have not yet shown that standards of justification are conventional (i.e. they are social institutions) and that all social institutions are created and maintained by communication. This is the task of Chapter 5. But it should be clear that *if* I am right in this claim, then quietism and contextualism are the only correct positions concerning the justification of testimony. Quietism and contextualism are two sides of the same coin: quietism regarding testimony is the view that global justifications of testimony are impossible; contextualism is the thesis that all justification is local and contextual.

My communitarian epistemology does not just oppose reductionism. It also rejects 'non-reductive' justifications of testimony, for example those offered by Thomas Reid, Alvin Plantinga, and Anthony Coady.[7] The non-reductivist, or fundamentalist, agrees with the quietist that our reliance upon testimony cannot be justified in terms of the deliveries of the other three sources of knowledge. Testimony is as fundamental a source of knowledge as are perception, memory, and inference. Nevertheless, the fundamentalist does not draw the quietist's conclusion; he does not stop seeking to justify our general reliance upon testimony. Instead, he seeks a new form of justification; a justification independent of reduction.

Hume's great opponent Thomas Reid defended our reliance on testimony by invoking 'the wise and beneficent Author of Nature':

---

[7] The classic defence of fundamentalism is Reid (1966: VI. xxiv). A closely related form of fundamentalism can be found in Plantinga (1993*b*).

A different form of fundamentalism relies on the 'parity argument':

> *Premise 1*: I am right to trust my own beliefs.
> *Premise 2*: Others' beliefs are as worthy of my trust as are my own beliefs.
> *Conclusion*: I am right to trust others' beliefs.

Versions of this argument have been endorsed by Keith Lehrer and Allan Gibbard (see Lehrer 1997: 127; Gibbard 1990: 179–81). I find Schmitt's criticism convincing (see Schmitt, forthcoming).

Another important form of fundamentalism has been presented by Tyler Burge. It is based on the ideas, first, that whatever is intelligible is likely to come from a rational source, and, second, that rational sources, by their very nature, tend towards the truth. I lack Burge's optimism regarding the link between rationality and truthfulness. For discussion, see Bezuidenhout (1998); Burge (1993, 1997); Christensen and Kornblith (1997); Faulkner (2000).

Hilary Kornblith's naturalistic defence of trust in testimony (1987) is also a form of non-reductionism.

The wise and beneficent Author of Nature, who intended that we should be social creatures, and that we should receive the greatest and most important part of our knowledge by the information of others, hath, for these purposes, implanted in our natures two principles that tally with each other. The first [is] ... a propensity to speak the truth ... Another original principle implanted in us by the Supreme Being, is a disposition to confide in the veracity of others ... (Reid 1966: VI. xxiv)

The problem with this fundamentalist justification is obvious: how does Reid know about the actions and intentions of the wise and beneficent Author of Nature?[8]

Coady's fundamentalism is much more sophisticated. Coady offers two non-reductive arguments for the reliability of testimony. The first is close in spirit to what Fricker calls 'the internal vindication' of testimony (Coady 1992: 169–73). Coady suggests that our beliefs are integrated on two levels. The first level concerns the way in which single beliefs are formed. Typically, different 'informational routes' (perception, memory, inference, testimony) are integrated in the formation of a belief; and this integration amounts to the formation of a coherent whole. For instance, in forming the belief that my mother is at the other end of the phone, I integrate perceptual information with memories, testimony, and inferences. Coady speaks of this integration as 'cohesion'. He saves the term 'coherence' for the second level of integration: different types of beliefs, including those based primarily on testimony, generally fit in with one another. This then is Coady's first non-reductive vindication of testimony: testimony must be reliable since its deliveries cohere both with input from other informational routes in the formation of single beliefs, and with other types of beliefs in the formation of systems of belief.

Since Coady's first argument is a close relative to Fricker's internal vindication, I need not criticize it here. The criticism I directed against Fricker at the end of the last section also applies to Coady. Testimony is too central to the constitution of our frameworks for justification; it therefore cannot be justified within them. Note also the curious coincidence of Coady's and Fricker's projects for the justification of testimony. What

---

[8] The same question can be used to weaken our confidence in Alvin Plantinga's talk of 'the design plan for the human cognitive situation', a plan that allegedly 'does not involve us merely as individuals; our cognitive systems are designed to work together in a certain way' (Plantinga 1993*b*: 82).

Fricker sees as the most moderate form of reductionism Coady sees as a form of non-reductionism. Perhaps this coincidence is an additional reason to see both reductionism and fundamentalism as two positions that we had best give up together. The position to which they naturally seem to gravitate is the coherentist justification of testimony proposed by both Coady and Fricker. But this position is deeply unsatisfactory, relying, as it does, on an individualistic model of justification in which we are expected to recommit ourselves to testimony using only on-board resources.

Coady has a second non-reductive argument for the reliability of testimony (1992: 152–69). This argument draws on a much discussed set of ideas put forward by Donald Davidson.[9] These ideas have to do with conditions of the possibility of understanding other speakers. I shall begin by explaining Davidson's train of thought in six steps.

Step 1. Our linguistic behaviour is, in good part, the effect of two causes. The first cause is that specific sounds carry specific meanings. The second cause is that we have beliefs—some of which we wish to make known to others. Why does a Finn make the sounds 'tämä on koira' when standing in front of a dog? There is a good likelihood that she does so because she happens to *believe* that there is a dog in front of her; and because the sounds 'tämä on koira' happen to *mean* 'there is a dog'.

Step 2. It often happens that we do not know, but wish to find out about, the beliefs of our interlocutors. How do we find out about their beliefs? In many cases we simply ask them. And since our interlocutors usually speak the same language as we do, they can tell us what their beliefs are. Thus, if you want to find out what sorts of beliefs I hold about the monarchy, you only need to ask. My words will teach you about my beliefs.

Step 3. Sometimes things are the other way round. We know what someone's beliefs are, but we do not know which meanings to attach to the noises coming from their mouth—we do not know the language they speak. Here is an example of how we deal with such cases. I have a friend who speaks English and Spanish. She is a great admirer of Diego Velazquez's *Las Meninas*. She has lectured to me about the painting many times, and thus I have come to know her views (i.e. beliefs) about every aspect of the painting.

---

[9] Davidson's ideas concerning radical interpretation can be found, for example, in Davidson (1989a). His position is criticized in Plantinga (1993b, ch. 4) and in Haack (1993, ch. 3).

Fortunately, she has done the lecturing in English, since, sadly, I do not understand a word of Spanish. Suppose now that my friend is visiting the Prado with me and a Spanish relative of hers; we are standing in front of *Las Meninas*, and my friend (pointing at different parts of the painting) is lecturing to her relative in Spanish. I am standing next to the two, trying to guess what my friend is saying. I know what she thinks about Velazquez's dress: that he had no right to paint himself dressed in the uniform of the Order of St John. As she points at the uniform, I hear Spanish-sounding noises coming from her mouth. And I have a pretty good guess what these noises mean. In this case then I can work my way towards knowing what the noises mean, starting from a prior knowledge of my friend's beliefs.

Step 4. If we know someone's language, then we have a way of determining what they believe. And if we know what someone's beliefs are, we can figure out what their sounds mean. This leaves the case where we know neither beliefs nor meanings. According to Davidson, we can eventually find out the speaker's meanings and beliefs even in such extreme or 'radical' situations: 'radical interpretation' is possible. Suppose that you find yourself alone on a remote island with a native; the two of you share no language; and you have no inkling as to what sort of belief system your new neighbour possesses. The way to make progress in this case, Davidson says, is to exercise 'charity': attribute to your neighbour the sorts of beliefs you would have in like circumstances. So if the native is standing in front of a dog, pointing at the dog while looking at you, and uttering the same sound repeatedly, say 'tämä on koira', then attribute to him the intention of teaching you how to express the belief 'this is a dog'. If you do so successfully—and Davidson might well allow that you will make frequent misattributions—then you will find yourself back in the situation of Step 3: you will know the beliefs, and you can work your way from beliefs to meanings. Note, furthermore, that to explicitly attribute one belief involves the implicit attribution of many more beliefs. In the above situation, for example, you are also implicitly attributing to the native beliefs like the following: that you can be taught; that dogs can be picked out from the environment; that you are not blind; etc. The key to the enterprise then is to attribute true beliefs, beliefs that you deem true, to the native. You can make sense of his verbal and non-verbal behaviour only if you attribute to him a system of beliefs that largely coincides with your own.

Step 5. Radical interpretation begins at home. The case described in the last section differs only in degree, but not in kind, from the everyday contexts we find ourselves in. We encounter other speakers who do not have full command of our language; we meet people who employ technical vocabularies; and we come upon interlocutors who make up new words, combine old words in new ways, or pronounce words in unusual ways. And in most such cases we do not have the benefit that I had above with my Spanish–English friend and *Las Meninas*. We do not have the speakers' beliefs ready in our memories. Thus we are forced to engage in radical interpretation: assume agreement in beliefs between yourself and the other, and then work your way from the attributed beliefs to the speaker's meanings.

Step 6. Up to this point the argument shows that if I want to interpret the words of another speaker, then I had better attribute a good deal of my own beliefs to her. In a controversial final twist to the argument, Davidson takes the further step of trying to convince us that agreement yields truth. That is, he seeks to show that we can get from agreement in beliefs to the truth of these beliefs. Without this additional twist, agreement in beliefs is compatible with all (or some majority) of the beliefs involved being false. Nothing has been said so far that rules out the possibility that the interpreter's beliefs are all (or mostly) false. Interpreter and speaker could end up agreeing, and interpretation might be possible, but they end up without truth. Davidson thinks he can assure us that this scenario is impossible. Here goes:

imagine for a moment an interpreter who is omniscient about any sentence in his (potentially) unlimited repertoire. The omniscient interpreter, using the same method as the fallible interpreter, finds the fallible speaker largely consistent and correct. By his own standards, of course, but since these are objectively correct, the fallible speaker is seen to be largely correct and consistent by objective standards. We may also, if we want, let the omniscient interpreter turn his attention to the fallible interpreter of the fallible speaker. It turns out that the fallible interpreter can be wrong about some things, but not in general; and so he cannot share universal error with the agent he is interpreting. Once we agree to the general method of interpretation I have sketched, it becomes impossible correctly to hold that anyone could be mostly wrong about how things are. (Davidson 1989a: 317)

What follows from all this for the reliability of testimony? If the argument were to go through, then most people would have to have true beliefs most of the time. And, presumably, if most people had mostly true beliefs most of the time, then most of their testimony would have to be true as well.

Alas, there are severe problems with Davidson's argument. To begin with, it is not clear at all that the inevitability of *having mostly true beliefs* implies the inevitability of *mostly speaking the truth*. Fricker puts this point well:

The great mass of a person's beliefs which must mainly be true . . . concern what is too boringly obvious and familiar to be worth asserting. We only bother to say what is—relatively—surprising and controversial. Thus there is no implication from the truth-in-the-main of beliefs to truth-in-the-main of assertions. (1995: 410)

Moreover, Davidson's crucial step from agreement to truth—bringing in the omniscient interpreter in Step 6—is entirely unconvincing.[10] First of all, note that the argument is hypothetical. It says: *if* there were an omniscient interpreter, *then* most of our beliefs would be true. But that is not enough for justifying the belief that most of our beliefs are in fact true. The hypothetical argument can lead to this result only if we can show that the antecedent is true; that is to say, only if we have a proof of the existence of an omniscient interpreter. Davidson provides no such proof.

Second, one might reasonably doubt the coherence of the notion of an 'omniscient interpreter'. The need for interpretation arises where knowledge has not yet been achieved, or where knowledge is impossible to gain. If the psychiatrist knows the problems and symptoms of her patient, then she need not interpret the latter. If the detective knows all about the evidence and the suspect's deeds, then he need not interpret the evidence. Or, to take a case where knowledge (in any strict sense) is impossible, the reader of a poem must interpret it since there is no way of knowing what all the poem might be taken to mean. An omniscient interpreter knows everything and yet is meant to interpret. It is hard to see why such interpretation would be necessary and how it could lead to an improvement in knowledge.

Third, the very idea of omniscience is dubious, at least for the communitarian epistemologist. As this book as a whole will argue, knowing is a social state, and knowledge is a social status. In calling a belief or statement 'knowledge', we ascribe it a certain position in a social network of exchange, argument, and justification. Such network fulfils the needs of beings that are not omniscient. Indeed, it is hard to see how an omniscient being could fit

---

[10] Davidson has come round to the same view. See Genova (1999) and Davidson (1999*a*).

into such network. And outside this network the concept has no clear application.

Coady is largely happy with what I have labelled as Davidson's Steps 1 to 5. Nevertheless, he introduces two modifications. The first is that he replaces 'system of belief' with 'communality of constitution' (1992: 167). The second is that he emphasizes the importance of both communality and difference:

If we require the outlooks of others to be too like our own we lose part of the capacity to learn from them; if we insist on their dramatic dissimilarity we lose our capacity to understand them at all.... We must take it that the aliens inhabit the same physical universe as we do and are creatures evolved in broadly similar ways, whatever their cultural idiosyncrasies.... This communality of constitution gives rise to some basic similarity of outlook and hence a considerable communality of beliefs and interests which, as Davidson remarks, is so obvious and banal in its operation as normally to merit no comment. (1992: 168)

In Coady's view, this communality ultimately underwrites the belief in the reliability of testimony. Davidson's argument at Steps 1 to 5, appropriately modified, 'strongly suggests a reasonable degree of reliability about the testimony of others, whether they be aliens or natives' (1992: 168).

It is questionable, however, just how 'strong' this suggestion really is. By dropping Davidson's Step 6, and by replacing agreement in beliefs with communality of constitution, Coady has perhaps made Davidson's argument more palatable. But he also has made the argument too weak for it to be able to have much bearing on the reliability of testimony. It is not clear at all whether a common constitution really must lead to 'a considerable community of beliefs and interests'.

QUIETISM AND CONTEXTUALISM

In the last two sections I have tried to show that no one has to date succeeded in putting forward a successful and informative general justification for our reliance on testimony. Granted, I have only discussed three such projects, but I hope at least to have chosen the strongest candidates. The positions I have reviewed were either variants of reductionism and foundationalism; or else variants of fundamentalism and coherentism. Both should be given up as forms of epistemological individualism, and both should be replaced with a communitarian quietism.

To urge quietism with respect to the general justification of our reliance on testimony is of course not to deny that we often justify to ourselves and others our acceptance of the testimony of a given speaker, or why we prefer to distrust another. Such justifications are pervasive, and to ignore them would be unacceptable. But it should be apparent that such contextual questions about specific kinds of testimony are different from in-principle questions about testimony as such. In a nutshell: as reductionism stands to foundationalism, and fundamentalism relates to coherentism, so quietism combines with contextualism.[11]

---

[11] My quietism and contextualism is influenced by John McDowell and Michael Williams, who argue for counterparts of these views in other domains of epistemology (see McDowell 1994; Michael Williams 1991, 1999a,b).

Chapter 5

TESTIMONY IN COMMUNITARIAN EPISTEMOLOGY

The epistemology of testimony has been dominated by the two debates covered in the last two chapters: the controversy between inferentialists and their opponents, and the dispute between reductionists and fundamentalists. No doubt, the issues raised in these two debates concern deep and fundamental questions, and to study them is richly rewarding. And yet, too much of these debates has the nature of abstract theorizing concerning the parallels, differences, and interrelations between our four sources of knowledge. We learn too little about the role of testimony in everyday life and in science; and too little about how testimony both constitutes and presupposes epistemic communities. These are of course topics close to the heart of the communitarian epistemologist; they should be of interest to anyone trying to understand the nature of testimony.

In this chapter I turn to these communitarian themes. I shall begin by explaining the ideas of two authors, John Hardwig and Michael Welbourne. Hardwig and Welbourne first introduced communitarian themes into the epistemology of testimony. Unfortunately their work has not been discussed as widely as it should have been. I shall indicate what I regard as the strengths and weaknesses of their respective proposals, and I shall try to build my own theory upon their strengths. At this point I thus move from criticizing individualism in the epistemology of testimony to developing a communitarian perspective.

TEAMS, TRUST, AND TESTIMONY

Strange as it may seem to the non-philosopher, mainstream epistemologists pay little attention to work done in the history and philosophy of science, not to mention the sociology of scientific knowledge.[1] They do so to their detriment. I do not need to give an argument for this assessment in the abstract. Hardwig's work on testimony and trust in science demonstrates beautifully just how much epistemologists can learn from reflecting on scientific practices.[2]

The starting point of Hardwig's overall argument is an attack on an individualistic conception of evidence. According to this notion, I can only have good reasons for a belief, say, that p, if I have 'evidence' for it; and evidence is 'anything that counts toward establishing the truth of p (i.e., sound arguments as well as factual argumentation)' (1985: 336). Suppose now that my trusted doctor of many years tells me that I have a rare medical condition in my foot. Let us imagine that she has good evidence for her claims: given her years of training and experience on the job, she is able to form a reliable judgement by studying X-rays of my foot, and by observing how I walk. Assume finally that I feel no pain, do not observe any irregularity in my walk, and find nothing surprising in the X-rays (medical layman that I am). In the imagined situation, my doctor then has good reasons to believe that I have the condition. Moreover, since I trust her, I have good reasons to believe that she has good reasons to believe that I have the condition. But do my good reasons constitute evidence for the truth of the claim that I have the condition? On an individualistic understanding of evidence, the answer must be negative. My having good reasons for trusting my doctor's good reasons (for believing that I have the medical condition) does not amount to my having my doctor's good reasons (for believing that I have the medical condition). As the individualist sees it, my doctor's good reasons cannot cross over a bridge of trust. The individualist insists that my reasons to believe that I have the condition are no stronger *after* I have been told about it than they were *before* I was informed of it (Hardwig 1985: 337).

---

[1] In my estimation card-carrying epistemologists have written far more about religion than about science.

[2] Hardwig has developed his position in Hardwig (1985, 1991). His views are critically discussed in Adler (1994), Blais (1985, 1990), and Woods (1989). Hardwig's work has also been influential in feminist epistemology; see especially Code (1987).

According to Hardwig, this narrow conception of evidence conflicts with common sense. And thus he urges us to widen our concept of evidence to include second-hand evidence. On this wider conception the fact that I have been told about my condition by a trusted source constitutes evidence for my having the condition. Hardwig warns us of the consequences if we refuse this widening: refusal to accept it would lead to a severe mismatch of philosophical theory with intuitions about the scope of rational belief. It would force us to say that most of what we believe we believe in an irrational way. An epistemology issuing such a verdict would itself be suspect. We believe countless expert claims without being able to check their truth and accuracy; and in many cases we lack the necessary competence not only accidentally but necessarily (we simply do not have the talents for acquiring it). We have some obligation to check experts' credentials, usually against the judgements of other experts. But we have no obligation to always think for ourselves (1985: 339).

Believing the experts is not only an epistemic right; in many cases it might even be a duty. If my child suffers from a serious illness, I have, *ceteris paribus*, the duty to believe the doctors regarding what would be the best treatment. At least this is what we would all naturally assume. This is not to deny that the rational layperson is entitled to engage the experts in argument. She is also entitled to reject scientists' claims once there are grounds to suspect the distorting influence of political biases and interests. In the absence of reasons for doubt, however, she is ultimately obliged to admit to her 'rational inferiority'. Hardwig 'see[s] no way to avoid the conclusion . . . that the rational layman will recognise that, in matters about which there is good reason to believe that there is expert opinion, he ought (methodologically) not to make up his own mind' (1985: 344).

It is not just 'rational belief' that can be based on an appeal to authority; Hardwig makes the same claim for knowledge. Again he argues from the idea that the best available evidence might be testimonial:

belief based on testimony is often epistemically superior to belief based on entirely direct, non-testimonial evidence. For [one person] *b*'s reasons for believing *p* will often be epistemically better than any [other person] *a* would/could come up with on her own. If the best reasons for believing *p* are sometimes primarily testimonial reasons, if knowing requires having the best reasons for believing, and if *p* can be known, then knowledge will also sometimes rest on testimony. (1991: 698)

Hardwig supports this abstract claim with observations on modern science. Scientists routinely form 'teams', and such teams are formed on the basis of testimony and trust. Take the case of modern, high-energy physics. Hardwig reports on an experiment done in the early 1980s:

> After it was funded, about 50 man/years were spent making the needed equipment and the necessary improvements in the Stanford Linear Accelerator. Then approximately 50 physicists worked perhaps 50 man/years collecting the data for the experiment. When the data were in, the experimenters divided into five geographical groups to analyze the data, a process which involved looking at 2.5 million pictures, making measurements on 300,000 interesting events, and running the results through computers ... The 'West Coast group' that analyzed about a third of the data included 40 physicists and technicians who spent about 60 man/years on their analysis. (1985: 347)

The research resulted in an article with ninety-nine co-authors, many of whom will 'not even know how a given number in the article was arrived at'. Needless to say, producing the data for such a joint paper presupposes that scientists exchange information, and that they take each other's reports concerning measurements as evidence for these measurements. Empirically, it could not be otherwise. It is clear that such experiments could not be done by one person. None of the participating physicists could replace his knowledge based on testimony with knowledge based on perception: to do so would require too many lifetimes (1985: 347).

Hardwig insists that this kind of 'epistemic dependence' is not unique to modern experimental physics; it can also be found in mathematics. He refers us to the proof of a famous mathematical conjecture (de Branges' proof of the Bieberbach conjecture), a proof that involved mathematicians with very different forms of specialization (1991: 695–6).

Hardwig brings out the importance of 'epistemic dependence' to knowledge by asking *who* should be said to *know* the results reported in the co-authored physics paper. There seem to be three alternatives. Hardwig does not label them; I suggest 'strict individualism', 'relaxed individualism', and 'communitarianism'. Strict individualism insists that knowledge is the possession of the individual, and that knowledge presupposes evidence based on one's own 'on-board resources'. A philosopher adopting this option would have to deny that *anyone* knows the results of the physicists' paper. Relaxed individualism allows that individuals know 'vicariously', that is, 'without possessing the evidence for the truth of what [they] know, and perhaps without even fully understanding what [they] know'. Communitarianism sees the community as the primary knower (1985: 349). Thus it is the community of physicists, perhaps the ninety-nine co-authors, that is the epistemic subject of the knowledge reported in the paper. Communitarianism allows us to retain the idea that a knower must be in 'direct' possession of the evidence but it breaks with the assumption that such a knower must be, or can be, an individual. It is not altogether clear which position Hardwig favours. But he seems to tend towards communitarianism:

Unless we maintain that most of our scientific research and scholarship could *never*, because of the co-operative methodology of the enterprise, result in knowledge, I submit that we must say that . . . someone can know 'vicariously'—i.e. without possessing the evidence for the truth of what he knows, perhaps without even fully understanding what he knows. . . . If the conclusion is unpalatable, another is possible. Perhaps that *p* is known, not by any one person, but by the *community* . . . Perhaps [individual group members] are not entitled to say, 'I know that *p*', but only, 'We know that *p*'. This community is not reducible to a class of individuals, for no one individual and no one individually knows that *p*. If we take this tack, we could retain the idea that the knower must understand and have evidence for the truth of what he knows, but in doing so we deny that the knower is always an individual or even a class of individuals. . . . The latter conclusion may be the more epistemologically palatable; for it enabled us to save the old and important idea that *knowing* a proposition required understanding the proposition and possessing the relevant evidence for its truth. (1985: 349)

Finally, Hardwig suggests a restructuring not just of epistemology but of philosophy more widely. He makes explicit what all other theories of testimony have left largely undeveloped: testimony is an area in which epistemology meets ethics. Whether or not the expert's reporting that *p* will give the recipient good reasons for believing *p* will depend on the recipient's perception of the reliability of the expert's testimony, which in turn will depend on an assessment of the expert's character (1991: 700). Has the expert been responsible enough to keep herself informed of developments in the field? Has she been conscientious, and realistic in her self-assessment of how reliable a judgement she is able to produce? To answer such questions is to make a statement about both moral and epistemic character. Hardwig concludes:

It remains true . . . that ethical claims must meet epistemological standards. But if much of our knowledge rests on trust in the moral character of the testifiers, then knowledge depends on morality and epistemology also requires ethics. In order to qualify as knowledge (or even as rational belief), many epistemic claims must meet ethical standards. If they can't pass the ethical muster, they fail epistemologically. (1991: 708)

Hardwig's contribution to the discussion of testimony is noteworthy for more than one reason. First and foremost, his penetrating observations show that the verdicts of individualistic philosophical epistemology do not match our intuitions concerning the extension of 'knowledge'. In particular, they do not match our intuitive verdicts regarding expert scientific knowledge. And Hardwig suggests that we can fix the shortcomings of philosophical epistemology in two ways. The first, communitarian, way is to permit 'teams' to figure as epistemic subjects. To relax our epistemology in this way is both revolutionary and conservative. It is revolutionary in so far as, in doing so, we are breaking with the assumption that only individuals can be knowers. But it is conservative in another sense: it allows us to retain the intuition that knowers must have—'within themselves'— all of the needed evidence. The second way is that of relaxed individualism. It too is both revolutionary and conservative. It is revolutionary in thinking that the individual knower need not have direct evidence for her knowledge, but conservative in maintaining that only individuals possess knowledge.

Moreover, Hardwig is to be commended for his analysis of testimony in science. The position of science vis-à-vis social dimensions of knowledge in general, and testimony in particular, is of course deeply ambivalent. On the one hand, many myths about the lonely scientific genius underwrite epistemological individualism. On the other hand, it is hard to think of a form of life in our culture that is second to science in its reliance upon testimony. All the more reason then for epistemologists of testimony to focus on trust and testimony in scientific communities. Fortunately, in the year 2000 epistemologists no longer need to rely (like Hardwig) on a single source of information on how trust and testimony function in modern science. Since the publication of Hardwig's first article on the subject in 1985, historians and sociologists of science have produced a number of detailed studies documenting many of Hardwig's themes in fascinating detail. For instance, studies of past and present high-energy physics by Peter Galison (1997) and Karin Knorr Cetina (1995, 1999) describe in detail how particle-accelerator experiments involving up to 2,000 physicists are organized, and how the trustworthiness of individuals and groups is assessed. And Simon Schaffer and Steven Shapin have provided us both with a detailed description of how trust was managed among natural philosophers in seventeenth-century England, and with a sociology of scientific trust (Shapin and Schaffer 1985; Shapin 1994).

Turning to Hardwig's second example, mathematical proof, recent work by Donald MacKenzie (1999) follows the history of attempts to prove the four colour theorem[3] and shows how only close cooperation between men of very different professional backgrounds (pure and applied mathematicians, computer scientists) was able to succeed. What is more, the 'successful' proof by Appel and Haken continues to be controversial since it involves the use of computers. If computers are needed for proving mathematical truths, then we have to give up a natural and traditional way of thinking about mathematical knowledge. According to this way of thinking, one fully knows a mathematical truth only if one is able to prove it on one's own (with one's on-board resources). Standing within this tradition, Bernard Williams has argued that there is a clear distinction between knowing a mathematical truth on the basis of one's own proving, and knowing a mathematical proof on the basis of testimony (Williams 1972). If computers are essential to proving theorems, then Williams's boundary will dissolve. (Coady 1992, ch. 14 makes this point with great force.)

One important aspect of this work on testimony in modern science is that it provides us with empirical arguments for granting testimony the status of a *generative* source of knowledge. The view that testimony can merely transmit knowledge seems plausible from cases of simple one-off exchanges. An example might be asking the bus-driver whether he will be able to take us to a certain destination. It might perhaps even make sense in Alvin Plantinga's example of a crew of geographers that together produce a map of the coastline of Australia, each one working on one stretch of the coast (1993b: 87). But given the fast and endless cycles of discussion and

[3] The theorem states that every map on a plane or sphere can be coloured with no more than four colours in such a way that neighbouring regions are never coloured alike.

information exchange in, say, a place like CERN,[4] the thesis that testimony is not *generative* loses all plausibility. Reports coming from other teams, the work of one's own primary team, and finally one's own work (usually itself part of a joint action with someone else) are so tightly interwoven that it is impossible to say where others' input ends and one's own processing starts.

Hardwig's work is also helpful is drawing out some of the links between epistemology and ethics. A normative communitarian epistemology must indeed link epistemology to ethics and to normative political philosophy.[5] (A descriptive communitarian epistemology can make do with sociology and anthropology.) After all, questions of testimony, expertise, and trust are intertwined with issues of power and privilege. The powerless in society are not usually taken to be trustworthy witnesses even when it comes to providing information about their own lives.

Some of Hardwig's critics have taken issue with his claims concerning the link between epistemology and ethics. They argue that trust in science is prudential rather than moral. As Michael Blais sees it, the normal scientist is honest, abstains from fraud, and aims to produce good data, because he is interested in durable cooperation with other scientists. Failure to deliver good data might result in their refusal to cooperate with him in the future ('tit-for-tat'). In the case of fraud, they might even expel him from the scientific community altogether. In Blais's own words: 'moral trust is not a necessary foundation for the reliability of the accumulating knowledge afforded by the methods of cooperative scientific investigation' (1990: 374). Blais's alternative to Hardwig will work only if, first, scientists are able to detect non-cooperative behaviour in their colleagues; and if, second, the punishment for non-cooperative behaviour is indeed severe enough to act as a deterrent. Hardwig rightly doubts both assumptions: scientists rarely replicate their colleagues' experiments, and expulsions from the scientific community are extremely rare even in cases of serious and publicized fraud (1991: 703–5).

Despite their many strengths, Hardwig's proposals also have some short-comings. One such problem is the way in which Hardwig derives his

---

[4] The European Laboratory for Particle Physics in Switzerland.

[5] For an interesting attempt to combine political philosophy and the epistemology of testimony, see M. Fricker (1998).

conclusions from his examples of experiments in high-energy physics and proofs in mathematics. The key passages sound as if Hardwig's call for rejecting strict individualism is confined to modern science. We speak of teams of physicists and biologists working on a given problem and finding out things about the world. But we would not generally say that we 'form a team' with bus-drivers who tell us where the bus is going. Hardwig's criterion for an epistemic community is inadequate. His criterion is that the community is whatever possesses the evidence required to establish the truth of some given, and formerly desired, claim or belief. This criterion does not cover the interaction with the bus-driver. In the physics case it is hard to see where to draw the line. Surely it is inadequate to include only the ninety-nine physicists and technicians. Each one of them used equipment, calculations, and theories that were not of their own making. But treating the whole past and present 'community' of physicists as the relevant 'epistemic community' seems unsatisfactory too.

Besides, it is disappointing that Hardwig leaves open the choice between relaxed individualism and communitarianism. There is, after all, a big difference between restricting knowledge to individuals and dropping that restriction in favour of groups. Relaxed individualism does the former, communitarianism the latter.

Another odd aspect of Hardwig's theory is the way in which he relies on the idea that knowledge is true belief based on evidence. Hardwig uses this idea to motivate his rejection of strict individualism: first, he observes that individuals can have sufficient evidence only if testimonial evidence is permitted; and second, he suggests that only teams have sufficient direct evidence. It is the second step that should raise a few eyebrows. On the one hand, any given team of scientists is likely to depend, for some of its claims, on the evidence of other teams. And, on the other hand, the claim that the evidence possessed by a team is somehow 'non-testimonial' needs more elaboration. Surely a team's non-testimonial possession of evidence is not like an individual's non-testimonial possession of evidence. At least, it is not like the latter if we follow Hardwig in denying that teams have mental states of their own (over and above those of the team's members).

Finally, note that the assumption according to which knowledge is true belief based on evidence is not uncontroversial. Many epistemologists now hold that knowledge is neither 'justified true belief', nor 'true belief based on evidence', but 'true belief reliably produced'.[6] (Other epistemologists deny altogether that knowledge is a species of belief.) 'Reliabilism' allows me to say that you somehow 'know' when it will rain even if you are unable to give any evidence or justification for your belief to that effect. It is sufficient that your true belief is produced by some epistemically 'virtuous' process, like perception or memory. I am not suggesting, of course, that Hardwig is obliged to adopt reliabilism. Furthermore, adopting reliabilism does not automatically commit one to the rejection of epistemological communitarianism. But Hardwig's complete silence on the issue is a bit disappointing.

TESTIMONY AND THE COMMUNITY OF KNOWLEDGE

Michael Welbourne's book *The Community of Knowledge* (1993) offers a communitarian account of testimony. In Welbourne's work epistemological communitarianism is not based on the observation that individuals almost always have to rely epistemically on others. This was Hardwig's line of thought. In Welbourne's book communitarianism arises from noting the normative commitments created by talking to others.

Welbourne's starting point is what we might call our 'folk epistemology' of how one learns something from a knowledgeable source.[7] According to Welbourne, our folk epistemology of the prototypical case of knowledge-transmission goes like this. Knowledge can be transmitted from speaker to hearer provided that the following conditions are met: first, the speaker has the knowledge in question and is honest; second, the speaker communicates the knowledge to the hearer via an appropriate speech-act of telling; and third, the hearer both believes and understands the speaker. 'Believing the speaker' means believing that the speaker is imparting knowledge through his speech-act; and 'understanding' involves understanding his words, understanding what he is talking about, and understanding the nature of his speech-act as one of telling. Our folk epistemology assumes that knowledge is transmitted without being removed from its source; speakers retain the knowledge they pass on to others. Moreover, our folk epistemology gives special importance to the recipient's attitude towards the

---

[6] I shall discuss reliabilism in Ch. 9.

[7] By 'folk epistemology' I mean common-sense assumptions about knowledge; these assumptions are reflected in recurring patterns of everyday talk about knowledge.

speaker; no knowledge can be transmitted unless the hearer has the special attitude of 'believing' towards the speaker. Even if you tell me all that there is to know about quantum theory, and even if I can later remember every word you said, and even if I understood what you said—if I did not believe you, then no knowledge was transmitted from you to me (1993: 13).

Going beyond Welbourne, one might suggest that our folk epistemology conceives of knowledge on the model of a substance that can expand in volume without losing its density and quality. This substance expands through channels (of communication) from person to person, provided only that recipients keep their end of the channel open. To believe a speaker is to keep open the channel that connects one to her. Finally, channels are many, but the expanding substance is one; 'belief' is a countable noun, but 'knowledge' is a *singulare tantum*.

Welbourne suggests that common sense does not connect knowledge and belief in the way in which most philosophers do. Philosophers standardly treat knowledge as a species of belief, for instance as 'justified true belief' or as 'reliably generated true belief'. Welbourne, on behalf of common sense, disagrees. The transmission of knowledge is not a transmission of belief. Nevertheless, belief enters the frame in two ways. On the one hand, believing the speaker (i.e. an open channel) is necessary in order to receive knowledge from her. On the other hand, believing is the attitude of taking something to be true. People usually have this attitude towards their knowledge. But this does not mean that this attitude constitutes or defines their knowledge. To use an analogy (mine, not Welbourne's): I can be the owner of a £10 note without believing that paper money is proper money. It suffices that I live in a society where others count the note as a £10 note. Likewise, we can have knowledge that *p* without believing that *p*. It is enough that others credit us with the knowledge (1993: 84).

Welbourne does not deny that our folk epistemology permits us to talk of the transmission of beliefs as well as of the transmission of knowledge. But folk epistemology seems to speak of the spreading of beliefs first and foremost where the transmission of knowledge has failed. When the conditions for the transmission of knowledge are not fulfilled (for instance, when the speaker is not competent on the issue at hand), then it is proper to speak of the transmission of (mere) belief. Here the transmission of belief is a transmission of something principally distinct from knowledge.

Welbourne rejects what he calls 'the evidence theory' of testimony (1993: 31). According to this theory, knowledge results from testimony through the following chain of events. First, the speaker possesses a piece of knowledge. Second, the speaker couches his piece of knowledge in words. Third, the recipient hears the words and understands their content. Fourth, the recipient takes the content as one input into the process of forming a belief. And fifth, if the resulting belief is true and justified, then the recipient possesses a piece of knowledge. This will be the same piece of knowledge as the one possessed by the speaker, provided the two pieces are sufficiently similar. Welbourne insists that this picture does not conform to our folk epistemology:

It is usual in these matters to speak of the *transmission* of knowledge. But for those who subscribe to the evidence-theory, this must be a misnomer. . . . Rather there is a new beginning of knowledge in the hearer. . . . It is not, as I would have it, that knowledge in the speaker's possession has been made available to the hearer and received by him as knowledge. . . . [According to the evidence theory] the world contains innumerable separate believers . . . but no proper *communities* of knowledge. (1993: 34)

The opposite of the evidence theory is 'the authority theory' (1993: 34). This is the folk-epistemological view of testimony described above: knowledge can be transmitted by say-so. The authority theory is not a defence of blanket gullibility, however. It is not the case that the authority theory denies what the evidence theory affirms, namely that we often deliberate on who to believe and what to believe. Rather, evidence theory and authority theory locate the deliberation differently:

The difference between the two theories appears in their different perception of the goal of deliberation. For the authority-theorist I am deliberating whether to believe the speaker or not; that is, whether to regard his utterance as genuinely knowledge-bearing or merely purporting or not even purporting to be such. For the evidence-theorist the speaker's utterance *that p* is just one among the pieces of evidence I weigh in considering whether *that p* is a conclusion warranted by the evidence. On this view, even if I reach the conclusion that the utterance represents knowledge in the speaker's possession I may need more justification before I know. (1993: 35)

Welbourne also notes other features of our everyday use of the words 'to know' and 'to believe'. One such feature is that 'to know' and 'to believe' function differently with respect to transmission and commitment (1993: 3). You might believe that I believe that this book will be a bestseller. This belief of yours is—alas—fully compatible with your further belief that this book will not be bought by anyone. But if you believe that I know that this book will be a bestseller, then—on pain of irrationality—you cannot maintain that this book will not sell.

Moreover, the verb 'to know' is often complemented with that-clauses and with interrogative constructions. 'To believe' only takes that-clauses. It is grammatically correct to say that 'you know that this book will be a success', or that 'you know whether this book will be a success'. But it is incorrect to replace 'know' with 'believe' in the last expression. The fact that 'know' accepts interrogative clauses suggests to Welbourne that

we use the notion of knowledge in describing our aims when we address questions to other people, when, so to speak, we engage in 'market-place' inquiries. It seems that we naturally assume that knowledge may sometimes be had for the asking. . . . The upshot of all of this is that the verb *know*, but not the verb *believe*, has the characteristics which the idea of inquiry requires of any word which is to be capable of expressing the goals and achievements of inquiry. (1993: 9)

Perhaps the most important claim of Welbourne's epistemology is to do with the concept of 'the community of knowledge'. Welbourne holds that acts of transmitting knowledge from one person to another create 'a primitive community of knowledge': 'A primitive community [of knowledge] consists of two people knowing the same thing and recognising each other as sharers in that knowledge; so each can act on the assumption of knowledge in the other and they will be able to act co-operatively' (1993: 25). If two people, say a and b, form such a community with respect to an item of knowledge, say p, then each will know that p; each will know that the other knows that p; and each will know that the other knows that the other knows that p. Moreover, the community will have a 'dynamic quality' (1993: 26). That is to say, the community of a and b will be recognized by a and b as the product of an act of communication. Furthermore, a and b will regard themselves as 'sharing' in this knowledge, and as committed to teaching p as a fact, and as a truth. And finally, a and b will accept that they can be criticized if they later on fail to reckon with p. p will acquire the status of *what is known* in their community, and in this role it will mark an 'external, objective standpoint' (1993: 52).

Welbourne distinguishes such a 'community of knowledge' from 'the community of belief' (1993: 26). The members of a community of belief coincide in the contents of their beliefs only accidentally. For instance, the passengers on the bus I took this morning all believed that the bus would take them to their destination. But they each arrived at this belief independently of one another; and they felt no commitment to pass their beliefs on to others.

Welbourne emphasizes that (according to our folk epistemology) knowledge, the transmission of knowledge, and the community of knowledge are all inseparable. Knowledge is what it is only in so far as it is transmitted to others, thereby creating, and enlarging, communities of knowledge. It follows from this that knowledge is never—at least not in the prototypical cases—a possession or property of individuals in isolation; it is a property of 'members of some actual or possible community [of knowledge]'. It is therefore wrong to insist that an individual could be a knower even though no one accepts his say-so as knowledge:

The supposed solitary knower whose say-so is not accepted by anyone is rather like a man with a £10 note in a community which has no use for money. It is senseless to insist that what he has is worth £10 in this context. And it would be equally pointless to insist that [a] solitary [individual] knows, when his say-so is universally rejected. (1993: 84)

As I have already indicated, Welbourne's work is an invaluable resource for developing a communitarian epistemology. It is unfortunate that it has not attracted wider attention among epistemologists.

Welbourne's epistemology is a reconstruction of our folk epistemology as this folk epistemology is found in salient patterns of our talk about knowledge and its transmission. Welbourne is not trying to revise our everyday understanding of knowledge; he is aiming to assert the right of our common-sense understanding of knowledge against mainstream epistemology. If epistemology is about codifying our pre-theoretical intuitions about knowledge into theory proper, then (if Welbourne's analysis is correct) epistemology has failed in its task.

Here it is interesting to note that our folk epistemology and our mainstream philosophical epistemology fall on different sides of the divide between communitarianism and individualism. While our folk epistemology is centred around the idea of a community of knowledge, our philosophical epistemology is based on the idea of the solitary knower. This observation raises the interesting historical question of how an attempt to do justice to (folk-)epistemological intuitions could have ended up in individualism. And it provides a justification for the attempt to rebuild philosophical epistemology along communitarian lines.

Welbourne's way of analysing the relationship between knowledge and belief is interesting. A number of other epistemologists have also advised against the analysis of knowledge as a form of belief, most notably Edward Craig, Karl Popper, Colin Radford, Zeno Vendler, and Timothy Williamson.[8] But it may well be doubted whether Welbourne has clinched the point. Take, for instance, Welbourne's suggestion according to which belief is an attitude (of taking something to be true) that people take towards their knowledge. This is one-sided. It does not do justice to the fact that we also talk of beliefs as objects ('I have had this belief for a long time') and that we also speak of knowledge as an attitude ('I know that she is here'). Or consider Welbourne's analysis according to which 'to know' allows for syntactic structures not shared by 'to believe'. This will not impress the defender of the traditional view. He will regard such differences as superficial and as perfectly consistent with the idea of knowledge as a species of belief.

Welbourne's most important contribution to epistemology is his defence of the idea that the community is central to our idea of knowledge. It seems right to say that sharing knowledge with others amounts to sharing entitlements and commitments with them.[9] At least this is so in many prototypical cases of knowledge. The entitlements include drawing on this knowledge as premises in arguments, or referring to this knowledge as an objective and external standard for what others ought to reckon with. Commitments include answering to others' entitlements, building further upon this knowledge, and seeking to spread new items of knowledge to interested others. Assume that I claim to know how long it takes to travel from Cambridge to Edinburgh; I tell you, and you believe me and tell me so. In doing so, we agree that we should not consent to anyone who suggests a different travel period, that we shall inform each other in case it turns out

[8] Craig (1990); Popper (1972); Radford (1970); Vendler (1972); Williamson (1995, 2000).
[9] I adopt the terms 'entitlement' and 'commitment' from Brandom (1994).

that we did not possess knowledge after all, that we shall let this information figure in an unchallenged way in travel plans, and so on.

We can perhaps go beyond Welbourne by saying that the sharing of knowledge creates a *new subject of knowledge*: the community. And, once this community is constituted, it is epistemically prior to the individual member. This is so since the individual community members' entitlement and commitment to claiming this knowledge derive from their membership in this community. The individual knows as 'one of us', in a way similar to how I get married as 'one of a couple', or how I play football as 'one of a team'.

At the same time, it must be acknowledged that Welbourne has given only a partial defence of communitarianism. In particular, he does not take on alternative individualistic views in any detail. No individualist will be impressed by Welbourne's insistence that the solitary knower cannot know. Welbourne appeals to the intuition according to which the solitary knower is like the man with a £10 note in a community that has no use for money. This intuition is not widely shared, however. Why can't we say that Robinson Crusoe comes to know the fauna on his island, and even before Friday joined him? And do we not frequently attribute knowledge to animals and machines? These knowers are clearly non-social. It is disappointing that Welbourne does not tackle such prima facie counter-examples to his claims. (In Part II I shall suggest how these cases can be handled by the communitarian.)

It is also doubtful whether Welbourne has done enough in order to distinguish his authority theory of testimony from the evidence theory. Welbourne needs to tell us what 'deliberation about whether to believe a speaker or not' means other than determining whether or not what the speaker tells you is to be accepted. Perhaps the difference comes down to the distinction between the scope of deliberation. According to the authority theorist we do not deliberate on each given piece of evidence; once we have decided to make some person our authority we take their word on trust. The evidence theorist insists that such procedure is never acceptable; each token of a claim has to be considered on its merit.

Note also that Welbourne focuses mainly on cases where one individual already in the know transmits her knowledge to another individual. This makes it appear as if individual knowledge is after all primary with respect to the knowledge of the community. Here we had better use Welbourne's analogy of the £10 note to protect his most valuable insights from epistemo-logical individualism. The £10 note becomes legal currency only once others accept it as such. It does not constitute money prior to their acceptance. Likewise, we should say that (at least in the two-person scenario) a claim does not constitute knowledge until it has been accepted, in the appropriate way, by the recipient.

There are other ways too in which Welbourne's focus on a two-person scenario is potentially misleading. On the one hand, it does not distinguish the case where a claim first acquires the status of knowledge from the case where a piece of already accredited knowledge is passed on. On the other hand, Welbourne's scenario, and his analysis of it, fail to explain the background against which communities of knowledge are formed. The two complaints are interconnected. Usually when something is trans-mitted as knowledge, speaker and recipient are already standing in a normative context. Take the teacher–student relationship for example. While it is true that the teacher's transmission of (a given piece of) know-ledge to the student creates a new set of commitments between them—a community of knowledge, if you will—these commitments, and this com-munity, build upon a whole nexus of prior entitlements and commitments. Moreover, whatever the teacher transmits as claims to knowledge *is* know-ledge; these claims do not first *become* knowledge because of the student's agreement. In teaching the student, the teacher enlarges, much more than creates, a community of knowledge. And he can bring the student into this community since the student usually already shares a prior community of knowledge with the teacher.

Welbourne's lack of interest in the background of knowledge transmis-sion can explain why his concept 'believing the speaker' remains somewhat thin and uninformative. Indeed, the concept remains a primitive term in Welbourne's analysis. How do we know which speakers to believe? And what kind of attitude is the attitude of 'believing someone'—rather than 'believ-ing something'? To answer the first question first, it seems clear that in many cases it is 'common knowledge' who best to believe. That is to say, know-ledge about authoritative sources results from the same kinds of processes as the knowledge that these authorities transmit. This shows that the forma-tion of a community of knowledge presupposes prior communities of knowledge.

Turning to the second question (i.e. what kind of attitude is believing someone?), I wonder whether Welbourne's 'believing someone' is not best captured with concepts like 'trust' or 'participant stance'. Trust in a person's word is more than simple reliance; trust among people has a moral quality. As Richard Holton puts it in a different context:

I think that the difference between trust and reliance is that trust involves something like a participant stance towards the person you are trusting. When you trust someone to do something, you rely on them to do it, and you regard that reliance in a certain way: you have a readiness to feel betrayal should it be disappointed, and gratitude should it be upheld. . . . When the car breaks down we might be angry; but when a friend lets us down we feel betrayed. . . . trusting someone is one way of treating them as a person. (1994: 67)[10]

Here 'participant stance' contrasts with the 'objective stance'; within the latter we treat the person as an object of intervention rather than as a co-subject.

Finally, pushing Welbourne's analysis to its natural conclusion, and thus further than he seems willing to go, we can formulate the resulting position as follows: 'knowledge' is a social status like money, and thus it only exists in so far as there are items upon which we are willing to impose the status. And the collective imposition of the status happens in and through local transmissions, first of knowledge-claims, and later of accredited knowledge-items. To put things in this way indicates what is needed in order to underwrite this theory: a richer theory of social institutions and social statuses—a theory that brings out the performative aspect implicit in all offering and accepting of testimony.

PERFORMATIVES AND THE COMMUNITARIAN EPISTEMOLOGY OF TESTIMONY

The communitarian approaches of both Hardwig and Welbourne make clear that testimony is a generative source of knowledge. Hardwig focuses more on the object of knowledge; how the pooling of evidence enables teams to know more about the world. Welbourne concentrates more on the subject of knowledge; how testimony constitutes knowers with specific commitments and entitlements. In what follows, I shall try to bring both sides, the subject and

---

[10]   Holton's argument builds on earlier work by Strawson (1974) and Baier (1986).

the object, under one theoretical roof. I shall show that the communicative generation of new communal subjects of knowledge is due to the same type of process that also generates (aspects of) objects of knowledge. And I shall make explicit how testimony is linked both to the generation of the social status 'knowledge' in general, and to the imposition of that status in particular circumstances. I would not be able to promise all this were it not for a theory of social institutions developed by Barry Barnes, David Bloor, and John Searle.[11]

Since my argument will be a bit complex, it is perhaps best if I provide a structured preview. My argument has five steps: *Step 1* argues that performative testimony is a generative source of knowledge. *Step 2* introduces 'communal performatives'; these are performative utterances, carried out by a collective 'we'. They have the form 'We (the community) hereby take these discs to be coins'. Communal performatives help us understand how social institutions and social statuses are constituted. Communal performatives are of course fictitious; in reality, communal performatives exist only in a fragmented and widely distributed form. And the fragments of communal performatives are carried by other forms of testimony. *Step 3* draws the natural consequence from the earlier considerations and insists that (almost) all testimony is involved in constituting social institutions. In *Step 4* I establish that 'knowledge' is itself a social status. I do so by contrasting 'knowledge' with 'natural kinds' like 'elephant', 'artificial kinds' like 'typewriter', and 'social kinds' like 'money'. I also explain how the status 'knowledge' is attached to particular claims, and what role agreement plays in such processes of attribution. Finally, *Step 5* deals with the ways in which our belonging to epistemic communities informs our choice of testifiers, and how and why we tend to 'repair' speakers' truthfulness and trustworthiness. Throughout this argument I am using 'testimony' in the sense of 'utterances we can learn from'.

Performative Testimony

The easiest way for me to lay the foundations of my communitarian theory of testimony is to return to my insistence, early on in this chapter, that

---

[11] My specific use of the constative–performative distinction owes less to Austin than to Kent Bach, Barry Barnes, David Bloor, and John Searle. See Bach (1975); B. Barnes (1983b, 1988, 1995); Bloor (1996, 1997); Searle (1995). Compare also Itkonen (1978); Lagerspetz (1995); Tuomela (1995).

performative speech-acts had better be included within the category of testimony. I defended this claim by saying that performative speech-acts are ubiquitous in everyday life, and that they are, indirectly or implicitly, involved even in other forms of talk. I maintained, furthermore, that if we allow for 'performative say-so' to count as testimony, then testimony is a generative source of knowledge. I shall now argue for these ideas in more detail.

We can bring performative testimony into sharp relief by contrasting it with the way in which traditional epistemology of testimony thinks of past-tense constative say-so. (Below I shall offer a new interpretation of constative say-so, an interpretation that combines constative and performative elements.) Let us take the latter case first (Fig. 5.1). A state of affairs, say p, obtains, from some time in the past onwards; say, from $time_1$ onwards. The person who will eventually testify that p, say person a, acquires that knowledge sometime after $time_1$, say, at $time_2$. At a still later stage ($time_3$), a tells another person, b, that p. And on that basis b knows that p. The obtaining of p and the telling that p are independent events. a's knowing and b's knowing are not fully independent events, since b's knowing is due to a's knowing. But the link is only external or accidental. b could have found out that p some other way. Indeed, on the traditional view, b would have been epistemically better off if she had found out that p directly, and on her own. Moreover, after a has told b that p their interaction ends. There is no room in the traditional picture for a nexus of obligations and rights between a and b either before or after a's telling b that p. And finally, it is easy to see how this picture motivates the view according to which testimony is not a

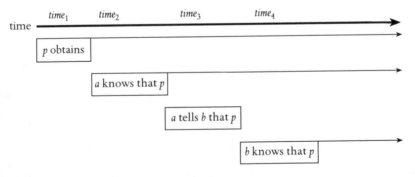

FIG. 5.1. The traditional model of constative testimony

generative source of knowledge. Although *a* has passed knowledge on to *b*, no new knowledge has been created. One reason why this intuition is so strong is that 'knowledge' is a *singulare tantum*. We cannot increase the overall amount of water by pouring it into many rather than one bottle. And we cannot increase the overall amount of knowledge by pouring it into many rather than a single mind.

The case of performative testimony is different in almost all of these respects. Again it might help to start by considering a graphical representation (Fig. 5.2). Performative testimony does not allow us to think of the state of affairs *p*, the telling, and the knowing as discrete, sequential, and independent events. The registrar *a* tells the couple *b* that they have now entered a legally binding relationship of marriage; and by telling them so, and their understanding what he tells them, the registrar makes it so that they *are* in the legally binding relationship of marriage. For the registrar's action to succeed, the couple has to know that they are being married through his say-so, and he has to know that his action of telling does have this effect. Moreover, *a* and *b* form a community of knowledge in so far as their jointly knowing that *p* is essential for *p* to obtain. That is to say, *a* and *b* enter into a nexus of entitlements and commitments, and it is this nexus

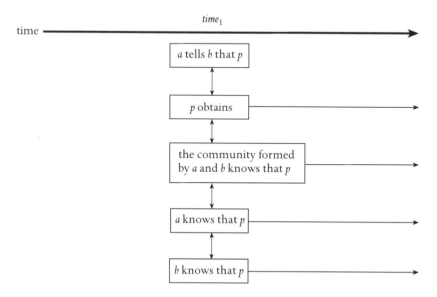

FIG. 5.2. Performative testimony

that makes it so that each one of them is entitled to claim that p. The registrar has to use certain formulas ('By the powers invested in me by the state of California . . . ' etc.), bride and groom have to confine themselves to certain expressions (a simple 'yes' will do fine), and each one commits himself or herself, and entitles the other, to refer to p as a fact subsequently. More principally, we might say that 'getting married' is an action that one cannot do on one's own (or just with one's partner). It is an action that is primarily performed by a 'we'.

In the case of performative testimony, there is no better way for the recipient to find out that p than being told that p. There is *no other* way, and thus *no better* way, of getting married than to be declared married by an appropriate official. It is only via the performative telling ('I hereby declare you . . . ' etc.) that one enters into the relationship. Performative testimony is thus a generative source of knowledge: the knowledge that p simply does not exist prior to the telling.

There are two important features of performatives that I want to emphasize here in particular. Performatives are 'self-referring' and 'self-validating' utterances. A performative utterance like 'I hereby declare you . . . ' refers to itself in so far as it announces what it does. It does not simply go ahead with the declaring; it tells you that it is doing the declaring by using the phrase 'I hereby declare you . . . '. In the right circumstances a performative utterance is also 'self-validating'. That is to say, although the performative utterance is not true of an independent reality prior to it, it is true of a reality that it itself creates. And thus we might say that (when carried out successfully) performative utterances make themselves true.[12] The self-referential and self-validating character of performative testimony explains how it can be a generative source of knowledge.

Communal Performative Testimony

In the above example the registrar's performative testimony brings about a new social fact, the fact that bride and groom acquire the social statuses of 'being legally married'. We might say that the registrar 'imposes' this social status upon bride and groom by his performative say-so. In having a social

---

[12] Of course, performative utterances can be successful only given an institutional setting. Performatives do not just constitute social institutions, they presuppose them as well.

status imposed upon them by performative testimony, our fictitious couple is not alone. All social statuses, and all social institutions, are due to performative testimony.[13] This is obvious, say, for the case of the registrar: he will have been appointed through someone's performative say-so. Some higher-up official will have said, or written, at some point something like 'By the power invested in me by the Queen, I hereby declare you a registrar of the Crown'.

Things get more complicated, however, as we turn to social institutions more generally, especially to social institutions not anchored in law. What about a social institution like greeting people? Or what about the social institution of the family? In other words, what about social institutions and statuses that do not owe their existence to an individual's performative say-so?

I propose that we should think of such institutions and statuses in analogy to the case in which an individual generates a social status. Institutions and statuses need not be created by the speech-act of a single individual; they may well be created by the speech-act of a community. Such speech-act has the form 'We hereby declare it right to greet people known to us'. The individual subject is replaced with a communal one. Of course, such communal speech-acts are fictitious; we do not create social institutions by speaking in chorus. What happens instead is that the communal institution-creating performative testimony is typically *fragmented and widely distributed over other speech-acts*. The communal performative is never explicitly made; it is only made implicitly or indirectly. It is carried out by people when they do other things: when they talk about greeting their colleague on the way to work; when they actually greet their colleague; when they criticize others for not having greeted them back; or when they chastize others for not having greeted them first. All these other speech-acts—most of which are in fact constatives—'carry' the relevant communal performative.

This is of great importance for the epistemology of testimony. Testimony, even past-tense constative say-so, is always in part performative, never mind whether we are dealing with physicists at CERN or with bus-drivers in Edinburgh. Almost all testimony carries parts of widely distributed communal performatives. Almost all testimony is *in part* performative;

---

[13] Again, since I am not here concerned to explain the ultimate origins of social institutions, I neglect the fact that usually performatives presuppose as well as create social institutions.

thus almost all testimony is generative of knowledge; and thus almost all testimony is involved in the constitution of social institutions.

Whether one finds the last claim plausible or not will depend on one's conception of a social institution. The claim will be palatable only once it is accepted that there are more social institutions in heaven and earth than are dreamed of in many traditional forms of sociology and philosophy. The definition adopted here is broad: whatever is created and maintained by a widely distributed communal performative is best thought of as a social institution. The extension of this concept of social institution includes the old favourites of the sociology of institutions—the family, the state, and the church—but it also leaves room for authorities, rules, taxonomies, knowers, and the category of knowledge itself.

The fact that communal performatives are fragmented and widely distributed over other speech-acts does not alter the fact that they are self-referring and self-validating. What creates, or constitutes, a social institution is the communal performative. As a widely distributed performative it is carried out in and through the entire gamut of references to the social institution. But ultimately this entire gamut of references has no other referent than itself. Summed up, *per impossibile*, in a single communal performative, it says: 'We hereby declare that it is correct to greet people one knows'. And this communal performative is as self-referential and self-validating as any performative ever could be. This does not mean that every *fragment* of a communal performative is fully self-referential or self-validating. No fragment can constitute the institution as a whole; and thus it refers to the social institution as an 'almost' or 'semi-' independent entity.

Constative Testimony as Performative Testimony

The social institutions that I have used as examples up to this point have been money and marriage. 'Money' and 'marriage' we might call 'social kinds' and distinguish them from 'natural kinds' like 'rose' or 'elephant', and 'artificial kinds' like 'typewriter' or 'table'.[14] All three kinds of kinds owe their existence to widely distributed communal performatives, but there are, nevertheless, important differences between them. Take away all talk,

---

[14] I have developed the concept of 'artificial kinds' in Kusch (1999). My analysis of natural and social kinds follows B. Barnes (1983*b*).

and whatever is referred to as a social kind ceases to exist. That should occasion no surprise: in the case of social kinds, the talk, ultimately, is the referent itself. The case of natural kinds is not equally straightforward: take away all talk, and the *category* 'elephant' disappears. What so disappears is our communally instituted and maintained taxonomy of animals and our exemplars and prototypes for what elephants look like. But whatever it was that we formerly referred to as 'elephants' will still be there. Finally, turning to the case of typewriters, once we withdraw the talk and the performatives, typewriters *qua* typewriters will cease to exist. But we shall leave behind a changed physical world.

The cases differ, but performative testimony is involved in the constitution of all three kinds of entities: the social institutions of, say, money and marriage; the communally instituted and maintained taxonomies and exemplars of, say, elephants; and the communally instituted and physically created artefacts of, say, office machines. All constative or performative testimony relating to marriage is involved in the constitution of the social institution of marriage. Every constative testimony about elephants carries part of the communal performative speech-act which constitutes the category of elephants, and in doing so, re-enforces the conventional ways of delimiting this category, and helps to entrench the conventional exemplars. And every constative testimony about typewriters supports the communal performative speech-act which constitutes the category of typewriters.[15]

The relationship between constative and communal performative testimony is thus intriguingly complex. On the one hand, constatives *presuppose* communal performatives. We can make claims about marriages, elephants, or typewriters only because our communal performatives have constituted the taxonomies and exemplars needed for making such claims. On the other hand, constatives *perform* (i.e. partially constitute) communal performatives. They carry out the fragments of widely distributed communal performatives.

Above I wrote that 'almost every' piece of constative testimony supports some communal performative or other. Let me add a word on the 'almost'. We had better leave room for the possibility that testimony is rejected. In

---

[15] All this is not a statement of anti-realism. One can take systems of classification as social institutions even if one believes that the categories cut nature at its joints. I shall argue against both realism and anti-realism in Part III.

some cases of rejection it seems reasonable to assume that the rejected testimony will not be part of a communal performative. If someone called 'rhinoceroses' what her peers call 'elephants', then her talk would not help to entrench the category of elephants. Put differently, testimony can constitute statuses like 'wife' or 'elephant' only if it is accepted by the recipient(s).

Knowledge as a Social Institution

We have now seen that a performative dimension is involved in all testimony, indeed, in all telling and talking. In good part, therefore, testimony is generative of its referents and generative of knowledge about these referents. Even if we left things here, we would have arrived at a theory of testimony that breaks with the traditional individualistic picture and shows that constative and performative testimony are usually mixed together in a way that rules out the simplifications of Figure 5.1. But we cannot stop here. A communitarian epistemology worth its salt must not leave the concept 'knowledge' unaccounted for. The status 'knowledge' itself needs to be brought under the theoretical umbrella suggested above.

Is 'knowledge' a natural kind term like 'elephant', a social kind term like 'wife', or an artificial kind term like 'typewriter?'[16] In a way only the whole of this book can give an answer to this question. But given the question's importance it is good to take a first stab at it here. (And then return to it in greater detail in Part II.) At this point, let us look only at cases of testimonial knowledge, and ignore the cases of animals and the social isolates. I cannot think of any better way to decide this question than to apply the existence test introduced above. We have to choose between these three options:

(1) 'Knowledge' is like 'elephant'. Whatever it is that we are picking out as knowledge, it can continue to exist (though not *as* knowledge) when we cease to maintain the communal performative (that institutes the animal taxonomy and exemplars of 'being an elephant').

(2) 'Knowledge' marks a social status like 'money' or 'marriage'. The social institution of knowledge disappears when the communal performative disappears.

---

[16] My discussion of different ways of construing the concept of knowledge has been helped by reading Zagzebski (1999).

(3) 'Knowledge' is like 'typewriter'. The physical or mental entity or process that we produce and label 'knowledge' can continue to exist (though not so labelled) when we cease to maintain the communal performative (that institutes the relevant taxonomy and exemplars for 'being a typewriter').

Option (2) surely is most in line with our intuitions about knowledge by say-so; and it is strongly suggested by Welbourne's analysis of our folk epistemology. Note, however, that even if we opt for treating knowledge as a natural kind we will have to understand knowledge on the basis of a communal performative: just as the category of elephant has its communally instituted and maintained exemplars and models, so too has the category of knowledge.

Knowledge then is a social status; and it is constituted by a communal performative ('We hereby declare that there is a unique, commendable way of possessing the truth, and we hereby call this way "knowledge" '). Knowledge is a social referent created by references to it; and these references occur in testimony—as well as in other forms of talk. Such talk includes claiming that something is knowledge, challenging knowledge, testifying to knowledge, questioning knowledge, and so on through the entire gamut of possible references. Knowledge as a status to which testimony can aspire is constituted in and through more testimony. Knowledge by say-so is a social status to which we can lay claim. But we can do so only because direct and indirect reference is made to this status in endless instances of constative and performative testimony; and it is this direct and indirect reference that creates knowledge as a status.

Of course, we do not lay claim to this status in general; we lay claim to it in connection with specific claims. Knowledge as a social status is constituted by the widely distributed communal performative. How are we to think about cases where we lay claim to the status knowledge for specific claims? What about the claim of the no. 17 bus-driver that his route takes me past the Festival Theater? And what about the claim by the biologist that he has discovered a new species—similar to, and yet distinct from, elephants? My answer will not come as a surprise, given my earlier discussion of Welbourne's work. These instances of testimony will acquire the status 'knowledge' for those that are willing to join the testifier in a nexus of epistemic

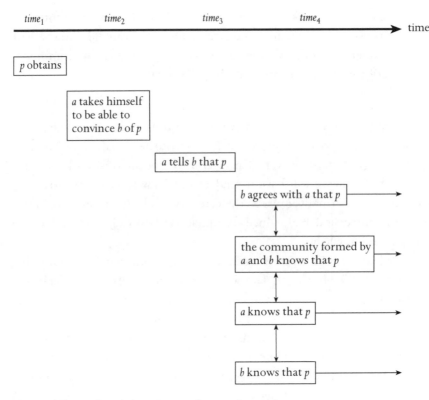

time₁   time₂   time₃   time₄

time

p obtains

a takes himself
to be able to
convince b of p

a tells b that p

b agrees with a that p

the community formed by
a and b knows that p

a knows that p

b knows that p

FIG. 5.3. The performative aspects of constative testimony

commitments and entitlements; they will acquire the status 'knowledge' for those that join the testifier in a 'community of knowledge'.

Perhaps Figure 5.3 might help to bring out how, on the theory I have been developing, the formation of a community of knowledge is related to testimony. It might also help to see which elements of the traditional picture (of Fig. 5.1) I retain.[17] The state of affairs p that the testifier a reports to the recipient b might well obtain before a's telling. The second stage in my theory is not, however, that a knows that p, but merely that a takes himself to be able to convince b of p. This is to signal that although individuals can lay claim to the social status in isolation, they cannot actually be granted this status.

[17] Needless to say, we are concerned only with the performativity involved in attaching the social status of 'knowledge' to specific claims. The figure does not cover the communal performative constituting knowledge as a social status in general; and it does not cover the performatives that constitute (aspects of) the object of knowledge.

Moreover, the second stage is optional; it need not occur for testimony to be possible. At *time₃* *a* tells *b* that *p* and during *time₄* *a* and *b* constitute a community of knowledge. It is at this stage that performativity enters into the fray. *b*'s agreement with *a* as to whether *p* constitutes them as a community of knowledge. And forming this community is tantamount to initiating and maintaining the communal performative 'We hereby declare ourselves to be the epistemic subject of *p* and are thereby committed and entitled to use *p* in the ways in which the general institution of knowledge suggests'. Of course, in practice this communal performative is fragmented and widely distributed over all the references that *a* and *b* make to *p* in their talk and actions. The important point is that *a* (or *b*) knows that *p* only in so far as she is a member of the communal knowledge-constituting *we*. She knows because she has a social status within that *we*. And she cannot acquire that status on her own.

Of course there are situations where *a*'s claims do already have the status of knowledge, and where *b* is more or less obliged to form a community with *a*. In such a teaching context *p* is 'taught as a fact'. And finally, there are naturally cases in which knowledge is attributed to someone who is not a member of the community of knowledge. *a* and *b* might decide that *c* is a reliable testifier—and knower—as to what the weather will be like tomorrow, even if *c* doubts that he has any such ability (he might think he is just guessing). In such cases the entitlements and commitments are carried by *a* and *b* alone.

Background Communities

Agreeing with the testifier need not take a very explicit form, and it can be the outcome of a wide variety of different attitudes. Such attitudes range from a critical examination of the testifier all the way to accepting her testimony on the basis of blind trust. Different situations and different claims call for different attitudes. Which attitude is appropriate in which context is something that most of us know on the basis of our experiences with different types of people and situations. Often it will be the social status of the testifier—as, say, bus-driver, teacher, or car salesman—that will indicate to us which attitude is appropriate. Or our socialization might include the teaching of maxims as to how to assess testimony. Here, for instance, is a list of maxims that Steven Shapin finds in the seventeenth-century literature on our topic:

(i) assent to testimony which is plausible; (ii) assent to testimony which is multiple [i.e. which has multiple sources]; (iii) assent to testimony which is consistent; (iv) assent to testimony which is immediate [rather than given a long time after the reported event]; (v) assent to testimony from knowledgeable or skilled sources; (vi) assent to testimony given in a manner which inspires just confidence; and (vii) assent to testimony from sources of acknowledged integrity and disinterested-ness. (Shapin 1994: 232)

If such rules are accepted and widely referred to as rules in talking and telling, and thus in testimony, then naturally they will themselves become social institutions. And as such they will be products of, as well as influences upon, social interaction; they will be both products of testimony and influences upon the reception of testimony.

Of course, knowledge of such rules cannot ever secure a unique verdict: the seven maxims are not independent of one another; they can be priori-tized in different ways, and there might even be inevitable circularities in their application. In the end there is no escape from the fact that the knowledge of the social world that we acquire in our socialization has in good part the character of 'a tacit skill': we get things roughly right but we are unable to say how exactly we manage to do so.[18]

Focusing on the ways in which we know or decide whom to trust may help to deflect one important worry. According to this worry, my account follows Welbourne in being too preoccupied with the ways in which testimony *creates* communities, and too little concerned with the ways in which testimony *presupposes* communities. I feel entitled to plead 'not guilty' to this charge; after all, I have emphasized all along that all testimony presupposes the prior existence of social institutions like taxonomies and exemplars. But perhaps it is worth while to conclude by bringing to the fore a different way in which testimony presupposes and involves communities.

Social institutions are not created once and for all. Their persistence over time is dependent upon the constant intervention of participants. Up to this point I have captured this 'constant intervention' only somewhat one-dimensionally. That is to say, I have talked about the need for repeated and continuous references to the institution in participants' talk. But this perspective misses something important about social institutions in general,

---

[18] For skill and socialization, see Collins (1985, 1990) and Collins and Kusch (1998).

and the social institution of testimony, or 'telling how things are', in particular. What it misses is the role of 'repair' in the constitution of communities. The repair work I have in mind protects a social institution by giving its members reasons not to opt out of, or disrupt, its functioning. Humans do this routinely; given what kinds of creatures we are, and whatever we happen to do, we cannot help building and rebuilding smooth social relations with the people around us.

Concerning the various institutions of telling and talking, this repair work takes the specific form of glossing speakers' utterances in a way that avoids accusations of dishonesty and incompetence. Such accusations are always explosive and endanger social institutions that are fundamental to much of our social life. We might get by without the social institution of the monarchy. We might even get by without the social institutions of money and marriage. But it is hard to imagine what life would be like without telling how things are. It is not surprising, therefore, that we protect the institutions surrounding telling and testimony especially carefully by ensuring that most speakers most of the time come out as speaking the truth. Our institutions perhaps do not presuppose general veracity. What they do presuppose is the general absence of challenges to claims of veracity.[19]

---

[19] Shapin (1994) has influenced my thinking about testimony generally. The same is true of Wittgenstein (1969) and Stroll (1994). Forrester (1997) prevented me from advocating the view that social life presupposes general veracity.

Chapter 6

SUMMARY

I have now completed the tasks of criticizing individualism in the epistemology of testimony, and of developing a communitarian viewpoint concerning knowledge and talk. Because it is all too easy to get lost in the nitty-gritty of arguments for and against specific claims, I conclude with a summary of the main claims and observations.

It is misleading to use 'testimony' as a covering term for our epistemic interdependence. It would be better to confine 'testimony' to its original legal context. Moreover, the narrow legal meaning of 'testimony' has acted as an unacknowledged 'intuition-pump'. Among other things, it is responsible for the mistaken individualistic view that testimony is not a generative source of knowledge. Epistemically relevant talk contains much more than the reporting of past events. Performatives are of particular importance not least because they are obviously a generative source of knowledge in the social world.

The debate for and against inferentialism has been damaged by an insufficient separation of phenomenological, psychological, pragmatic, and normative questions. For instance, inferentialists usually start from a contrast between perceptual belief as direct and testimonial belief as inferential. They also suggest that the inferences (or the monitoring) involved in the reception of testimony are often unconscious. But if the inferences are unconscious, then the contrast with perception is lost. Furthermore, participants in this controversy are sometimes guilty of psychological reification and social dilution. Alleged analyses of the phenomenology of testimony are really misbegotten studies of language games in which testimony is tested and invoked. And epistemologists tend to draw the wrong conclusion from the correct observation that contexts of testimony vary: they try to understand the variety of cases as mere variants of one or two extreme cases. A communitarian epistemology had better leave these projects behind.

In the dispute over the best global justification of testimony I rejected both of the salient solutions: reductionism and fundamentalism. I renounced reductionism as a form of foundationalism. Hume's reductionism is a non-starter. For instance, Hume is unable to produce a testimony-free stratum of beliefs in terms of which testimonial beliefs could be justified. I opposed fundamentalism as a form of coherentism. I considered two main fundamentalist arguments: the argument from the coherence of our sources of beliefs and the argument from radical interpretation. Both turned out to be insufficient. The coherence argument is too weak in two ways: it does nothing for the sceptic and nothing for the already convinced. The argument from radical interpretation failed to establish a link between agreement and truth. It also did not succeed in taking us from the truth of beliefs to the truth of testimony. Against both these individualistic contenders in the debate over justification I urged communitarian quietism and contextualism. Since testimony is constitutive of all forms of justification, it is senseless to provide a general justification for it. Only local and contextual justifications are meaningful.

I discussed two earlier projects for a communitarian epistemology of testimony and went on to develop my own. All three projects claim that the giving and receiving of testimony must be understood as a social–communal process. This process presupposes prior communities and it creates new ones. My own proposal relied heavily on the idea of social institutions as communal impositions of statuses. I argued that almost all testimony is generative of social statuses and that such statuses are involved in all forms of knowledge. Finally, I argued that knowledge itself is a social status, and that accepting another's testimony amounts to forming an epistemic community with them.

Appendix I.1
BAYESIANISM AND TESTIMONY

Treatments of testimony based on probability theory are not for every reader; and thus I shall deal with Alvin Goldman's recent work on testimony only in this appendix (Goldman 1999, ch. 4). Goldman is a self-proclaimed social epistemologist who wants his epistemology to help us evaluate 'social epistemic practices', that is, social practices in which knowledge is acquired and assessed. The yardstick is 'veritistic value'. It works as follows. Let 1 stand for 'true' and 0 for 'false'. And let individuals have 'degrees of belief' in propositions where degrees of belief range from 0 to 1. For instance, take the true proposition that this bus goes past the Festival Theater. And assume that you assign only a small degree of belief to this proposition, say 0.2. In this case the veritistic value of your belief is small. You are 0.8 away from the truth (i.e. from 1). I believe the proposition with a very high degree of confidence, say 0.9. Thus my veritistic value is higher than yours. Goldman wants to identify those social epistemic practices that will lead to an increase in the veritistic value of our social epistemic practices.

In particular, Goldman wants a new social epistemic practice for assessing the trustworthiness of testimony. His new method of assessment amounts to using a specific theorem from probability theory, called Bayes' theorem. This theorem defines how a rational reasoner would change his probability assignment to a hypothesis in light of new evidence. Here is an example of how this would work in the case of testimony.

Peter has two friends, John and Mary. Peter wonders whether John had a beer in the pub last night. Let us write this in abbreviated form as 'Peter wonders whether b'. As it happens, Peter does not deem it very likely: he knows that John rarely drinks beer and dislikes pubs anyway. In light of this, Peter assigns b a very low probability, 0.2. We can write this as:

$$p(b) = 0.2.$$

After Peter has decided on this value, Mary 'testifies' to him that John did have a beer in the pub last night. Abbreviated: $T[b]$. This poses a problem for Peter: how should he revise his 'prior probability' assignment for b in the light of $T[b]$, that is, in the light of Mary's report? Or, to use the language of probability theory, which probability should he assign to b, given that he now has got $T[b]$? In formal terms:

$$p(b/T[b])?$$

Obviously this will depend on whether or not Peter regards Mary as a competent and honest testifier. More specifically, it depends on what degrees of probability Peter assigns to the following two scenarios: that Mary would testify that b when b was the case, and that Mary would tell him b when b was not the case. Formally the two cases to be distinguished as:

$$p(T[b]/b)$$

and

$$p(T[b]/\sim b).$$

The 'likelihood ratio'

$$p(T[b]/b)$$
$$p(T[b]/\sim b)$$

determines whether Peter should revise $p(b)$ upwards or downwards in light of Mary's testimony. If $p(T[b]/b)$ is higher than $p(T[b]/\sim b)$, then he should revise $p(b)$ upwards; if $p(T[b]/b)$ is identical with $p(T[b]/\sim b)$, then he should leave $p(b)$ unchanged; and if $p(T[b]/b)$ is lower than $p(T[b]/\sim b)$, then he should revise $p(b)$ downwards.

Let us assume that Peter is fairly confident in Mary's trustworthiness, and that he assigns values as follows:

$$p(T[b]/b) : 0.7$$
$$p(T[b]/\sim b) : 0.3.$$

Bayes' theorem tells us how to combine all this information into one calculation for deciding in which direction Peter should revise his estimate for $p(b)$, given that he has received Mary's testimony:

$$p(b/T[b]) = \frac{p(b) \times p(T[b]/b)}{p(b) \times p(T[b]/b) + p(\sim b) \times p(T[b]/\sim b)}.$$

Inserting our numerical values, we get:

$$\frac{0.2 \times 0.7}{0.2 \times 0.7 + 0.2 \times 0.3} = \frac{0.14}{0.14 + 0.06} = 0.7.$$

Thus, in light of Mary's testimony that John had a beer last night, Peter's 'posterior probability' should be 0.7.

I shall not follow Goldman into the details of his proof that Bayesian inference 'has veritistic merit in *any* report environment, that is, regardless of the honesty or dishonesty, competence or incompetence of the witnesses' (1999: 115). Goldman shows that *if* the reasoner somehow gets the likelihood ratio right—surely a big 'if'—then there is a high probability that use of Bayes' theorem will move her degree of belief closer to the objectively correct value of either 0 or 1.

Goldman concludes that

> there is a social belief-forming practice—'social' because it operates on the reports of others—with positive V-value [i.e. veritistic value]. In saying that there 'is' such a practice, I do not mean that it is actually in use. I mean that we as theorists can specify such a *possible* practice and urge people to realize and conform to it as closely as possible. This illustrates in the domain of testimony how veritistic social episte-mology can identify social practices with good veritistic properties. (1999: 130)

Goldman's treatment of testimony is normative in a strong sense: he thinks that we should change the ways in which we adopt testimony. He is not interested in descriptive questions; his treatment of testimony tells us nothing of the role of performative testimony in the constitution of social institutions, nothing about social statuses, and nothing about the global justification of testimony. The rush to normativity has a price, however. The price is that Goldman remains tied to all of the traditional assumptions, including the mistaken belief that the prime case of testimony is the legal case. This is deeply disappointing coming from an author who promises to provide us with 'a general theory of societal knowledge' and with 'a philosopher's contribution to the shaping of an information-rich society'. Surely, the first step of such a general theory should have been a systematic broadening of the traditional narrow concept of testimony.

Moreover, even as a treatment of legal testimony Goldman's contribution is not really compelling. Here too the neglect of all descriptive and empirical issues is the culprit. Goldman does not seem to have been aware that the use of Bayesian inference has been considered by the courts (in Britain) between 1995 and 1996. In *Regina* v. *Denis John Adams*, a rape case, the defence sought to counter the prosecu-tion's DNA evidence with another 'scientific method': Bayesian inference. An expert witness instructed the jury in the use of the method. When the case eventually reached the Court of Appeal, the use of Bayesian inference became one of the central issues of contention. As reported by the sociologists Michael Lynch and Ruth McNally, the Court of Appeal rejected its use. The arguments of the Court are worth considering.[1]

---

[1] My excerpts of the judges' verdict come from Michael Lynch and Ruth McNally (forth-coming).

First, the judges pointed out that Bayes' theorem 'can only operate by giving to each separate piece of evidence a numerical percentage representing the ratio between the probability of the circumstance A and the probability of B, granted the existence of that evidence. The percentages chosen are matters of judgement: that is inevitable'. The judges expressed the worry that such 'objective figures' might easily 'conceal the element of judgement'.

Second, the judges suspected that the theorem's methodology requires too rigid an approach to evidence: 'the theorem's methodology requires . . . that items of evidence be assessed separately according to their bearing on the accused's guilt, before being combined in the overall formula'. As the judges saw it, the evidence that juries typically deal with cannot be divided up in this way: for instance, 'the cogency of . . . identification evidence may have to be assessed, at least in part, in the light of the chain of evidence of which it forms part'.

Third, the Appeal Court insisted that juries should not be constrained in their use of methods of evaluation: 'Jurors evaluate and reach a conclusion not only by means of a formula, mathematical or otherwise, but by the joint application of their individual common sense and knowledge of the world to the evidence before them.' The judges therefore rejected the idea that expert evidence should 'induce juries to attach mathematical values to probabilities arising from non-scientific evidence adduced to the trial'.

In short, the verdict says that credibility and plausibility (of evidence and witnesses) are not the sort of things that are best thought of in discrete quantities. The judges were also concerned to preserve the independence of the jury; they do not want expert witnesses that tell the jury how it would be most rational for them to calculate in questions of guilt and innocence. I find the judges' reasoning convincing. And I think that we should be suspicious of any Bayesian treatment of testimony assessment that does not discuss the judges' concerns. Of course, I do not mean to suggest that philosophers should abstain from contributing to normative issues relating to testimony assessment. But I suspect that any such treatment will only prove useful if it fulfils two conditions: it must be based on a descriptively adequate and context-sensitive account of testimony; and it must recognize the limitations of applying formalisms to human judgements.

Part II

Empirical Belief

Chapter 7

QUESTIONS ABOUT RATIONALITY

In Part I I argued that communitarianism is needed to develop an adequate epistemology of testimony. In Part II I shall propose that communitarianism must also be central in the epistemology of empirical knowledge. The argument of Part II is thus a generalization of the discussion of Part I.

In order for us to understand the primary concerns of the epistemology of empirical knowledge it is best to start from an analogy. Take the moves in a game of chess. Of any given move we can ask: 'Is it rational or irrational to make this move at this stage in the game?' Let us call such a query a 'first-order question'. First-order questions in chess request a judgement on whether a specific move deserves to be called rational or irrational. They are answered with reference to specific positions on the chessboard, with reference to specific players and their abilities, and with reference to specific earlier and possible later moves. Stepping back from individual moves and games, we can also pose much more principled 'second-order' questions about the rationality of chess moves. Such second-order questions include the following:

> Why is it that the dichotomy 'rational versus irrational' can be applied to chess moves? Are there constraints on possible chess moves in virtue of which some chess moves are rational and others are irrational? Are chess moves rationally constrained? Is there a boundary within the realm of possible chess moves that divides the rational from the irrational moves? And what constitutes this boundary?

Answers to second-order questions differ from responses to the first-order question. Answers to second-order questions describe and explain general features of the game of chess: its rules for moving the pieces; its rules for determining winner and loser; the ways in which moves can link together tactically and strategically; the role of psychology in the choice of strategies, and so on.

The epistemology of empirical knowledge focuses on second-order questions with respect to empirical belief. Matters are more complicated in this realm, however, since we can ask two different kinds of first- and second-order questions regarding empirical beliefs. We can ask about truth and we can ask about rationality:

First-order Question about Truth. Is this empirical belief true or false?

Second-order Questions about Truth. Why is it that the dichotomy 'true versus false' can be applied to empirical beliefs? Are there constraints on possible empirical beliefs in virtue of which some empirical beliefs are true and others are false? Is there a boundary within the realm of possible empirical beliefs, a boundary that separates true empirical beliefs from false empirical beliefs? And what constitutes this boundary?

First-order Question about Rationality. Is it rational or irrational to hold (or form) this empirical belief?

Second-order Questions about Rationality. Why is it that the dichotomy 'rational versus irrational' can be applied to empirical beliefs? Are there constraints on possible empirical beliefs in virtue of which some empirical beliefs are rational and others are irrational? Are empirical beliefs rationally constrained? Is there a boundary within the realm of possible empirical beliefs that divides the rational from the irrational empirical beliefs? And what constitutes this boundary?

The epistemology of empirical knowledge does not focus on second-order questions about truth. Most authors assume some version of the correspondence theory of truth, which suggests approximately the following answer to Second-order Questions about Truth: Empirical beliefs can be true or false since beliefs purport to be about states of affairs in the world. A belief is true if it corresponds to the state of affairs to which it refers; otherwise it is false. I shall scrutinize this view in Part III.

In this part I shall discuss a number of proposals on how to answer Second-order Questions about Rationality. These proposals claim that the rationality or irrationality of an empirical belief is a function of the belief's relation to

experience; and/or
other beliefs; and/or
the world; and/or
its (the belief's) causes; and/or
the ability of the believer to handle objections; and/or
social institutions.

In saying that the epistemology of empirical knowledge seeks to answer Second-order Questions about Rationality, I am imposing my own interpretation and terminology upon the field. Most epistemologists treat as the central dichotomy the opposition 'justified versus unjustified', rather than the contrast 'rational versus irrational'. I use the latter in order to bring otherwise distinct positions under the same heading. In my usage 'rational true belief' covers both 'justified true belief' and 'reliably caused true belief'.

I shall argue that none of the earlier proposals constitutes a successful answer to Second-order Questions about Rationality. Only the move to communitarian epistemology provides a solution. Communitarianism insists that empirical beliefs can be rational or irrational only in so far as the attributers of the respective beliefs are members of epistemic communities. Social relations between human beings are the only source of normativity and the only source of standards for rationality and irrationality. Non-communitarian views deny at least one of these claims. Some of them construe the natural world as a rational constraint on our empirical beliefs; others insist that communities are of no epistemic significance.

In thinking about the theories to be discussed in Part II, I have found it useful to resort to a rational reconstruction of the recent history of epistemology—taking great liberties with the actual history. The structure of Part II reflects this rational reconstruction. In order to highlight the advantages and strengths of communitarianism, I shall accentuate the shortcomings of six alternative views: foundationalism, coherentism, reliabilism, direct realism, consensualism, and interpretationalism.[1] (A seventh view, contextualism,

[1] There are many more epistemologies of 'empirical knowledge' than there are epistemologies of testimony. In consequence, I shall have to typify and select. I shall occasionally deal with types of doctrines rather than with individual theorists; and I shall be highly selective in my choice of representative authors. My selection of such authors is based on their importance in the

will be treated as a close relation of communitarianism.) I shall discuss the theories in pairs. Each pair can be thought of as an instance of the famous Hegelian structure of thesis and antithesis. (But no knowledge of Hegel is assumed!) The members of each pair are related in similar ways to earlier and later pairs; they stand at an equal distance to communitarianism; they are concerned with one common issue; and they seize upon opposite solutions to the same problem. At this point it perhaps suffices to present the positions in a picture (Fig. 7.1). Each pair will be explained in more detail in subsequent chapters.

At this juncture it is more urgent to take up one general worry. How do Second-order Questions about the Rationality of empirical belief stand with respect to the distinction between normative and descriptive epistemology? This question is indeed pressing. On the one hand, I have characterized communitarian epistemology as close to the descriptive project of the sociology of knowledge; on the other hand, several of the epistemological positions mentioned are generally regarded as normative projects. How can I take both sides as putative solutions to the same problem (i.e. to Second-order Questions about Rationality)?

The answer lies with the special character of Second-order Questions about Rationality. It is impossible to formulate a normative epistemological theory without giving at least an implicit answer to (some of) these questions. Consider what normative epistemologies of empirical belief do. Obviously, they tell us how we ought to justify our beliefs. For instance, they instruct us to justify our beliefs by showing that these beliefs form a coherent set. In doing so, normative epistemologies define constraints on rationally held beliefs. Normative epistemologists insist that, say, coherence ought to be such a rational constraint for us. This involves at least two strands of commitments to descriptive accuracy. On the one hand, normative epistemologists usually appeal to human psychology in defending their normative recommendations. They suggest that we have been using coherence all along as our epistemic standard for justified empirical belief. We just did not formulate it clearly enough. On the other hand, normative epistemologists do not just want to formulate abstract ideals; they want their epistemic standards to be achievable for us. It follows that normative epistemologists

contemporary debate, on the accessibility of their writings, and on the strength of their arguments.

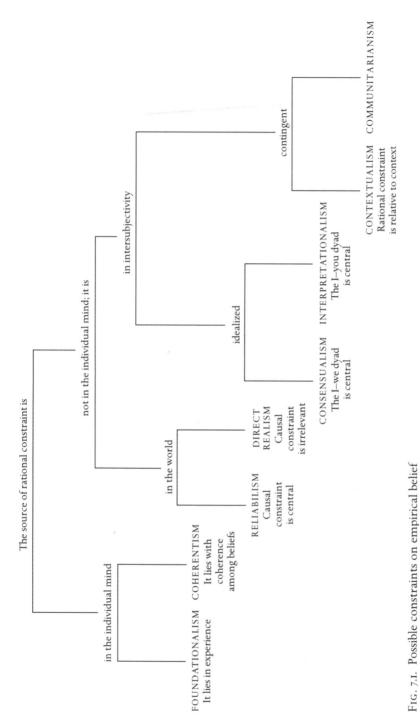

The source of rational constraint is

in the individual mind

not in the individual mind; it is

in the world

in intersubjectivity

idealized

contingent

FOUNDATIONALISM
It lies in experience

COHERENTISM
It lies with coherence among beliefs

RELIABILISM
Causal constraint is central

DIRECT REALISM
Causal constraint is irrelevant

CONSENSUALISM
The I–we dyad is central

INTERPRETATIONALISM
The I–you dyad is central

CONTEXTUALISM
Rational constraint is relative to context

COMMUNITARIANISM

Fig. 7.1. Possible constraints on empirical belief

cannot avoid commitments to views on who we are: we are the kind of creature for whom adherence to their normative principles is possible. Sometimes these commitments are stated explicitly; sometimes they can be easily identified. In considering explicitly normative theories of empirical belief alongside more descriptive theories, I am thus not comparing apples and oranges; I am comparing explicitly descriptive theories with the descriptive commitments of normative theories.

Chapter 8

FOUNDATIONALISM
AND COHERENTISM

Twentieth-century Anglophone epistemology has been dominated by debates between (various versions of) foundationalism and (different forms of) coherentism. An analysis of the recurring features of these debates is essential for motivating the communitarian project.

Prolonged debate between two positions is possible only if they share a good number of assumptions. The argument between foundationalists and coherentists is a case in point. A first common idea is the classic conception of knowledge as justified true belief. I have already mentioned that this conception has its opponents: philosophers who deny that knowledge is a species of belief, and philosophers who reject justification as a necessary condition for knowledge. Our current pair is united in opposing, or ignoring, such deviations from the traditional view. Moreover, most versions of foundationalism and coherentism are individualistic and internalistic. On the one hand, they focus on the knowledge or justification possessed by an individual. On the other hand, they demand that the knower (or justified believer) be aware of the reasons for her belief, and base her belief explicitly upon these reasons. Put differently, foundationalists and coherentists take *self-attribution* as the central case of knowledge attribution. And finally, foundationalism and coherentism approach the issue of rational constraint on empirical beliefs in similar ways. Both have a two-step model. The first step consists of worldly processes causing certain events in the individual mind. In the second step, these *intra*-mental events (and the relations between them) rationally constrain beliefs about the world.

INTRODUCING FOUNDATIONALISM AND COHERENTISM

It is hard not to feel the intuitive appeal of both foundationalism and coherentism.[1] Put in a nutshell, the foundationalist claims that our empirical beliefs should be founded upon our experience of the world. Only my experience can justify my beliefs. Equally plausibly, the coherentist suggests that only a belief can justify another belief. It is hard to see how a mere sensation could justify anything. Justification is a relation between propositional (sentential) items.

As clear-cut as these intuitions are, it has proved difficult to work them out in detail. What follows is a bird's-eye view of both positions. The main ingredients of the two positions, their differences and their common features, are perhaps best summed up by means of diagrams.[2] These diagrams are based on the conventions illustrated in Figure 8.1.

Imagine the mind of the epistemic subject (as Realm$_2$ and Realm$_3$) embedded in the world (as Realm$_1$). The inner circle (Realm$_3$) is the realm of beliefs. The contents of beliefs are 'propositions'. That is to say, the contents of beliefs are statement-like and candidates for being true or false. Propositions are *what* we believe. We believe, for instance, that grass is green, that Mary is smart, or that $2 \times 2 = 5$. Each belief's content is either true or false. Propositional contents contrast with non-propositional contents. The latter are not candidates for truth or falsehood. But they are candidates for existence or non-existence. An example of a non-propositional content is the experience (i.e. sensation) of an itch. The itch either exists (obtains) at a given time or it does not; but it cannot be either true or false. Realm$_2$ is the realm of non-propositional experiences. Foundationalism, coherentism,

---

[1] Clear statements and defences of the foundationalist position are Audi (1988), Chisholm (1989), Lewis (1946), Moser (1989), and Bonjour (1999). All of these texts attack coherentism and other alternatives of foundationalism. A fine review is Triplett (1990). Early attacks on foundationalism include Sellars (1997) and Austin (1964). More recent criticisms are Bonjour (1985) and Roth (1991) (this is a review of Moser 1989); Plantinga 1993a; Rescher 1973, 1974; Michael Williams 1999a. Of these texts Sellars (1997), Bonjour (1985), and Rescher (1973) defend coherentism. Another important defender of coherentism is Lehrer (1986, 1990a,b, 1997). Donald Davidson is sometimes regarded as an advocate of coherentism; see e.g. Davidson (1989a). For an excellent anthology of critical reactions to recent versions of coherentism, see Bender (1989). For a useful critical survey of both positions, see Haack (1993). A very influential paper on the relationship between foundationalism and coherentism is Sosa (1991b). See also McDowell (1994).

[2] Diagrams close to these are invoked, but not actually drawn, in McDowell (1994).

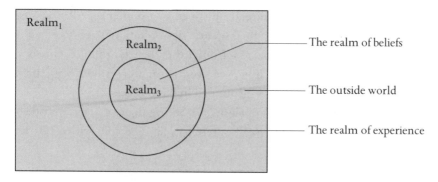

Fig. 8.1. Conventions for diagrams

direct realism, and reliabilism all distinguish between these three realms, but they differ in how they conceive of their interactions and their respective contents. They place relations of causation and justification at different boundaries, and they situate reasons and concepts in different realms. In my use of the term, an experience is within the 'space of concepts' if it essentially involves a concept. For instance, one cannot experience a piece of music as 'jazz of the 1940s' unless one has at least the concepts 'jazz' and '1940s'. Foundationalists believe, however, that there are also non-conceptual experiences; itches, for example. Finally, the 'space of reasons' captures all those entities that can stand for X and/or Y in the formula 'X justifies Y'.[3]

Foundationalism is represented in Figure 8.2. The external world impinges causally on the realm of experience, thereby causing the subject to have non-propositional experiences. Realm$_2$ is taken to be non-conceptual. Realm$_2$ contains what is 'given' in experience prior to the imposition of any conceptual or propositional structure. Elements of the realm of experience (Realm$_2$) justify (or 'make right') beliefs in Realm$_3$. Hence the space of reasons covers both the realm of experience (i.e. Realm$_2$) and the realm of beliefs (i.e. Realm$_3$). Elements of the realm of experience justify beliefs in two ways, depending on whether the beliefs in question are 'basic' or 'non-basic'. Think of basic beliefs as making up the boundary of the inner

---

[3] The term 'space of reasons' goes back to Wilfrid Sellars. He writes that 'in characterizing an episode or state as that of *knowing*, we are not giving an empirical description of that episode or state; we are placing it in the logical space of reasons, of justifying and being able to justify what one says'. Sellars is a coherentist but using his term does not commit us to siding with coherentism. See Sellars (1997: 76).

circle. A belief is basic if it is directly justified by experience. All non-basic beliefs, that is, all beliefs inside Realm₃, are 'right', 'rational', or 'justified' if, and only if, they can be inferred from other beliefs. Infinite chains of inference are not acceptable, however. And thus, all (justificatory) chains of inference must ultimately be grounded in basic beliefs.

Coherentism is represented in Figure 8.3. Seeing the two diagrams side by side should clarify where the main differences lie. The coherentist restricts

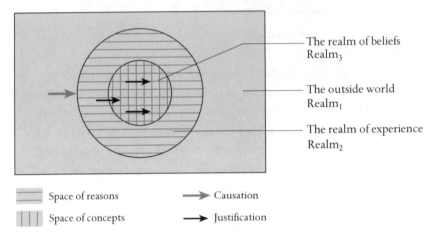

FIG. 8.2. A diagrammatic representation of foundationalism

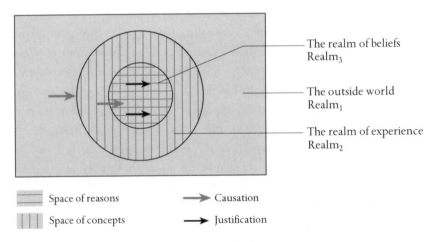

FIG. 8.3. A diagrammatic representation of coherentism

the space of reasons to the realm of beliefs, and she reduces the realm of experience (or sensations) to the same 'a-rational' status as the external world. But the realm of experience is conceptual. Realm₁ and Realm₂ work as causal rather than rational constraints on Realm₃. The external world causes sensations, and these sensations in turn cause beliefs. Once the beliefs have been produced, they can then be evaluated epistemically as 'justified' or 'unjustified'. And such evaluation amounts to determining their 'fit' with other, earlier beliefs. According to the coherentist, 'nothing can count as a reason for holding a belief except another belief'. Thus all and only beliefs are within the space of reasons. Most coherentists also disagree with the foundationalist over the role of concepts in experience. They assume that experience is conceptual. (Ergo Realm₂ has horizontal lines.) But this does not mean that Realm₂ is propositional. Finally, since no belief is ever justified by experience, the coherentist has no need for the foundationalist's basic beliefs. Of course, the coherentist need not assume that all beliefs are equally distant from experience; but proximity to sensations is a causal, not a rational, measure.[4]

There is a second short cut to the essentials of foundationalism and coherentism. It is helpful to use types of social structure as models for foundationalists' and coherentists' conceptions of the epistemic mind (cf. Rescher 1973: 332). The foundationalist view of the epistemic subject is

---

[4] My diagram does not of course capture all elements of coherentism. First of all, it does not tell us what coherentists mean by 'coherence'. The minimal requirement is 'logical consistency'. A set of beliefs is logically consistent if all its members can jointly be true. Stronger requirements are 'inferential and explanatory connectedness'. Beliefs are inferentially connected if they follow from one another; they are connected by relations of explanation if they explain one another. (What I believe about the heart fits with what I believe about the blood and its circulation; the function of the heart explains the circulation of blood around my body.) Moreover, most coherentists insist that justification has a 'non-linear' and 'holistic character'. Justification would be 'linear' if it proceeded from one belief to the next, and so on, one by one. Coherentists maintain that a given belief is hardly ever justified by just one other belief. Instead, justification has to do with the 'mutual support' that beliefs give one another. Coherentists reject 'linear' justification not least in order to escape the so-called 'regress argument'. This foundationalist argument insists that every line of justification must terminate somewhere; and for that termination not to be dogmatic, it had better be in the realm of basic beliefs. Making justification non-linear disarms this argument. Furthermore, coherentists claim that coherence is the *only* source of justification for a belief. It is this that sets them apart from foundationalists, who sometimes allow that the coherence among beliefs provides an additional source of justification for them. Finally, the coherentist proposes that single beliefs are justified by their membership in a coherent whole. Wholes are justified if their elements cohere with each other to a high degree.

'theocratic'. Each member of the society of beliefs has its rank 'by birth'. That is to say, to be basic or non-basic are intrinsic properties of beliefs. Basic beliefs are the pillars of society; they are the foundations upon which the social fabric rests. They owe their special status to the fact that they provide the link to 'the world beyond (beliefs)'; in this, they remind one of the priests of a theocratic society. Just as the priests are closer to God than any lay folk, so basic beliefs are closer to experience than any other beliefs. We might push the metaphor even further by imagining that the priests of a theocratic society owe their position to their reports of apparitions. This strengthens the parallel between priest and basic belief; the basic belief owes its status to its special proximity to what is 'given' in perceptual experience. And the congregation of non-basic beliefs can be connected to 'the world beyond', to 'the given', only through the mediation of basic beliefs.

Coherentism's image of the mind is reminiscent of an egalitarian society. At least it does not know of apparitions as forms of legitimization. In the coherentist society of beliefs, positions of leadership must be earned. What makes one belief more important than another is that it is involved in, and presupposed by, a greater number of different groups in society. At the same time, the coherentist society does not tolerate disagreement; meta-beliefs police society and make sure that every belief fits in with every other belief. Spontaneity is allowed, perhaps even encouraged, but only if it ultimately accords with established laws and traditions. Different schools of coherentism have developed this basic social scenario into different directions. Some have emphasized the harmony that results once all beliefs cohere with all others. Others have put more stress on the competitive element. New beliefs have to compete for a place in society by 'networking'. In the case of conflict the better-connected belief always wins.

A COMMUNITARIAN CRITIQUE OF
FOUNDATIONALISM AND COHERENTISM

Foundationalism and coherentism both try to make sense of the possibility of rational constraint on empirical beliefs. I now want to argue that they do not have the resources needed for explaining this possibility. Neither foundationalism nor coherentism has the resources to answer Second-order Questions about Rationality.

My point is simple. Rational constraint cannot be found where both positions are looking for it. It cannot be found among elements in the depth of the individual mind—whatever the route by which the elements have entered. It is not that foundationalism or coherentism has not yet found the appropriate elements. It is that individual-psychological facts or worldly facts on their own are not normative. No fact or event can rationally constrain a mind; only norms can. A norm might demand that the presence of a certain fact should give rise to some action. But without such a norm there is no obligation and no duty.

It will not do to defend our pair by saying that they simply take the norms for granted, or that they are providing us with rational reconstructions of the norms that we always already follow. Even if this were the case, we would still have to chastise both positions for failing to explain how such norms exist, how they govern the individual mind, how they change, and how they are sanctioned. But things are in fact worse than this. Foundationalism and coherentism make it impossible for any such norms to take effect.

At this point we need to remember Wittgenstein's important lesson (Wittgenstein 1968). Wittgenstein famously pointed out that no account of rightness is adequate unless it is able to show how 'being right' differs from 'seeming to be right'. No one has a concept of 'right' unless she understands statements of the form 'this action seems to me to be right, but I realize that it might well be wrong'. Put differently, the contrast between 'seems' and 'is' is central to the language games we play with 'right' and 'wrong'. It follows that any account that collapses 'is right' into 'seems to be right' is no account of rightness at all. Wittgenstein also showed that there was only one way to avoid such collapsing. Such collapsing can be evaded by showing how an alleged 'is right' can be criticized and corrected by others as being merely a 'seems right'. The seems–is contrast is at the centre of our evaluations of how far, and whether, others deviate from our private and collective judgements.

Wittgenstein is not ruling out the possibility that an isolated individual might correct herself. We do so all the time. It seemed to me that the door was open (I heard noises), but now I realize that it is in fact shut. I thus have shifted from an 'is right' (it is right that the door is open), to a mere 'seems right' (it seemed to me to be right that the door is open). And I have done so in the light of what I now take to '*be* right'. Does this not prove that the distinction 'is right/seems right' can be drawn on the level of the individual? It does not. To see why, we only need to note that the 'is right' that we have invoked to correct a 'seems to be right' is itself only a new 'seems to be right'. I started with (*a*), and then moved to (*b*) in the light of (*c*):

(*a*) It is right that the door is open.

(*b*) It seems (or 'seemed') to be right that the door is (or 'was') open.

(*c*) It is right that the door is closed.

But this (*c*) is really in the same boat as (*a*): it too only states what seems to me to be right, (*d*):

(*d*) It seems to me to be right that the door is closed.

Instead of escaping the 'seems right' of (*b*) we have only arrived at the new 'seems right' of (*d*); instead of getting to an 'is' we have multiplied the 'seems to me'. The only way for me to escape from this iteration is to draw on a 'standard' of what is right. Such a normative standard must be (largely) independent of my individual judgements; otherwise it again collapses into a 'seems'. And it must be such that it can be used to evaluate my judgements. What can this standard be? It cannot be any fact or object in the world. Facts and objects are not normative in and of themselves. Nothing about a door fixes how it 'must' be viewed or understood. Facts and objects can figure as standards only when they have been adopted as standards. And such adoption had better 'be right' rather than 'seem right'! Since individual judgements and objective facts cannot provide the standards, what can? Only the community, suggests Wittgenstein. What seems right to almost everyone—that is, the collective 'seems right'—is the most we can get in terms of an 'is right'. It is a normative standard largely independent of my own judgement; and thus a foil against which I can draw the distinction between 'is right' and 'seems right'. This does not mean, of course, that the community might not sometimes turn out wrong. (I appreciate the need for further arguments in defence of what one might call 'the community thesis regarding normativity'. I return to it in much greater detail in Chapter 13.)

Neither foundationalism nor coherentism (in their typical individualistic garb) is able to draw the distinction between 'is right' and 'seems right'. Take foundationalism first. Foundationalists place the foundations of knowledge at a point where they are in principle accessible only to the individual knower. Non-conceptual experiences cannot be 'shared' with anyone; not with another person, and not with oneself at a later time. I can try to place you in the same location and make you look in the same direction; and yet there is no guarantee that your non-conceptual experiences will be anything like mine. Alternatively, I might try to describe my experiences to you. But in doing so I turn the non-conceptual into the conceptual, and transform ultimate foundations into hearsay. The same goes for the relation between me today and me tomorrow. Memory of, and testimony about, non-conceptual experiences are no substitute for those experiences themselves. Memories and reports lack the status of ultimate grounds. It is this inaccessibility of the foundationalist's grounds of knowledge that makes them unsuitable candidates for any involvement in rational and normative constraint. There is no space here for the distinction between 'is right' and 'seems right' to take any hold. Whatever seems right to the epistemic subject at a given time is right; there is no space here for correction by others or oneself. (Note that my point is not just that foundationalism fails to address issues like testimony or the formation of epistemic groups. My criticism is rather that foundationalism is unable to make sense of normativity even within its own chosen domain, the knowledge possessed by the individual.)

The same is true of individualistic versions of coherentism. These versions assume that a belief is justified if it fits with *all*, or *most*, of my contemporaneous other beliefs. But who has access to that totality? Who is able to judge whether my assessment of the fit is correct? Surely not another person—for it is of course impossible to convey to you the totality (or most) of my beliefs. And surely not to myself at another time, for similar reasons. And thus there is again no position from which the judgement of a given epistemic subject at a given time could be rationally assessed or corrected. Again we get no distinction between 'seems right' and 'is right'.

All this is doubly devastating. Foundationalism and coherentism are unable to account for rational constraint, and they are unable to defend the intuition that knowledge can be shared through communication. It comes as no surprise, therefore, that twentieth-century epistemology has had so little to say about testimony.

There is a second communitarian criticism of both positions that is worth introducing at this point. This criticism turns against the 'invariantism' and 'psychologism' of our pair.[5] Foundationalism and coherentism are 'invariantist' in so far as they ignore the contextual nature of justification. We all know that types of justification vary with contexts; that different contexts have their own peculiar and characteristic forms of obligation, challenge, and defence. Take a claim like 'there is a shadow in the middle of this X-ray photo'. How far such a claim needs to be justified depends on whether one is confronted by groups of laypersons, of GPs, of X-ray specialists, of journalists, or transient acquaintances in a bar. And how one ought to defend the claim is prescribed by one's role and profession as medical doctor, physiologist, or layman. Foundationalists and coherentists are unable to account for such relativity. Foundationalists do not just say that in each context some beliefs or other are fundamental. (That would be like saying that any layperson can be a priest.) They say that some beliefs are fundamental, whatever the contexts happen to be. And coherentists do not suggest that coherence has local parameters, or that it is a matter only of subsets of beliefs—maybe subsets distributed over different persons. Coherentism demands that a given set of beliefs must cohere with all (or most) beliefs of a subject at a time.

Invariantism goes hand in hand with psychologism. Since foundationalism and coherentism fail to account for varying contexts, they also fail to reckon with the social nature of justification. And this leads them to rely on psychology in their attempt to describe epistemically virtuous states of mind. This is a mistake. We learn what it is to justify a belief by engaging in language games in which specific types of beliefs are justified according to specific epistemic standards. It is these language games that fix our understanding and our intuitions regarding justification. The social nature of justification is apparent even in situations when we investigate our own beliefs in social isolation. In such cases we simply simulate, or 'pretend-talk', language games of justification. (That's what I do anyway.) Foundationalism and coherentism bypass all this by asking 'how must a belief be related to other beliefs (and non-conceptual content) for the belief to be justified?' And this question is understood as demanding a psychological answer: a list of those psychological types of relations among beliefs to which we (episte-

[5] The charge of invariantism is central in Michael Williams (1991). For a survey of different uses of 'psychologism', see Kusch (1995).

mologists) attach high epistemic status. To specify epistemically virtuous states is, for foundationalism, to enumerate specific ways in which beliefs of one kind (e.g. basic beliefs) relate to beliefs of another kind (non-basic beliefs). And each of these two kinds can be described with the tools of the introspective psychologist. The coherentist identifies constellations of beliefs, again placing his hopes on psychology. If contextualism and communitarianism are right, then this is a fruitless endeavour. Epistemically virtuous states are social states, not psychological states. And as social states they are variable and contextual.

Chapter 9

DIRECT REALISM AND RELIABILISM

INTRODUCING THE POSITIONS

I shall take John McDowell's recent work as representative of direct realism (McDowell 1994). McDowell's direct realism can best be understood through his opposition to foundationalism and coherentism. McDowell rejects one central assumption common to both: the assumption that the border between the epistemic subject and the external world can be crossed only by causes. The direct realist's alternative tears down all frontier barriers and controls. He does so by arguing that on both sides of both borders—inner circle and outer circle in our diagrams—we find entities of the same kind: concepts and propositions. Once the barriers are down, the world's rational control over empirical beliefs is no longer a difficult issue. An empirical belief is right if it fits with the way the world is. The difficult problems concerning causality disappear. Figure 9.1 represents this view.

The reliabilist's criticism of foundationalism and coherentism is the mirror image of the criticism advanced by the direct realist. Like the direct realist, the reliabilist is also dissatisfied with the dualism of causal and rational constraint. But whereas the direct realist promotes a monism of rational constraint, reliabilism tends towards a causal monism. That is to say, the reliabilist has no need for a space of reasons; and he lets causality rule supreme. A belief is rational if and only if it has been produced by a reliable method—a method that produces (or would produce) a high frequency of true beliefs in a long series of applications. Whether or not the epistemic subject is even aware of this is irrelevant. As the reliabilist sees it, rational constraint simply is causal constraint, and it is nothing else. Figure 9.2 seeks to capture this position by getting rid of the space of reasons, while retaining the arrow of justification. Arrow of justification and arrow of causation fuse into one. (I have not marked the 'space of concepts' either, since such space has no special significance to the reliabilist.)

Direct realism and reliabilism are perhaps further apart than foundationalism and coherentism. Both constitute different 'slides' away from the

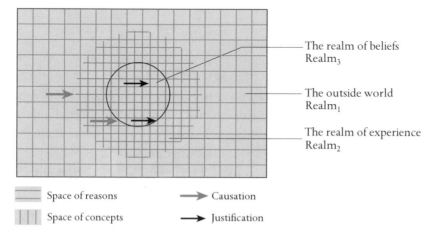

FIG. 9.1 A diagrammatic representation of direct realism

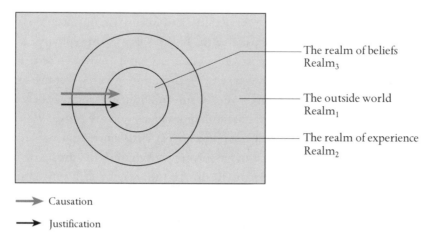

FIG. 9.2. A diagrammatic representation of reliabilism

traditional way of rendering the problem of the epistemology of empirical knowledge. This might explain why to date there has not been much debate between them. Nothing could be more obscure to the reliabilist than the idea of the world possessing a conceptual and propositional structure. And nothing could be more mysterious to the direct realist than the idea of an epistemology without spaces of reasons. Before taking up these critical themes, we need to study both direct realism and reliabilism in slightly greater depth.

DIRECT REALISM

McDowell's central aim is to give us epistemological tranquillity.[1] We need not fear that our beliefs about the world are all false, or that the world lies hidden behind a wall of causes. Direct realism allows us to see that rational contact with the world is not a problem. The mind always already makes such contact. And it is the conceptual structure of the world itself that enables the mind to do so. No doubt this will sound a bit bizarre to common sense. Here is my attempt to reconstruct McDowell's train of thought.

The first step is an argument to the effect that all experience is conceptual, that is, that 'conceptual capacities are drawn into operation' in experience. There are no non-conceptual contents of the sort the foundationalist assumes. The details of this argument need not detain us here (McDowell 1994: 3–23).

Second, the distinction between Realm$_2$ and Realm$_3$ (in our diagrams) is best couched in Kantian terms; Realm$_2$ is the space of 'receptivity' and 'passivity', Realm$_3$ is the region of 'spontaneity' and 'activity' (1994: 12). That is to say, in experience we 'take in' information, we are receptive and passive in so far as we do not 'make up' the information. In forming beliefs, in thinking and justifying, we exercise our spontaneity and are active. We are creative. McDowell gives this distinction a novel twist. Conceptual capacities are involved both in experience and in forming beliefs. But they are involved in two different modes. Experience (Realm$_2$) is the area in which conceptual capacities are involved in a *passive* mode; the realm of beliefs (Realm$_3$) is the

---

[1] McDowell develops his position most clearly in his *Mind and World* (McDowell 1994). Important criticism can be found in Gibson (1999), Davidson (1999*b*), Friedman (1996), Rorty (1998*b*), Michael Williams (1999*a*,*b*), and Brewer (1999).

area where they are *active*. Moreover, we are able to identify conceptual capacities in experience (i.e. when they are involved in a passive mode) only because we are familiar with them from their role in thought (i.e. when they are involved in an active mode). McDowell emphasizes the merely passive involvement of conceptual capacities in experience in order to give the world rational control over the contents of our beliefs. If conceptual capacities were active in experience, then we could not 'find' ourselves with beliefs about the world. If our conceptual capacities were actively rather than passively involved in experience, then we would be in danger of losing rational constraint from the outside. And McDowell wants to make room for the possibility that networks of beliefs are changed precisely from outside our beliefs: 'The conceptual capacities that are passively drawn into play in experience belong to a network of capacities for active thought . . . And part of the point of the idea that the understanding is a faculty of spontaneity . . . is that the network, as an individual thinker finds it governing her thinking, is not sacrosanct' (1994: 12). Experience can thus constitute a 'tribunal' for our beliefs; our thinking is 'answerable to the empirical world' and the relation between mind and world is 'normative'. The way the world is sets the standard for what it is to think rationally (1994: 10).

Third, since experience is conceptual through and through, we never encounter the world in anything but a conceptual form. McDowell asks us to take this observation seriously. To him doing so involves rejecting any opposition between our concepts *qua* form and an unconceptualized world *qua* matter. Since the world 'comes to us' in conceptual form, we must accept that the world 'has' a conceptual form. The claim that the conceptual realm has no boundary is of course reminiscent of absolute idealism. McDowell is not embarrassed; he happily embraces absolute idealism as an ally: 'It is central to Absolute Idealism to reject the idea that the conceptual realm has an outer boundary, and we have arrived at a point from which we could start to domesticate the rhetoric of that philosophy . . . the conceptual is unbounded; there is nothing outside it' (1994: 44).

Fourth, what McDowell appreciates most about absolute idealism is that it supports direct realism. If everything is conceptual, then there is no real boundary between the knowing mind and the known world. The process of my coming to know something about the world involves, as it were, no change of medium, and no gaps that need to be bridged by causes. If only the subject has the right kind of openness, then she will be able to get 'glimpses of the world' and take in 'the way the world is' (1994: 12).

Finally, McDowell needs to tell us where the individual acquires the concepts that link her to the world. This is where tradition and education come in. Through education and membership in a cultural tradition we have acquired conceptual capacities and the ability to move in the space of reasons. McDowell criticizes individualism as a form of philosophy that fails to appreciate the role of tradition. He also establishes a link between this individualism and philosophers' alleged blindness concerning the passive role of conceptual capacities in experience. The link is an excessive emphasis on the spontaneity and activity of the individual mind:

What results from this devaluation of tradition is an outlook in which individual reason is sovereign. And that is hard to combine with the idea that reason might be operative in states or occurrences of sheer passivity, which would make it indebted to the world. So what starts as a loss of the idea that reason might owe its being to a place in a tradition shows up as a strain on the idea that reason might owe anything to impacts from the world. (1994: 99)

RELIABILISM

The starting point of reliabilism is the idea that a belief is knowledge if it is true *in a non-accidental way*.[2] I might currently believe that the British Prime Minister is talking to the US President at this very moment; and this belief might in fact be true. And yet I could not be said to know this fact if my belief was due to pure guesswork, wishful thinking, or hallucination. Why not? The reliabilist's answer is that pure guesswork, wishful thinking, and hallucination are not—epistemically speaking—'reliable processes'. They do not usually lead to true beliefs.

Alvin Goldman has worked out a version of reliabilism that focuses on 'reliable processes'. According to his theory, someone knows a proposition,

---

[2]   Classical statements of the reliabilist position are Armstrong (1973) and Goldman (1985, 1992, 1993, 1999). Sosa seeks to combine reliabilism with coherentism (Sosa 1991*b*). A naturalistic version of reliabilism is advocated by Kornblith (1987, 1994, 1997*b*, 1999). Criticisms of reliabilism can be found in most recent contributions to foundationalism and coherentism. I have especially learned from Brandom (1994, ch. 4) and Haack (1993, chs. 7 and 8). See also Fumerton (1988). Important criticisms of naturalized epistemology are Kim (1997) and Moore (1991).

say p, if, and only if, she believes p on the basis of a method that causes beliefs that p only (or mostly) in circumstances in which p is the case. For instance, my belief that the computer screen is situated one metre from my eyes constitutes knowledge by this criterion. This belief has been produced by my visual system. And my visual system usually produces beliefs that p only in cases where p obtains. Or, take my belief that I saw my favourite comedian on television last night. This belief constitutes knowledge since it was produced by my long-term memory. For my long-term memory is in general a reliable process for transmitting the information that p from one day to the next (Goldman 1985).

Process reliabilism is sometimes subsumed under the label 'virtue episte-mology'. Virtue epistemology privileges concepts like 'epistemic', 'intellec-tual', or 'cognitive virtue'. It is easy to see how process reliabilism can come under this label. We might think of processes as 'epistemically virtuous' in the case when they lead mostly to true beliefs. Thus Goldman suggests that we 'identify the concept of justified belief with the concept of belief acquired through the exercise of intellectual virtues'. For Goldman, the 'virtues' in question are processes like perception, memory, or reasoning (1992: 157). They are not what Aristotle and his contemporary followers mean by intellectual virtues, that is, qualities of character like inquisitiveness, atten-tiveness, circumspection, or open-mindedness.[3]

What makes reliabilism a provocative doctrine is the idea that one can attribute knowledge to another person even if that person is unaware of the grounds of their true belief. If my memory is reliable, then the beliefs produced by my memory constitute knowledge. And this is true even if I do not know that my memory is reliable. The same goes for perception. If my perceptual system is reliable, then my perceptual beliefs constitute knowledge whatever I happen to think about my perceptual system and its reliability. It is easy to see how the reliabilist convinces herself of the superiority of her position, compared with the other three. Since justifica-tion (by the epistemic subject herself) matters little, most of the problems that haunted foundationalism, coherentism, and direct realism disappear. The reliabilist need not concern herself with questions of how basic beliefs,

[3] There is a separate research programme in epistemology around these Aristotelian virtues. I shall not go into this programme here. See Greco (1993); Axtell (1997); Kvanvig (1992); Zagzebski (1996).

features of experience, or properties of whole belief systems are accessible to the epistemic subject.

Many reliabilists emphasize the 'naturalistic' qualities of their approach to knowledge. As they see it, determining the reliability of a given method of belief-acquisition can be accomplished by scientific—for instance, experimental-psychological—inquiry. Epistemology can be brought from speculation and conceptual analysis 'down to the earth' of the psychological institute. This naturalistic approach to knowledge suggests to some reliabilists that knowledge is most profitably regarded as a natural kind. Since it can be studied like other natural phenomena, there is no reason why it should not be regarded as a natural phenomenon itself. Here is a clear statement of this position by Hilary Kornblith:

The goal of a naturalistic theory of knowledge, as I see it, is not to provide an account of our concept of knowledge, but instead to provide an account of a certain natural phenomenon, namely, knowledge itself.... What we seek is an adequate account of knowledge, and in order to develop such an account we must investigate the phenomenon of knowledge itself. We may do this by examining apparently clear cases of knowledge to see what it is that they have in common, just as an attempt to understand what aluminium is would begin by collecting apparently clear cases of the stuff in order to see what it is that they have in common. (1999: 161–2)

A COMMUNITARIAN CRITIQUE OF DIRECT REALISM AND RELIABILISM

Do direct realism and reliabilism constitute an advance over foundationalism and coherentism? In particular, do they provide us with satisfactory answers to Second-order Questions about the Rationality of empirical beliefs? Do they explain how it is possible for our empirical beliefs to be rationally constrained?

There are certainly respects in which the present duo marks progress relative to foundationalism and coherentism. They both show some awareness of the importance of the social, albeit in a vague or obscure form. The important truth in reliabilism is its externalism: that is, its insistence that in order to qualify as a knower one need not have first-person access to the justification of one's true belief. You could attribute to me the knowledge of how to distinguish between paintings of the two Brueghels even though I myself were to doubt that my beliefs were non-accidentally true; it would suffice that you had noticed my beliefs in this matter to be reliable. And to insist on this point is to see that the basic epistemic scenario must contain at least two persons: the 'attributer' and the 'attributee'.

And yet, reliabilism contains this insight only in a half-blind fashion. Reliabilism is 'epistemology with the view from nowhere'. That is to say, it systematically treats the attributer of knowledge as a *resource of*, rather than as a *topic for*, epistemological inquiry. It does not inquire into the space of reasons that you enter when you attribute knowledge to me. Instead, reliabilism concerns itself only with the fact that I—as the attributee—need not make contact with the space of reasons. Although the latter is true, it is merely a half-truth about the process of knowledge attribution as a whole. For the normative context—and thus the community—is still crucial; but it is crucial for the attributer rather than for the attributee.

This is the point at which we need to revisit my very first characterization of communitarian epistemology (in the Introduction). According to this characterization, communitarian epistemology is based on two ideas: that knowledge is a social status, and that usually the knower is plural rather than singular. Reliabilism points us to the exceptions regarding the second claim. The above-mentioned example (concerning my beliefs regarding the paintings of the Brueghel brothers) is one such case. This case does not show that knowledge is not a social status, of course; but it does show that there are situations where you could attribute knowledge to me even though you do not form any kind of epistemic community with me.

Lest the existence of such situations is counted as a major blow to communitarian epistemology, it is important to note immediately two things about them. The first observation is that such cases are relatively rare. Cases where reliable true believers are ignorant of, and sceptical regarding, their epistemic reliability are not widespread. Reliable true believers usually are well aware of their degree of reliability (Brandom 2000: 104). And thus they are able to argue about their reliability, convince others of it, and share their reliable beliefs with others. In other words, reliable true believers generally are able to enter into systems of entitlements and commitments, and thereby form epistemic communities with their interlocutors.

Second, epistemic communities are of crucial significance even in the rare cases where reliable true believers are ignorant of, and sceptical regarding, their own epistemic reliability. In claiming that my beliefs are reliably true, you are laying claim to an epistemic social status both for my beliefs and for your beliefs regarding my beliefs. For the latter to constitute knowledge you have to form an epistemic community with others—along the model described in Part I (and to be elaborated later in this Part II). And *if* you are successful in forming such a community regarding your beliefs about my beliefs, *then* my beliefs can partake of the same status. In this case my beliefs do have a plural subject: you, your interlocutors, and I all share the same belief. But only you and your interlocutors form an interacting epistemic community.

All this is invisible to reliabilism since it fails to turn the attributer of knowledge into a topic. And thus the social dimension is again moved out of sight. The importance of this step cannot be exaggerated. This is the crucial but unargued premiss of reliabilism. With this move all questions of negotiation and justification are moved backstage; anything that could be regarded as social is removed from sight. It is thus hardly surprising that knowledge appears to the reliabilist as a natural thing like aluminium.

Reliabilism has not provided us with an account of normativity. It does not show how our empirical beliefs are rationally constrained by the world, by other epistemic subjects, or some combination of natural and social factors. We can bring this point into still sharper relief by considering the favourite metaphor of reliabilists, the thermometer. (Just as a thermometer reliably indicates the temperature, so a reliable belief indicates the truth.) Reliabilists feel drawn to this comparison because of the lawful connection between temperature and the height of the mercury column. And yet there is more to be said about thermometers than this! Thermometers are calibrated against one another; they are accepted or rejected in different communities; they are judged as 'good enough' or 'too precise' for given purposes; and they are evaluated as to whether they are 'behaving as they should'. All these are precisely the thorny normative issues about which reliabilists are frustratingly silent.

In McDowell's case too we can applaud the presence of some communitarian elements.[4] I am referring here to his emphasis on tradition as a precondition for our openness to the world. McDowell is right about this point, but he fails to capitalize on it. He tells us little more than that enculturation and socialization bring us into the space of reasons, and refers us to Hans-Georg Gadamer's 40-year-old Hegelian ideas about language and tradition—as if Gadamer's position had not itself been challenged for silence or vagueness on all these very same questions!

McDowell's explanation of normativity and rational constraint centres on the relationship between the individual, her tradition, and the world. The world constrains the empirical beliefs of the individual; and the individual recognizes such constraint provided she has been properly socialized into the space of reasons. This could all be counted as being on the right track except that McDowell repeatedly talks as if the natural world itself was both judge and expert witness regarding the individual's beliefs. On the one hand, the world is the judge who decides whether our beliefs are correct or incorrect. The world exerts rational and normative control over us. On the other hand, the world is something like the (infallible) expert witness whose reports we had better accept passively and uncritically. I cannot help thinking that McDowell has put the poor world in an impossible position! And as if this were not bad enough, are there not strong resonances of foundationalism in all this? Is not McDowell's world as expert witness remarkably similar to the foundationalist's priestly apparitions? The only difference is that McDowell has got rid of the priest as an intermediary. In his scenario God (or the world) speaks to all beliefs directly and without any mediation. (The theology of direct realism is Protestant, whereas the theology of foundationalism is Catholic.)

---

[4] There is a further point of contact between McDowell's direct realism and communitarianism that is worth mentioning. Both McDowell and the communitarian urge quietism concerning projects of global justification. (See Ch. 4, 'Quietism and Contextualism'.) For the communitarian, however, such quietism is the result of contextualism; that is, the insight that global justification assumes invariant contexts for justification. One of the many oddities of McDowell's position is that he advocates epistemological quietism without adopting contextualism. He rejects as nonsensical the question of whether our belief system as a whole is justified. At the same time, however, he assures us that if only we are properly receptive we shall get glimpses of the world. Why is this not the sketch of a global justification?

Ultimately I am unconvinced by McDowell's arguments in favour of treating the world as itself conceptual. Granted that our experience is conceptual in quality; it still does not follow that the world itself is conceptual. Unfortunately, the lack of clarity on McDowell's part makes it hard to be sure exactly what his position comes down to. So perhaps the best way to sum up my discomfort is by means of a choice. *Either* McDowell merely means to say that the world *of our experience* is conceptual. This may well be so, but it does not give McDowell what he needs—for it still leaves open the question concerning the boundary between the world outside, and the world within, our experience. *Or* he wants us to accept that the world itself is reason-providing and conceptual. But what could possibly underwrite such panpsychism? Only the mistaken view that equates reality with how it appears to us.

To sum up: Direct realism and reliabilism constitute opposite attempts to solve the problems central to the earlier debate between foundationalism and coherentism. To the extent that the two sides introduce—albeit in an almost blind fashion—intersubjective elements into the explication of constraint, they are ahead of the earlier see-saw. And yet, a full understanding of normativity presupposes an adequate analysis of how individuals interact in epistemic communities, and how epistemic statuses are constituted in and through such interaction. Neither direct realism nor reliabilism have the resources for taking this step.

Chapter 10

CONSENSUALISM AND INTERPRETATIONALISM

DUALISM AND DUETTISM

Direct realism and reliabilism do not emphasize the epistemic significance of intersubjectivity. Nevertheless, they do contain hints concerning its import-ance: McDowell's direct realism alludes to the importance of the group for the individual; and reliabilism implies the epistemic indispensability of the second person (i.e. the attributer). Taking some liberties with the actual historical development, we might regard the two positions of this chapter as developments of these two hints. 'Consensualism' highlights the relations of 'I' to 'we'; 'interpretationalism' focuses on the dyad formed by 'I' and 'you'.

The positions studied in the two earlier chapters all had their well-established labels. 'Consensualism' and 'interpretationalism', however, are my own terms of art for the views of Keith Lehrer and Donald Davidson, respectively. These terms are meant to capture the roles of consensus in Lehrer and interpretation in Davidson. I shall also use a second classification in this chapter. Consensualism is a form of epistemological dualism, whereas interpretationalism is a version of duettism.[1]

I call an epistemology 'dualistic' if it is subdivided into the two branches of individual and social epistemology. Dualistic epistemologies are developed on the basis of individualistic forms of reliabilism or coherentism. The individualistic version is maintained under the rubric of 'individual' or 'personal' epistemology. 'Social epistemology' is constructed using the

---

[1] I adopt the term 'duettism' from Hacking (1989).

global 'find and replace' command. Where the key definitions of the individualistic version contained 'I' or 'he', the central definitions of social epistemology carry a 'we' or 'they'. Dualistic social epistemology is thus characterized by an abrupt, 'abstract' juxtaposition of the individual and the group. We do not learn how the communication among individuals constitutes group phenomena, or how social facts shape individuals and their interaction. Dualistic epistemology is a conservative extension of traditional epistemology. It is the simultaneous attempt to preserve the tradition *and* use it for the 'social aspects' of knowledge. Dualistic epistemologists take it that the tradition was more or less right about individual knowledge. But they feel that the tradition fails to tell us enough about the social side. Social epistemology fills the gap. This kind of view is now widespread among contemporary epistemologists and philosophers of science. It is advocated, among others, by Alvin Goldman, Philip Kitcher, Hilary Kornblith, and Keith Lehrer.[2]

The difference between dualism and duettism can perhaps most easily be grasped in terms of our earlier diagrams. Dualism results from a juxtaposition of two readings of Figure 8.3 or Figure 9.2, depending on whether or not the dualistic epistemology in question is coherentist or reliabilist. The two-circle structure is read as representing either the individual or the group. Duettism works without groups. It sticks to individuals. But it drops the constraint on a single individual. Duettists insist that the dyad of attributer and attributee is the basic unit of epistemology. Thus we end up with two individuals facing each other. These two individuals might again be the ones of Figure 8.3 or Figure 9.2.

Interpretationalism is the most important form of such duettism. It is built around a particular type of paradigmatic situation, in which an interpreter tries to assign a meaning to the utterance of a speaker. Interpretationalists believe that reflection on this situation teaches us important lessons about how we attribute beliefs, about how belief and truth are linked, and about how central intersubjectivity is to knowledge. The best-known advocate of such epistemology today is Donald Davidson. One characteristic feature of interpretationalist epistemology is its proximity to the philosophy of language and the philosophy of mind. Since the paradigmatic situation

---

[2] Goldman (1999); Kitcher (1993); Kornblith (1994); Lehrer (1987).

concerns the interpretation of utterances, the philosophy of language cannot be far off. And since interpretation involves assigning beliefs and desires, the philosophy of psychology is always lurking in the background.

It is a central tenet of this chapter than neither epistemological dualism nor epistemological duettism enables us to understand how empirical beliefs can be right or wrong. It is erroneous to assume that we can understand normativity through a study of I–we relations, and it is incorrect to suppose that we can comprehend normativity on the basis of an investigation into I–you relations. Neither type of relations can be reduced to the other, and neither is more fundamental than the other. The key to understanding normativity is to recognize that both types of relations are inextricably intertwined. At the same time there is much to be learned from both Lehrer and Davidson; it will thus be useful to discuss their respective views in some detail. I begin with dualism in general and Lehrer in particular.

CONSENSUALISM

I am sceptical about any epistemology that is subdivided into individual and social branches. If the arguments of Part I and Chapter 7 are anywhere near their target, then traditional epistemology is mistaken in conceiving of knowledge as a primarily individual phenomenon. It is misleading to say that traditional epistemology is right about the individual's knowledge but negligent of social aspects of knowledge. The fault runs deeper than this. Traditional epistemology is based on the assumption that isolated individuals can possess knowledge. And to reject this assumption is to give up the idea that there can be an independent epistemology of the individual. The epistemology of the individual knower is but a chapter in the epistemology of the group.

We need to be highly sceptical also about a second feature of dualism. I am referring to the tendency of 'social epistemologists' to confine themselves exclusively to normative issues. (By 'social epistemologists' I mean epistemological dualists working on the social branch of their epistemology.) Social epistemologists eagerly set norms for groups and interacting individuals, but they never stop to ponder the nature of norms, standards, institutions, or groups. Social epistemologists are happy to leave all such issues to sociology and the philosophy of the social sciences. This practice contrasts sharply with that followed in individual epistemology. In the latter field epistemologists are always prepared to advance detailed phenomenological and psychological descriptions. Indeed, in this day and age they go to great lengths to prove their scientific credentials by linking their work to recent advances in cognitive psychology, evolutionary biology, or artificial intelligence. Nothing of the sort can be found in the work of social epistemologists. They make only very occasional contact with the research literature in the social sciences, and on the few occasions when they do, their main concern is to distance themselves from what they regard as irrational and relativistic tendencies among sociologists. Unsurprisingly, I again beg to differ. Social epistemology without social ontology is both blind and empty. I take Part I to have proved this point; it is useless to set norms for practices that are poorly understood.

All these shortcomings can be demonstrated clearly in Lehrer's case. But before I continue my critique, Lehrer's epistemology needs to be introduced in more detail.[3] Lehrer's epistemology is a version of the coherence theory of knowledge. Coherence is the central concept for understanding the knowledge possessed by groups ('social knowledge') and for understanding the knowledge possessed by individuals ('individual knowledge'). Lehrer's version of coherentism differs slightly from the one introduced in Chapter 1.

To begin with, Lehrer replaces talk of 'belief' with talk of 'acceptance'. He thus speaks of 'the acceptance system' of (a subject) S, rather than of the 'belief system of S'. For our concerns this difference does not matter, and thus I shall use both terms interchangeably. Moreover, Lehrer distinguishes between 'the acceptance system of S' and 'the verific system of S'. The latter results from the former by removing all falsehoods. The verific system is central in Lehrer's account of being 'objectively justified'. To be 'objectively justified' is to be either 'verifically' or 'completely' justified:

> S is *personally* justified in accepting that p if and only if p coheres with the acceptance system of S.

> S is *verifically* justified in accepting that p if and only if p coheres with the verific system of S.

[3] Lehrer and Wagner (1981); Lehrer (1986, 1987, 1990a,b, 1997). For criticism of Lehrer's work, see Bender (1989).

S is *completely* justified in accepting that p if and only if S is personally justified in accepting that p and S is verifically justified in accepting that p. (Lehrer 1986: 8)

To give an example, assume I am paranoid and have many false beliefs about bus-drivers trying to kidnap me and to take me to Antarctica. I am getting on the bus one morning and form the belief that the driver is one of those people who want to condemn all communitarian epistemologists to the cold. Given my acceptance–belief system (me as a paranoid person) I am *personally* justified in my belief. My current belief coheres very well with my other paranoid beliefs. However, remove all of my false paranoid beliefs about bus-drivers from my belief system, and my current belief will no longer be acceptable. It is not *verifically* justified. And thus it is not *completely* justified either. Compare this with the belief that I have blue eyes. That belief coheres both with my personal acceptance system and with my verific acceptance system. And thus I am completely justified in accepting it.

Lehrer's social epistemology is constructed on the model of individual epistemology. In the case of groups too we can distinguish between 'consensual acceptance systems' and 'verific acceptance systems'. Group beliefs can be 'consensually', 'verifically', and 'completely' justified. For instance:

We are completely justified in accepting that *p* if and only if we are consensually justified in accepting that *p* (that is, *p* coheres with our consensual acceptance system), and we are verifically justified in accepting that *p* (that *p* coheres with the subsystem of our consensual acceptance system in which what is accepted is also true, our social verific system). (Lehrer 1987: 91)

All this fits of course with my characterization of the epistemological dualist as someone who introduces group phenomena in direct ('abstract') analogy to individual phenomena. But here I must tread carefully and report fairly. Unlike most dualists, Lehrer does make an extended effort to overcome a simple juxtaposition of group and individual. (No doubt the Lehrer aficionados among my readers will have wanted to insist on this since the beginning of this chapter.) I acknowledge this effort by calling Lehrer's view 'consensualism'. For it is the concept of 'consensus' that lies at the heart of his project. And yet, as we shall see, Lehrer does not escape the criticism that his epistemology is too abstract and insufficiently sensitive to the social nature of knowledge.

Lehrer has developed a normative theory of consensus formation; this theory is meant to generate 'a coherent probability assignment from conflicting information'. Lehrer himself has worked out this theory in a fairly informal form; his collaborator and co-author Carl Wagner has given the theory mathematical elegance (Lehrer and Wagner 1981). Since a fairly non-technical characterization will suffice for my limited purposes, I shall refer in general only to Lehrer.

Lehrer's technique to get disagreeing individuals to form a 'rational consensus' is meant to take hold in a rather specific situation. This is the situation of 'dialectical equilibrium'. A group of arguers is in dialectical equilibrium once 'all empirical data and theoretical ratiocination has been communicated ... [and] further discussion would not change the opinion of any member of the group' (Lehrer and Wagner 1981: 19). Lehrer makes two assumptions about the individuals in such a situation. The first assumption is that each individual assigns some probability value to the idea or claim under dispute. The second assumption is that each individual attaches some weight to the opinions of others, regardless of whether or not they agree with her (1981: 19–22).

Imagine that John, Peter, and Mary disagree over the question of how probable it is that a vegetarian dinner tonight would be the best way of preparing for tomorrow's marathon run. John gives the proposition the probability 0.3, Peter 0.6, and Mary 0.9. (This is the first assumption.) Assume, furthermore, that each member of our threesome assigns degrees of expertise or credibility to one another. (This is the second assumption.) Lehrer suggests capturing these 'weights' numerically. Values for epistemic weight lie in the interval between 0 and 1; and each individual must divide up unity weight between herself and others. To assign weight 0 to another individual is to ignore her; it is to regard her as inevitably wrong in her beliefs. And to assign weight 1 is to take her to be infallible. The following matrix might be thought of as an example of such distribution:

	John	Peter	Mary
John	0.4	0.2	0.4
Peter	0.2	0.7	0.1
Mary	0.3	0.3	0.4

Lehrer tells us that in order to be fully rational each one of the three should multiply weight and probability for each of the three persons, and then add the resulting values. This gives us:

John: $0.4(0.3) + 0.2(0.6) + 0.4(0.9) = 0.66$
Peter: $0.2(0.3) + 0.7(0.6) + 0.1(0.9) = 0.57$
Mary: $0.3(0.3) + 0.3(0.6) + 0.4(0.9) = 0.63$

Note here that the three values now all lie between 0.57 and 0.66, whereas they originally lay between 0.3 and 0.6. (The values are the probabilities concerning the statement that a vegetarian dinner tonight is beneficial for the marathon run tomorrow.) The convergence continues to grow as the same procedure is reiterated with the new values 0.66, 0.57, and 0.63 taking the place of 0.3, 0.6, and 0.9. After a second round the values are 0.63, 0.59, and 0.62, and after a third round they are 0.62, 0.6, and 0.61. After a few more rounds they converge on the consensual probability 0.6.

This is rational consensus-formation with invariant weights. Lehrer also considers the possibility that individuals might want to reconsider their value assignment to others after each round (Lehrer and Wagner 1981, ch. 4). For instance, in the initial first round Mary's assignments of weight to John and Peter are based only on her assessment of their expertise in questions of nutrition. After the first round of calculations is 'in', however, Mary has more information about her two friends. She now also knows how they assigned weight to her and to each other. And this might well influence how she assigns weight to them in the following round. She might, for instance, lower their weights on the ground that they—in her opinion—proved themselves rather incompetent as judges of others' competence. The fact that Peter only gave her 0.1 weight might well prove to Mary that he is a bad judge of judges. And thus she might assign only 0.1 to him in the second round of calculations.

Lehrer shows that a rational consensus is possible even when weight assignments vary for a few rounds. After all, it is likely that they would eventually settle. It is unlikely that Mary's assessment of John's competence as a judge of judges of judges of judges of judges of competence differs from her assessment of John's competence as a judge of judges of judges of judges of competence. In all likelihood her weight for John from round three onwards would be constant. And then the above method of amalgamation would lead to a coherent or consensual assignment of probability.

Lehrer claims that his method leads to a 'rational consensus'. The reason is that

The justification for averaging when I assign positive weights to others is that the refusal to average is mathematically equivalent to assigning everyone else a weight of zero and averaging. If I assign them a positive weight, then an interest in consistency provides an argument for averaging. Averaging is rational. The argument extends, of course, to all members of the group. . . . if a single averaging by all members of the group does not produce consensus, all members will, provided they continue to assign positive weight to others, have the same argument for averaging again. (Lehrer 1987: 99)

Finally, Lehrer claims that wherever such rational consensus on a question is available, individuals must not deviate from it. In other words, as long as John is aware of the dialectical equilibrium and the consensus value, he must stick to the latter. Any deviation from this value would make his belief lack justification (Lehrer and Wagner 1981: 62–4).

A COMMUNITARIAN CRITIQUE OF CONSENSUALISM

At this point we can revert from description back to critical evaluation. I applaud Lehrer's central intuition concerning the importance of understanding consensus-formation. Indeed, consensus is central also in my communitarian epistemology. But I do not think that Lehrer's work is helpful for understanding and answering Second-order Questions about Rationality.

To this it might be objected that Lehrer has no intention of doing any such thing; his goal is merely to formulate a normative theory. I am not convinced, however, that this reply gets Lehrer off the hook. (I have already discussed this issue in Chapter 7 but a brief recap will perhaps be helpful.) First of all, if indeed Lehrer offers nothing in answer to descriptive Second-order Questions about Rationality, then there is a bad lacuna in his social epistemology. After all, these questions have not been made central by communitarian epistemology; they have guided decades of epistemological work. If Lehrer wants his social epistemology to be (or contain) a social epistemology of empirical knowledge, then he *should have* something to say about the descriptive questions. Second, a normative theory defines an idealized practice; and such practice should be familiar to us at least in a non-idealized form. A normative theory for choosing job applicants defines an idealized practice for selecting job applicants. The practice the theory defines should still be recognizable to us as a practice for choosing job applicants; it should have similarities with our current practices in this area. If the gap between the practice and the ideal is too wide, then the normative theory might simply be irrelevant. To avoid such failings, the normative theorist had better do some of the descriptive homework. Third, a closely related point is that a normative epistemological theory should be clear on the conditions of its own applicability. The theory should tell us what kind of individual or group is needed for it (that is, the theory) to be realizable. Fourth, and finally, even if none of this is acceptable, it might still be a useful exercise to see exactly why Lehrer's work fails as a descriptive theory in general, and as a theory that answers Second-order Questions about Rationality in particular. At least the contours of an adequate descriptive theory might thereby emerge more sharply.

The first point to note about Lehrer's consensualism is that it does not provide coherentism with any new defences. We are not told, in any case, why social coherentism (i.e. consensualism) constitutes an advance over traditional coherentism in this respect.

More importantly, I argued earlier that standard forms of coherentism are unable to account for normativity. This failure was due to their common individualism. Normativity cannot be generated within the isolated individual, or in the causal interaction between the world and the individual mind. Lehrer's social epistemology does not make progress with regard to this issue. Lehrer never even sees the problem since for him normativity is never a topic—normativity is presupposed as a resource. Lehrer gives us a theory of how the rational individual would amalgamate the empirical information shared by members of her group. This theory might be taken to answer the question of how an individual might go about such amalgamation, given that the individual wishes to be rational in Lehrer's sense. But taken as an answer to the guiding question of the epistemology of empirical knowledge, that is, as an answer to Second-order Questions about Rationality, this fails badly. Lehrer's theory does not illuminate the source or constitution of normativity.

Lehrer's normativism has detrimental effects not only concerning his ability to answer the Second-order Questions about Rationality. It also leads him to overlook alternative ways to think about consensus itself. Lehrer introduces his method for consensus-formation without any prior discussion of various types of consensus. This leads him to neglect an important distinction: the distinction between (what I suggest calling) 'external' and 'internal' forms of consensus. An external consensus is a mere coincidence in the view of several individuals. Take, for instance, the passengers on a normal city bus. Such passengers do not usually communicate with one another, and yet they all *agree* that the bus will stop at various points along the way. I call such consensus 'external'. Alternatively, think of a committee that after long and adversarial discussion adopts a compromise formula as *its* final decision. Each member of the committee commits herself to this compromise formula as the consensus view. Clearly such consensus deserves to be called 'internal'. Interaction is central to this second case, but it was irrelevant to the first. An internal consensus is a collective commitment. One important difference between the two cases is that an internal consensus creates mutual obligations between individuals. Having agreed in the company of the others, they have made an (implicit) promise not to deviate from the agreement.

Lehrer's consensus is close to the external model. The consensus in question is a coincidence of individual commitments to a specific degree of probability. But it is not a collective commitment. The individuals in question are not committed to honouring the probability value as the view of the group. And thus no commitments to other individuals have been generated. This is clear from the fact that the whole consensus-forming mechanism operates with minimal communication: the individuals only exchange their calculations. The calculations are interconnected, but the consensus value is arrived at 'behind each other's back', as it were. This is an interesting result given my general criticism of dualism. I claim that dualistic (I–we) theories are unable to connect properly the individual and the group. They merely juxtapose the two poles in an abrupt and abstract fashion. We can now see that this criticism applies to Lehrer despite his consensualism. For the kind of group that Lehrer's algorithm produces is merely external: we get a set of individuals that make calculations regarding one another, and that end up with an identical probability assignment for some initially controversial statement. But we do not actually get a group—at least not if by a group we mean a set of individuals with commitments and entitlements to, and regarding, one another.

It should also be clear that Lehrer's method for forming an external consensus presupposes an internal consensus. Lehrer's method can only be properly applied if the individuals in question commit themselves to playing by the rules: to being honest about having reached dialectical equilibrium, to assigning weights to others in a fair and 'disinterested' way, and to keeping others informed about their calculations. Lehrer makes it impossible for himself to see the need for this internal consensus since he turns commitment to his game into a demand of rationality as such.

Finally, it cannot be stressed too much that Lehrer's 'dialectical equilibrium' is a fiction. I cannot recall ever having found myself in an argument with someone else where all empirical data and theoretical ratiocination had been communicated and no further discussion would have changed the opinion of any participant. (The idea rings familiar only from my intrasubjective arguments with myself!) Lehrer hints that some disputes in science are occasionally at this point, but this is a dubious claim. There exists a plethora of case-studies on scientific controversies from physics to psychology, and from mathematics to physiology; not one of those known to me describes a situation where the Lehrer model would have been applicable. This suggests to me that Lehrer has developed a normative model of consensus without any useful application.

INTERPRETATIONALISM

Davidson's epistemology is inseparable from his philosophy of language in general, and his ideas of radical interpretation in particular.[4] (A reader unfamiliar with Davidson might profit from rereading my brief account of radical interpretation in Chapter 4, 'Fundamentalism'.) Davidson's epistemology has three main strands. The first is the anti-foundationalist theme

---

[4] Davidson's philosophy forms a complex whole. Anyone trying to familiarize himself or herself with Davidson's epistemology had better start from his philosophy of language, truth, action, and event (Davidson 1980, 1984a). Davidson's most important epistemological writings are Davidson (1989a,b, 1990, 1991). Davidson's epistemology is discussed by various writers in LePore (1989).

according to which only a belief can justify another belief. The second is the argument that most of our beliefs must be true. And the third strand concerns the claim that our three 'varieties' of knowledge are interconnected. By 'varieties of knowledge' Davidson means knowledge of the external world, knowledge of one's own mind, and knowledge of others' minds.

Here I shall concentrate on Davidson's third claim only. Davidson argues that none of these three forms of knowledge can be reduced to any of the others, and that they all presuppose one another. In defending this thesis, Davidson attacks epistemological individualism, internalism, and bold externalism. Epistemological individualism would be beaten if it could be shown that all forms of knowledge presuppose knowledge of other minds. Internalism would be defeated if knowledge of one's own mind presupposed other kinds of knowledge. And bold externalism would not survive the proof that all forms of knowledge presuppose knowledge of one's own mind. There can be no doubt that Davidson is chasing after very substantial game. Here is his argument in summary (Davidson 1991).

Davidson's argument is couched in terms of the paradigmatic situation of (radical) interpretation. Since his line of thought is far from simple, it will be helpful to return to our earlier example. Assume again that you are alone with a native on a remote (Finnish) island in front of a dog. The native points to the dog and utters the sounds 'tämä on koira'. You have not heard these words before. We already know what Davidson thinks about such situations: you as the interpreter can do no better than to start by attributing to the native beliefs that you would have in like circumstances. When *you* stand in front of a dog with a foreigner, point at the dog, and utter sounds, *you* usually mean to express the belief 'this is a dog'. Hence you attribute this belief, and this meaning, to the native's sounds. Here we can already see how one variety of knowledge presupposes another variety of knowledge. You cannot even begin to get knowledge of the native's mind unless you make use of knowledge about your own mind. Thus: *Knowledge of other minds presupposes knowledge of one's own mind.*

Moreover, interpretation cannot succeed without the interpreter's knowledge of the external world. To see this we need to re-examine your interpretation from a different angle. Imagine you had not yet settled on the hypothesis that the native is telling you that 'this is a dog'. All you have done so far is hear his sounds, and see the dog, as well as his pointing finger. In this situation you must decide this question: is the native trying to tell you something true, or is he trying to express something false (never mind whether the falsehood is due to lying or to an error)? Here you had better settle for truth. Your interpretation could not proceed at all if you opted for falsehood. Progress of interpretation is progress regarding the fit between utterance and situation. And empirical falsehoods do not fit empirical situations at all.

And so you opt for truth. However, although *the truth* is one, *truths* are many. There are many true things the native might be saying in this situation. Simply supposing that he is telling you 'the truth' does not yet provide you with an indication as to which truth he is trying to convey. It could be the truth that $2 + 2 = 4$; that there is a dog; or that Finland is cold in the winter. Therefore, you need a further constraint—a constraint in addition to the truth assumption. The needed further constraint links the *content* of the native's belief and utterance to what you assume to be its most likely *cause*. If you want to make progress with your interpretation, then you must suppose that the content of his belief is determined by its cause in the external world. Your reasoning should go something like this: there is the dog; there is his hand pointing to the dog; these are his sounds; ergo: his utterance is caused by the presence of the dog, and the content of his utterance (and his belief) is that there is a dog. To sum up this second step in the argument: *No knowledge of the external world, no knowledge of other minds.* You need to employ your knowledge about the dog, and about causes of beliefs, in order to get to a working hypothesis concerning the contents of other minds.

The next step in the argument undermines internalism and individualism. It is also the most difficult step. A crucial element in this part of the argument is Davidson's view of the holistic nature of beliefs and their attribution. Beliefs never come one by one. To believe one (first) thing is to believe a whole range of other things in support of the first. To believe the utterance 'this is a dog' (in English) is for you to believe that there are things called 'dogs', that one can speak about them, that one can refer to things by means of the word 'this', and so on. Likewise with interpretation. One can never attribute just one belief in isolation; one always has to attribute a whole number of beliefs at once. Say you are interpreting 'tämä on koira' as expressing the belief that this is a dog. In doing so, you are attributing to the native beliefs about this dog, some implicit beliefs about dogs in general, and some tacit beliefs about the conversational context. Beliefs that are jointly attributed (explicitly or implicitly) must fulfil an important requirement; they must form a logically consistent group or set. Suppose someone suggested to you the following as the best way of interpreting the native's action: the native believes you deaf and believes himself capable of teaching you how to express the belief 'this is a dog' in Finnish. Surely, this someone would be a lousy interpreter. The point holds in general and in principle: it is part of the essence of beliefs to be parts of consistent groups of beliefs.

Making this point about consistency is tantamount to establishing once more the importance of truth. After all, a set of sentences is logically consistent if the sentences can be true together. Above we saw that Davidson also has a more direct way of linking truth and belief. This is the idea that belief is by its nature 'veridical'; for the interpreter the default position regarding belief attribution is that the belief is true. Here it is important to add that by 'true' Davidson means 'true *simpliciter*', not 'true as it seems to me', or 'true as it seems to the native'. The seems-formulas allow for too much slack between the situation and the belief. To say that the attribution of beliefs to the native is constrained by 'what seems true to him' is to say that the attribution of beliefs to the native is not constrained at all. Any old falsehood might 'seem true to him'. This is not to say that the 'seems true to him' formula has no application in interpretation. You can attribute error and 'seem true to him' beliefs to the native once you have in place a substantial theory of his overall belief system. But such attributions only make sense against the backdrop of what is true in an unqualified sense. The same goes for the 'seems true for me' formula. Here the 'seems true' is parasitic upon the 'true' *simpliciter*. We speak of what 'seemed to us' when we correct ourselves in the light of what we now regard as true.

Beliefs come in consistent sets; beliefs are veridical; beliefs are mostly true. These are the lessons we learn from interpreting others. But they are more than that. They are also the preconditions for our being able to consider ourselves as believers, for our being able to consider ourselves as having beliefs. We learn about beliefs through interpreting the utterances of others. And the process of interpretation opens our eyes to the essential link between belief, truth, and consistency. In doing so, the process of interpreting others sets the benchmark for ourselves. If I want to consider myself as having beliefs, then I must strive for beliefs that are true and consistent. Unless we interpret the minds of others we cannot know how to be right in our own mind. In other words, unless we interpret the minds of others we are unable to know of the demands we have to honour in order to have beliefs at all: namely, the demands of truth (*simpliciter*) and consistency. Ergo: *Knowledge of one's own mind presupposes knowledge of other minds.* And since, as we already know, knowledge of other minds presupposes knowledge of the external world, we can add: *Knowledge of one's own mind presupposes knowledge of the external world.*

In order to close the triangle, it remains for Davidson to show how knowledge of the external world depends on knowledge of one's own and of other minds. Let us return once more to the native, his utterance, and the dog. Above we saw that you can use your knowledge of the dog in order to construct a hypothesis regarding the native's beliefs. The dog was what the native's utterance (and belief) was about; and the dog was the cause of the native's utterance (and belief). For this hypothesis to be possible, you must of course presuppose that the dog is something outside your own mind. The dog must not be something that is cognitively accessible only to you, or else it could not play the designated role of referent and cause of the native's belief. But what constitutes something as 'objective' or as 'outside your mind'? Or what is the difference between a sensation, experienced by you, and a physical object, observed by you? Davidson's answer is that an entity is objective in so far as it is intersubjective. In the paradigmatic situation of interpretation, the physical entity can function as cause and referent for the beliefs of more than one believer. It is possible to triangulate the native's belief, your belief, and the dog. Your sensation cannot take this role. It makes no sense for you to allege—in the situation described—that the cause of the native's utterance is your sensation. The sensation is subjective, not intersubjective. We might summarize this point by saying that objectivity *qua* mind-independence is intersubjectivity.

Objectivity has also a second meaning, however. This is 'objectivity *qua* standard of rightness or truth'. The dog is not just objective in so far as it causes both the native's and your belief. It is objective also in so far as its existence and location marks a boundary between true and false beliefs. The dog is objective in so far as it is the object of your and the native's true beliefs.

Putting these two elements of the final step together, we can say that it is the mark of the external world that it is objective; that objectivity presupposes intersubjectivity; and that intersubjectivity is constituted by the ways in which our own beliefs and the beliefs of others are intertwined. Ergo: *Knowledge of the external world presupposes knowledge of other minds and our own minds.*

A COMMUNITARIAN CRITIQUE OF INTERPRETATIONALISM

Davidson's argument is an impressive philosophical tour de force in favour of a social theory of knowledge. It establishes that in order to understand truth, belief, and objectivity we had better place them in the intersubjective context of interpretation. For it is in this context that we can see best how these concepts are linked together and dependent upon one another. Proving this point is perhaps one of the most important achievements of analytic philosophy of the last thirty years—at least judging from the perspective of social and communitarian epistemology. It is unfortunate that Davidson's message has not been heeded by many epistemologists. However, despite its many strengths, Davidson's line of argument also has some weaknesses. It is important to identify these somewhat ruthlessly for us to be able subsequently to strengthen and complement his general viewpoint.

First, Davidson's epistemology is somewhat limited in scope and formulated on a very abstract level. There is nothing to be learned from Davidson about the four sources of knowledge (perception, reason, memory, testimony), or about how we (should) justify empirical claims. Indeed, his epistemology is formulated at such an abstract level that these traditional questions can seem irrelevant. As far as Davidson is concerned, it does not matter which causal mechanisms cause us to have beliefs; his theory would not be affected by the discovery that we owe all our beliefs to telepathy or hypnosis. He regards this as a strength of his theory. But this is so only if we confine epistemology to his two epistemological concerns: the global justification of knowledge and the demonstration that the three varieties of knowledge are interrelated. There is no reason why we should accept this narrowing of the traditional problematic.

Second, Davidson's argument can be given two different readings. According to the weak reading, individuals first acquire the concepts of belief, truth, and objectivity in the context of interpretation. Once the concepts have been acquired, however, their subsequent use is no longer dependent upon interpretation. According to the strong reading, it is both the original acquisition, and the subsequent use, of these concepts that is dependent upon interpretation. Continuous interaction with others is essential to being able to use the concepts, and to being able to use them *correctly*. Which of the two readings one adopts will surely make a world of difference. The first reading treats social interaction as important in (child) development; the second conceives of the social as continuously constitutive of our concepts. The first reading might be regarded as compatible with many individualistic viewpoints; but only the second is compatible with the sociology of knowledge and with communitarian epistemology. To be ambiguous on such fundamental issues as this is absolutely intolerable. Imagine a theologian whose view of the relationship between God and world was completely ambiguous between deism and the theory of continuous creation. The epistemologist Davidson does no better than the theologian.

Third, and most importantly, we need to return to the most important characteristic of Davidson's position, his duettism. Does Davidsonian duettism succeed where the earlier pairs and where dualism failed? Does duettism give us a satisfactory answer to the question of how our beliefs are rationally constrained, or how right and wrong, rational and irrational, are possible in the realm of empirical belief? The answer is, I fear, negative. We cannot understand normativity without bringing in the 'we', that is, without bringing in the community. The distinction between 'is right', 'is wrong', and 'seems right' cannot be understood on the narrow basis of an interaction between two abstract individuals. In calling these individuals 'abstract' I am referring to the fact that they have no history and that their interaction is one-off. The interpreter can notice that the native does things *differently* from the way he, the interpreter, does them. But to identify beliefs as different is not to understand them as incorrect, as wrong, or as irrational. In order to get to the distinctions between 'is right' and 'seems right', right and wrong, rational and irrational, we need to bring in the interpreter's community and the ways in which communities create and maintain standards via communal performatives. In other words, to call something 'right' or 'rational' is to say that it accords with norms and standards that are *shared*. And sharing here means not an accidental coincidence of interpreter and native; it means a consensus-based coincidence of opinion and action within a wider community. Such standards would not exist unless different individuals in many different encounters referred to them over and over again.

I suspect that Davidson's focus on radical interpretation has made it hard for him to see the need for the 'we'. In his paradigm scenario the interpreter does of course already possess the standards of his culture, and so does the native. But Davidson slips from taking possession of these standards for granted to regarding these standards as somehow irrelevant. Perhaps he would have done better if he had heeded an important lesson from Wittgenstein: to wit, that philosophers should not live on too one-sided a diet of examples.

Chapter 11

CONTEXTUALISM AND COMMUNITARIANISM

Contextualism urges the epistemological significance of social context. Communitarianism insists on the epistemological importance of the group. Clearly the two positions are closely related. Contextualism and communitarianism could even be regarded as identical were it not for the fact that the best-known versions of contextualism tend to backtrack from their initial contextualist and relativist insights. I shall first introduce contextualism and then explicate the communitarian position.

CONTEXTUALISM

Contextualism is a fairly recent addition to the epistemology of empirical knowledge. The outstanding reference book for the field *A Companion to Epistemology* did not carry an entry for contextualism in its 1992 edition (Dancy and Sosa 1992). The label is currently appropriated by a number of authors. In my use of the term, 'contextualism' refers to the bundle of views that allow at least one epistemologically important element *to vary with social context*. Here 'epistemologically important elements' are justification and knowledge. I shall concentrate on two writers concerned with contextualism concerning justification.

Dialectical Justification

The most radical and provocative form of epistemological contextualism insists that all justification is 'dialectical'. That is to say, to be justified in one's belief is to be able to defend it against other members of one's own society. Richard Rorty once called this view 'epistemological behaviorism' and expressed it by suggesting that 'epistemic authority' had best be explained in terms of 'what society lets us say' (1980: 174). Michael Williams wrote in almost identical words 'that being justified consists in doing or saying what your conscience and your society let you get away with' (1999a: 115). The clearest formulation of dialectical justification, however, can be found in David Annis.[1]

Distinguish between two contexts: the context of the putative justified believer and the context of the attributer of the justification. To make the distinction more vivid, assume that the putative attributee is an Azande tribesman believing his neighbour to be a witch, and that the attributer is one of a group of Cambridge philosophy students. Under what circumstances are the Cambridge students entitled to regard the tribesman's belief as justified? Only if the tribesman is able to 'meet' the 'current objections' coming from an 'appropriate objector-group' as determined by the 'issue-context' (Annis 1978: 215). All of these conditions concern the context of the putative justified believer. The 'issue-context' is the conventional type of situation in which the belief is held or expressed. The relevant situations are those of the culture of the believer (i.e. the Azande) not those of the attributers (the Cambridge students). Imagine, for instance, that two important situations for the Azande are a light-hearted spring festival and a sombre necromancy.[2] In the first situation, accusing one's neighbour of being a witch is without much consequence; indeed it is part of the light-hearted nature of the event that tribesmen go around accusing others of being a witch. In the second setting, however, identifying a witch has enormous consequences for the success or failure of the ritual. In this case, one is entitled to call someone a witch only if one is able to meet various objections from the accused and his family. For the Azande to be justified in believing that his neighbour is a witch in the second context he

---

[1] Annis develops his positions in Annis (1978, 1982). The latter paper is a reply to Airaksinen (1982); Michael Williams's defence of contextualism can be found in Williams (1991, 1999a,b). Rorty discusses Williams's position in Rorty (1998a). Rorty's own conception of dialectical justification can be gleaned from Rorty (1980, 1982, 1991). Other versions of contextualism are Alston (1993), Cohen (1986, 1987), DeRose (1992, 1995, 1999), Dretske (1981), Lewis (1996), and Unger (1986).

[2] I am here taking liberties regarding the lives of the actual Azande.

must be able to meet these objections, provided only that the latter are not far-fetched or concerned with goals other than truth. Moreover, the objections must be local, concerned with specific and concrete error possibilities, and based on the currently available evidence. Finally, to 'meet' a given objection means 'to produce within the objecting group a general but not necessarily universal rejection [of the objection] or at least the general recognition of the diminished status of [the objection] as an objection' (Annis 1978: 214). We might picture the Azande objectors raising specific doubts about the accused's ancestry and the accuser defending himself by reporting on various accidents that have occurred since the new neighbour moved in.

Here then is a clear statement of the dialectical view of justification. Whether or not we are entitled to regard the tribesman as justified in his belief depends almost exclusively on the standing of his belief among his peers. It is not for the Cambridge students to judge whether the tribesman is answering the objections correctly, or whether his peers are correct in regarding an answer to a given objection as successful or not. It all depends on the Azande and their criteria. This is of course a radical perspective on justification and worth contrasting with the traditional view. For the traditional epistemologist there is no question as to whose standards we are to use in evaluating the justification of the tribesman's belief. We are to use the correct standards, and these better be ours—if we harbour any doubts on that score then we must redo our epistemology. Either the Azande is able to meet the universally correct criteria for justification, or he is not justified. Of course, the choice need not be simply between completely local and fully universal standards. For instance, one might suggest that all cultures share the same 'epistemological desiderata'— necessary though not sufficient marks of virtuous beliefs—but that different cultures give different weightings to different desiderata. Thus one culture might value the feeling of certainty where another attaches more importance to observed reliability. Some contextualists have tried this route. But this is not Annis's position. In his view justification is almost exclusively contextual.

I write 'almost exclusively contextual' since some elements of the assessment seem left to the Cambridge students after all. Annis implies that it is the attributer's privilege to decide whether or not the believer's peers' objections are local and current, based on real doubts, and concerned with the goal of truth (1978: 216). That seems to me to be insufficiently contextual and ad hoc. If we contextualists are willing to leave it up to the Azande to decide whether or not a given objection has been met, why should *we* want to pass judgement on what are the legitimate objections? It seems to me that Annis is losing his contextualist nerve at a decisive moment.

Communitarianism is also best kept free from Annis's version of epistemological tolerance. By epistemological tolerance I mean the view that believers belonging in other contexts or cultures have a right to be evaluated by their own peers and standards. Perhaps epistemological tolerance is, in many circumstances, a demand of fairness. But it does not follow from the observation that justification is contextual. To go from

(*a*) All beliefs are challenged and justified in local contexts

to

(*b*) No belief can be justified or challenged outside of its original context

clearly is a non sequitur. The step from (*a*) to (*b*) can be turned into a logical inference only by adding, as a further premiss (*c*), that all beliefs are internally related to their original context. (*c*) amounts to the claim that a belief only has meaning in its original setting. Is (*c*) plausible? I suspect not. Such contextualist essentialism contradicts our natural inclination to allow that the same belief can occur in different settings. Ergo, the communitarianism of this book is not tied to epistemological tolerance. The task is to understand the contextual nature of knowledge; the task is not to legislate who is entitled to evaluate which beliefs.[3]

Quietism

Contextualism is incompatible with projects of global justification. Such justification is justification of the totality of our beliefs. We found a clear example of such a project in Davidson, who undertook to show that most of our beliefs must be true. Classical foundationalism and coherentism also have global aspirations; they aim to outline what the overall structure of our system of beliefs must be like for that system to be justified. Foundationalism

---

[3] I will have much more to say about these matters in Part III.

insists on a proper grounding of non-basic beliefs in basic beliefs; and coherentism demands a mutually supporting set of beliefs. All such projects are doomed once the contextual nature of justification is taken on board. The very idea of a system of beliefs related to one another by relations of justification is wrong. For such a system makes sense only on the assumption that beliefs have a permanent position within a stable network of justifications. Contextualism teaches that such networks do not exist. Since all justification and evidence is fragmentary and perspectival, there is no permanent and stable network or space of reasons. Ergo: no stable network of reasons, no system of beliefs; no system of beliefs, no meaningful totality of beliefs; and no totality of beliefs, no global justification.

Annis has not much to say on global justification, but Williams's critique of it takes precisely the above form. Moreover, Williams draws the natural conclusion that talk of totalities like 'our knowledge of the external world' or 'our knowledge of experience' is deeply misleading. To make his point, he asks us to consider arbitrary aggregates like the objects in his study. Surely we do not expect one general blanket explanation as to why all of these objects happen to be in the study. We expect 'general intelligibility only with respect to kinds that exhibit some kind of theoretical integrity'. And diverse objects like chairs, pens, flowers, all the sorts of things that we can imagine at his place of work, do not exhibit such integrity. Williams's point is that the theoretical integrity of our various theories and beliefs about the external world is not greater than the theoretical integrity of the things in his study:

Consider our 'beliefs about the external world:' these include all of physics, all of history, all of biology, and so on indefinitely, not to mention every causal thought about the world around us. There is no theoretical unity, no genuine totality, here, only a vague and arbitrary assemblage. The demand for a blanket explanation of 'how we come to know such things' looks misplaced, if it is even intelligible. (1999b: 57)

Contextualism and Reliabilism

As far as the defence of quietism is concerned, the communitarian is a faithful follower of Williams's contextualism. In some other respects, however, I wish to distance myself from Williams's more recent writings. For these texts water down his original dialectical contextualism into a strange amalgam of contextualism and reliabilism. In his writing of the 1990s Williams contends that a 'purely dialectical conception of justification' on its own is insufficient. A dialectical conception of justification needs a reliabilist complement. In this spirit, he distinguishes between two concepts of justification: 'personal justification' and 'evidential justification'. Personal justification is an updated version of the old 'purely dialectical justification'. 'Evidential justification' is evidence to the effect that the belief has adequate grounds (1999*b*: 50).

In saying that personal justification is an 'updated version' of dialectical justification, I wish to stress that Williams has new and important things to say about it. He characterizes personal justification using terms like 'epistemic responsibility' and 'default-and-challenge structure' (1999*b*: 51). One acts epistemically responsibly if one is willing to defend one's beliefs against well-motivated challenges of one's peers. This means, at the same time, that beliefs are innocent until proved guilty. As long as no challenge has been presented, one is entitled to stick to one's beliefs. There is no requirement to seek grounds for unchallenged beliefs. Williams stresses that challenges have to be 'earned' (1999*b*: 52). The mere logical possibility of error is not enough; objectors must show that the mentioned error possibilities are real and relevant in the given context. One important consequence of this demand is that total scepticism cannot be stated in a coherent fashion. The sceptic cannot claim that nothing is ever known or justified. For in order to be entitled to make this claim, the sceptic has to invoke knowledge and justification himself.

'Evidential justification' is a different matter. In order to have this second type of justification, a belief must be based on adequate grounds. Williams claims that this type of justification is reliabilist and externalist. At the same time, however, he allows that the standards of evidential justification too are 'standards that we fix in the light of our interests, epistemic and otherwise' (1999*b*: 53).

Williams feels that personal and evidential justification are equally important since 'both [reliability without responsibility and responsibility without reliability] disqualify us from knowing':

we are very reluctant to ascribe knowledge to someone who has formed a belief by a method that he has good reason to think unreliable, even if he is wrong about his method's unreliability.... But we are equally reluctant to ascribe knowledge to someone who has formed a belief by an unreliable method, even if his circumstances render his use of the method epistemically blameless. (1999a: 187)

A further argument for combining personal and evidential justification is that challenges to personal justification 'arise out of suspicions concerning the objective adequacy of one's grounds' (1999a: 190). We start doubting that people have acted epistemically responsibly when we are convinced either that they have arrived at a false belief or that they have arrived at a true belief in an unreliable manner.

The ultimate motivation for the distinction, however, seems to lie with Williams's eagerness to distinguish contextualism from relativism:

We must not confuse contextualism with relativism. Contextualism is not the view that epistemic evaluations come with implicit subscripts, so that 'justified' really means 'justified in context C'. A belief is evidentially justified when it is supported by adequate evidence. But standards of adequacy depend on both the world and the dialectical environment and can shift with changes in either (and as a result of their interaction). (1999b: 53)

I am not convinced by Williams's way of using reliabilism to combat relativism. Judgements about reliability do not transcend 'the dialectical environment'. That is to say, the justification of beliefs about the reliability of belief-forming methods is every bit as contextual as is the justification of all other beliefs. Judgements about reliability too have to be earned, their justification has a default-and-challenge structure, and in making them we are again answerable to our peers. It is true that a given group of attributers might make a distinction between reliability and personal justification. Recall the earlier example of the two contexts: the context of the putative justified believer (e.g. the tribesman) and the context of the attributers of justification (e.g. the Cambridge students). We can easily imagine the students making two assessments: an assessment of the tribesman's way of answering objections and an assessment of the Azande's method of belief-formation. The first evaluation would then fall under personal justification, and the second under evidential justification. But it would be wrong to treat these two assessments as if the first was concerned with the relation of the tribesman's belief to other beliefs, and the second with the belief's relation to the world. This asymmetry is doubly unjustified. It is unjustified since the tribesman's peers' challenges might be equally concerned with the belief–world relation; and it is unjustified since the students' only way of judging the relation between belief and world is by bringing in their own beliefs about the world.

Williams seems to me to betray contextualism twice: by privileging one assessment over another, and by making judgements of reliability special. The last paragraph commented on the first move; here is my criticism of the second. Why should reliability have a special position among 'epistemological desiderata', that is, among circumstances and conditions that we regard as prima facie epistemically advantageous? Why value it more, for instance, than the believer's cognitive access to her reasons; or the belief's belonging to a coherent set of beliefs? If contextualism is to have real bite, it had better be able to survive the reflexive move. That is to say, which epistemological desiderata gain first prize in different epistemologies is itself a contextual matter. Ordinary folk invoke all sorts of different epistemological desiderata in everyday life. Some are referred to so persistently that they become obvious and intuitive. And yet, ordinary folk appeal to different desiderata in different circumstances, and they have no (strong) views about the order or rank of such desiderata. Epistemologists are uncomfortable with this untidiness. They fasten on one or two of these items and argue that these, and only these, are essential to justification and knowledge. Why they fasten on one condition rather than another is of course an intriguing question. It may be due to their degree of familiarity with different contexts—contexts in which different desiderata are central. This in turn might of course be a result of their own social position, their education, and their other philosophical commitments. The contextualist moral of this variation will not astonish: it is a mistake to assume that any one of the epistemic desiderata must trump the rest. Rather than pit intuitions against intuitions, epistemologists should give up on the whole debate and accept the variety of intuitions as beyond the need for repair.

Beyond Contextualism

The original contextualist insight into the local nature of all justification is worth preserving and defending—even against card-carrying contextualists. There are also other specific doctrines advanced by contextualists that are important to preserve; I have already adopted their attack on invariant and global justification, and their rejection of totalities like 'our knowledge of the external world'. To these we can add the idea, proposed by Annis and Williams, that our knowledge of justification is at least in part 'tacit', that is, impossible to reduce to rule. As Annis puts the point: 'Part of learning our epistemic standards, as is the case with both legal and moral standards, is learning the conditions of excusability. Such conditions are highly context dependent and it would be extremely difficult if not impossible to formulate rules to express them. In general, we learn the conditions of excusability case by case' (1978: 218).

I shall return to this topic in the next chapter. At this point it is more important to point out that Annis's and Williams's contextualism points beyond itself and towards communitarianism. The test question for contextualism is again its answer to Second-order Questions about Rationality, that is, the question how our empirical beliefs can be rational or irrational. Annis's answer to this question is simple and straightforward: empirical beliefs can be right or wrong, rational or irrational, since they are evaluated by communities rather than by isolated individuals. Williams's answer is more complicated in so far as he combines reliabilist and dialectical forms of justification. He suggests that beliefs can be rational or irrational in two ways: in so far as they are subject to evaluation and discussion with one's peers, and in so far as they are brought about in a reliable way. I have argued against reliabilism as an answer to our guiding question earlier and shall not rerun the argument here. But what about Annis's and Williams's ideas concerning dialectical (or personal) justification? Do these ideas answer Second-order Questions about Rationality? In a way they do. The insistence on community is very much on the right track, and so is the idea that the application of standards proceeds case by case, or context by context. And yet the answers that we get from the contextualists do not satisfy. They are simply too thin. They are far too sketchy to satisfy philosophical curiosity. This curiosity will only be satisfied once we have an understanding of how contexts and standards are created and maintained, how communal judgements are possible, or how consensus is achieved. These are questions that contextualism does not seek to answer. Communitarianism does.

COMMUNITARIANISM

The communitarian epistemology of empirical knowledge to be developed here is very much one with the communitarian epistemology of testimony presented at the end of Part I.[4] What I did there for testimony and speech-acts I do here for beliefs. I argued that performative testimony is an important but overlooked category of testimony, and that it is a necessary condition for the existence of constative testimony. Here I advance an analogous claim concerning the relationship between 'performative' and 'empirical' beliefs. Performative beliefs generate their referents; empirical beliefs do not.[5] Traditional versions of the epistemology of empirical knowledge fail as answers to Second-order Questions about Rationality because they overlook the importance of performative beliefs. Performative beliefs are not just an important category of beliefs; they make empirical beliefs possible.

I shall spell out communitarianism in seven steps. *Step 1* introduces the taxonomy of beliefs that forms the backbone of my theory. Central in this taxonomy is the distinction between performative and empirical beliefs, and the opposition between individual ('I') and communal ('we') beliefs. In *Step 2* I concentrate on the relationship between individual and communal empirical beliefs.[6] I argue that individual empirical beliefs typically acquire the status of knowledge by becoming communal beliefs. In *Step 3* I investigate communal performative beliefs. I suggest that communal performative beliefs presuppose individual beliefs of a special kind, and I ask how the latter are justified. In *Step 4* I turn to the issue of rational constraint on empirical belief. This part of my theory presents justification as dialectical and contextual. *Step 5* is concerned with the relationship between rational and causal constraints. I emphasize that these two constraints have to be

---

[4] Hence my intellectual debts are similar: Barnes's and Bloor's work in the sociology of knowledge, and Searle's work on social institutions. See also Gilbert (1989, 1996); Pettit (1993). My communitarianism in the epistemology of empirical knowledge is also influenced by work in the philosophy of action, where Annette Baier and Frederick Stoutland have defended 'communitarian' perspectives (my term, not theirs). See Baier (1997) and Stoutland (1997).

[5] My prime example of a communal performative belief is 'We communally believe these discs to be coins'. My paradigm of a communal empirical belief is 'We communally believe that there are nine major planets in our solar system'.

[6] That is, the distinction between the following two beliefs: 'We communally believe that there are nine major planets in our solar system'; 'I believe that there are nine major planets in our solar system'.

seen as intertwined. For instance, we often assess the rationality of beliefs on the basis of their causal history. In *Step 6* I look at ways in which the order of beliefs relates to the order of people. Finally, *Step 7* returns to the question of whether knowledge is a social kind.

Kinds of Beliefs

Two distinctions are important for my argument in this chapter: the distinction between 'performative' and 'empirical' beliefs, and the distinction between 'communal' and 'individual' beliefs. Like performative and constative speech-acts, performative and empirical beliefs can be told apart on the basis of their 'direction of fit'. Empirical beliefs aim to fit some aspect of the empirical world; performative beliefs create a psychological or social reality that accords with them. I speak of 'empirical' rather than 'constative' beliefs in order to stay close to the vocabulary of the traditional epistemology of empirical knowledge.

Communal beliefs are beliefs with a plural believer. Such beliefs can be performative or empirical. For instance, the beliefs listed under (*a*) are communal performative beliefs, whereas the beliefs mentioned under (*b*) are communal empirical beliefs:

(*a*) We believe these discs to be coins.
   We believe him to be a member of our group.
   We (the members of the International Astronomical Union) believe
      that in order to count as a 'major planet' of our solar system, a
      planet must have a diameter of at least 2000 km.
(*b*) We believe that these stones are emeralds.
   We believe that the bus goes up Leith Walk.
   We (the members of the International Astronomical Union) believe
      that object TO66 is not a major planet of our solar system.[7]

The general form of communal performative beliefs is 'we believe in, and thereby constitute, the social fact that *p*'. The general form of communal empirical beliefs is 'we believe, on the basis of experience, that *p*'.

---

[7] TO66 is an object in the Kuiper Belt, a swarm of Pluto-like objects beyond Neptune. TO66 was discovered in 1996. It is 800 km. in diameter. I have learned about the Kuiper Belt and related matters from the NASA website:
<http://science.nasa.gov/newhome/headlines/ast17feb99_1.htm>

Nothing in the term 'communal' forces us to think of the plural subject as a 'we' rather than a 'they' or 'you' (second-person plural), but I shall concentrate on the first person both in the communal and in the singular case. Moreover, in my use of the term 'communal belief' the 'we' in question refers to a community. The individuals making up this 'we' are thus much more than an aggregate of social isolates. That is to say, they are tied together by mutual commitments and entitlements. Each individual thinks of herself as a member of the community, accepts the other individuals as members of the community, and takes on commitments and entitlements. Commitments include: to defend the communal belief against critics, to sanction deviation by group members, or to hold the communal belief oneself. Entitlements are, among others: to draw on the communal belief in defence of other beliefs, or to endorse action on its basis.

Individual beliefs are beliefs with a (first-person) singular subject. Examples of individual empirical beliefs are easy to find; we only need to replace the 'we' in, say, the first two examples under (b) above, with an 'I'. The category of individual performative beliefs is much less straightforward. There is no direct analogue in the realm of beliefs for individual performative testimony of the form 'I hereby declare you husband and wife'. Utterances by individuals can—in the appropriate social circumstances—create social facts; beliefs, just by themselves, that is, unuttered, cannot.[8] The registrar must utter the magic words to constitute the marriage; her believing is not sufficient. This is not to deny that there are any individual beliefs that might perhaps be counted as individual performative beliefs. Perhaps one might count certain kinds of introspective beliefs as individual performative beliefs. In such beliefs the act of believing is also the content of the belief:

(c) I believe that I am having a belief. Or: I believe that I am a believer.
(d) I think that I am a thinker. Or: I think that I am having a thought.

These beliefs are self-referring and self-validating, and they also constitute something; namely the believer in (c) and the thinker in (d). I shall not discuss such beliefs here.

---

[8] Of course, the creation and maintenance of communal performative beliefs also demands communication.

Instead, let us focus on the question of how individual beliefs relate to communal beliefs. Here we need a further distinction between two kinds of individual beliefs. On the one hand, there are 'purely' individual beliefs. These are beliefs that are held by an individual without any direct reference to a community of 'co-believers'. Think of an individual in isolation, and a belief concerning the time of day, or the content of the fridge. On the other hand, there are 'group-involving' individual beliefs. These are beliefs where the singular first-person subject makes her group membership a part of the belief. In order to distinguish such group-involving beliefs from purely individual ones, we might suggest that they have a different 'logical form'. Compare (e) and (f) below. For our purposes (e) can be thought of as a *purely individual* belief while (f) should be taken as a *group-involving individual* belief.

(e) I believe that the fridge needs cleaning.
(f) I (as one of us) believe that the fridge needs cleaning.

The distinction between purely individual and group-involving individual beliefs is important for understanding the existence of communal beliefs. Communal beliefs are not the beliefs of some 'group mind' or 'community mind'. In other words, I do not claim that groups have beliefs in the same way that individuals do. Groups have no mental states over and above the mental states of their members. The assumption of communal beliefs does not commit me to the group-mind hypothesis. According to my taxonomy, only some beliefs, namely individual beliefs, are phenomena of the mind. Communal beliefs are not. They are social phenomena; phenomena constituted by group-involving individual beliefs. It is well worth putting my central point a bit technically:

(g) A communal belief 'that p' exists if and only if there exists a group of individuals such that each one of them believes 'that p' in a group-involving way.

Note the circularity of this suggestion—I am referring to community in both *definiens* and *definiendum*. I am not worried about this circularity. I am not trying to tell a genetic story of how communal beliefs originate; I am aiming to clarify a structure that maintains both communal beliefs and group-involving beliefs.

I have just insisted that communal beliefs are not the beliefs of a group mind. At the same time I also wish to emphasize that communal beliefs do not 'reduce' to individual beliefs per se. That is, communal beliefs do not reduce to purely individual beliefs. Communal beliefs exist as group-involving individual beliefs. Call this a reduction of communal beliefs to individual beliefs if you like. But do not overlook that this is not a smooth reduction; the individual beliefs all refer to a community of believers.

This chapter will say a lot about how individual beliefs relate to communal beliefs, and there is no need to anticipate all of the further developments here. Nevertheless, it is perhaps useful to return briefly to the issue of individual performative beliefs—an issue that I have already touched upon. The point I want to make here is that group-involving individual beliefs, regardless of whether they are empirical or performative, are not simply individual performative beliefs. Compare:

(h) I believe that I have beliefs.

(i) I (as a member of the International Astronomical Union) believe that Pluto is a planet.

(j) I (as a member of the International Astronomical Union) believe that in order to count as a 'major planet' of our solar system, a planet must have a diameter of at least 2,000 km.

Beliefs (i) and (j) are group-involving individual beliefs but they are not individual performatives. Or, to put it more technically, they are not cases that fit the scheme 'I believe that p. Therefore I constitute p. Therefore p'. Using the metaphor of fragments introduced in Part I, we might say that beliefs like (i) or (j) carry out a fragment of a (possibly widely) distributed communal belief. But, as we shall see below, acting as such a fragment involves elements of both empirical and performative belief.

Three more and—for my project—minor distinctions are worth mentioning to round things off. First, sometimes we have empirical beliefs about social matters, sometimes we have empirical beliefs about non-social matters. For instance, I might believe that Finland is a democracy, or I might believe that snow is white. Traditional epistemology of empirical knowledge is concerned only with knowledge of the latter kind. The context will make clear where I am using the term in the narrower or the wider sense. (The wider sense includes empirical beliefs about both social and non-social matters; the narrower includes only the former.)

Second, beliefs are usually thought of as involuntary rather than voluntary. We cannot decide what to believe in the way in which we can decide how to act. Changing our own beliefs involves bringing us into situations where our beliefs will change. For instance, can I decide to believe that smoking is good for you? No. But I can decide to spend the next two years reading nothing else but the glossy magazines published by the tobacco industry. Perhaps I shall then one day find myself believing in the virtues of tobacco. I have no objection to the thesis of the involuntariness of belief as long as we restrict it to individual empirical beliefs. Communal performative beliefs—*qua* communal stipulations—clearly are not involuntary. We can decide what view we wish to make the view of the group. The cases of other types of beliefs are, as we shall see, mixed.

Third, and finally, traditional epistemology opposed empirical beliefs not to performative but to 'a priori' beliefs. In other words, the tradition thought (and continues to think) that some beliefs are due to experience, and that some other beliefs are independent of experience and due only to reason. Moreover, sometimes the 'a priori' was, and is, taken to be a condition of the possibility of experience. How then does the a priori relate to the performative? Let a brief answer suffice. I shall argue later in this chapter that communal performative beliefs make all empirical know-ledge possible and that they are the condition of the possibility of rational assessment. I also have already said that performatives create rather than fit (some) realities. All this makes it reasonable to treat performative beliefs as a priori beliefs. 'A priori' here does not, however, refer to an invariant and non-historical structure. The very opposite is true. Communal performative beliefs change over time. Perhaps it would then be most adequate to speak of communal performative beliefs as 'the historical a priori'.[9]

Empirical Beliefs

In this section I follow the epistemological mainstream and take empirical beliefs to be beliefs about non-social matters. How do communal empirical

---

[9] A term that looms large in Michel Foucault's archaeology. See Foucault (1974).

beliefs relate to individual empirical beliefs? The obvious answer is: they relate to each other in more than one way.

To begin with, a purely individual belief can become a communal belief and thus a group-involving individual belief. I might start out being the only person who believes that the Kuiper Belt contains objects far bigger than Pluto. But perhaps one day the International Astronomical Union (IAU) will come round to sharing my view; from then on the belief in question will be communal and group-involving. Or an individual might learn and adopt the communal empirical beliefs of some group. This can happen in two ways. In both cases the individual ends up believing what the group believes, but in two different 'modalities'. If the individual joins the group, and is accepted into the group, she will end up having group-involving beliefs. If, on the other hand, the individual remains outside the group, she will only have purely individual beliefs. For instance, I am not an astronomer and not a member of the IAU. In order to have an astronomical example ready at hand, I have read about recent debates within the IAU over the status of objects in the Kuiper Belt. But that does not make me a member of the IAU—neither officially, nor implicitly. I have come to share the beliefs of IAU members (on a very small topic, anyway), but I have not entered into any entitlements or commitments regarding these beliefs. If (only!) the IAU accepted me as a member, and if I wished to join, things would be different. I would then believe, say, that Pluto is a planet 'as one of us (IAU members)'.

The above-mentioned relations between individual and communal empirical beliefs did not involve epistemologically important concepts, like justification or knowledge. We must now direct our attention to relations that do. It seems that challenges to, and justifications of, empirical beliefs usually involve communal empirical beliefs. We typically challenge new beliefs on the grounds that they do not mesh with beliefs that we all subscribe to. And usually we defend beliefs by showing that they follow from, or fit with, beliefs that we all share. To a considerable degree communal empirical beliefs thus are the touchstone for whether or not purely individual empirical beliefs rise to the status of communal beliefs. Of course, a communal belief is often not available *prior to* the situation in which an individual belief is challenged and defended. You tell me that we will be able to catch the bus despite the fact that we arrive late at the bus stop. I challenge you. You defend your belief by pointing over my shoulder to the bus that is stopping behind my back as I speak. Here too you are drawing on a communal belief. It is a communal belief that is formed as I turn round and see what you are seeing.

Furthermore, in order to become knowledge, a belief must become a communal belief. Being a *communal* belief is a necessary, though not sufficient, condition for knowledge.[10] It is not sufficient, since the community in question might well decide that it lacks evidence for its belief. But it is a necessary condition. The argument for this view has already been advanced in Part I and in earlier chapters in this part. According to our folk epistemology, knowledge is a social status, like 'married' or 'divorced'. Social statuses presuppose communities; social statuses can be imposed upon someone, or something, only by communities and their certified representatives. Individuals can lay claim to such statuses, but no one possesses a social status simply in virtue of having laid claim to it. And as far as the social status knowledge is concerned, to acquire this status for one of my beliefs is for this belief to be shared by others. And such sharing typically amounts to the formation of an epistemic community, a nexus of epistemic entitlements and commitments. At this point I wish to extend the argument from knowledge to justification. 'To be justified' is a social status, too.

A couple of examples might help with digesting my claim. Take the situation where I tell some friends about interplanetary object TO66, about current debates over the Kuiper Belt, and about Pluto's status as a major or minor planet. If my friends accept my reports, and if they act in accordance with our epistemic folkways, then they will regard me as someone who knows about these matters. Their willingness to grant me this status is of course dependent on a variety of factors; my trustworthiness, for example, and my ability to back up my claims about IAU matters with references to sources. In other words, it is dependent on my being able to justify my belief.

[10] Note that this also holds for cases dear to reliabilists. If you attribute to me the knowledge that this painting is by Pieter Brueghel the Younger, then you and I share the same belief. Moreover, for you to be able to lay claim successfully to the status of knowledge for this belief, you must be able to form an epistemic community (regarding this belief) with others. There is, however, a special case of beliefs to which my analysis does not apply. We might collectively agree that some genius (or some Robinson Crusoe) possesses an item of empirical knowledge the content of which is incomprehensible both to us and to any other epistemic community. Obviously, in this case the genius's belief is not shared, and yet is judged to be knowledge. I acknowledge the exception; but shall ignore it in what follows. Such cases are, in any case, very rare.

Again, for my friends to accept my justifications is for them to share them with me; it is for them to form with me an epistemic community around the belief and the justification.

What about cases where I am on my own? Can I not decide all by myself that I know about interplanetary object TO66, and without having consulted with anyone? Or, to pick a case of new rather than already accepted knowledge, can I not decide all on my own that my beliefs concerning epistemology constitute knowledge? Yes, of course I can. But to decide that my beliefs deserve to be regarded as knowledge is not yet for my beliefs actually to possess the status of knowledge. That status they can only acquire in interaction with others. I am, however, free to anticipate their success in such a forum and think of them as knowledge even prior to such testing. In thinking of my beliefs as knowledge I am making a prediction as to how they will fare. Note also what I must do in order to convince myself that my beliefs about epistemology do indeed deserve the status of knowledge. Clearly the rational way to convince myself is to have a '*pretend* challenge– defence discussion' with people I am familiar with. I imagine the objections that might be brought against my position by orthodox philosophers, by sociologists of knowledge, and by historians. And I become confident that I have got things right to the extent that I am able to fend off these imaginary objections. In other words, coming to convince myself is actually to form a pretend communal belief with pretend others. And this is clearly parasitic on the case where the others and their objections are real rather than imagined.

The claim then stands: individual beliefs cannot be justified since justification is a social status; and for something to be knowledge it must be the subject of a communal belief.

Performative Beliefs

In Part I, I suggested that communal performative testimony exists only in a widely distributed and fragmented way, and that the fragments are carried by individual performative and constative testimony. For instance, the fictitious communal performative 'We accept these discs as coins' is carried by all sorts of references to these discs as coins, in whatever kind of testimony they might appear. The analysis of performative testimony can serve as the model for the analysis of performative belief. Communal performative beliefs exist only in a widely distributed and fragmented form. The fragments can have the form of individual group-involving beliefs, but they can also be carried indirectly by various kinds of empirical beliefs. Thus, the communal belief (k) is realized by instances of individual group-involving beliefs (l), and by individual empirical beliefs (m) or (n).

(k) We believe that these discs are coins.

(l) I (as one of us) believe these discs to be coins.

(m) I believe that I can pay for this glass of wine with the change I've got in my pocket.

(n) I believe that you owe me these coins.

The individual beliefs (l), (m), and (n) are not fully performative beliefs; neither one of them creates a social reality on its own. They do, however, *participate in creating* and sustaining the social reality in question. The more individuals of a given aggregate of people form beliefs of form (l), (m), and (n), the more 'real' the 'coin status' of the discs will become. We might call this the 'performative element' of beliefs (l), (m), and (n). At the same time, beliefs like (l), (m), and (n) also have an 'empirical element'. They refer to a reality which is not (exclusively) of their making, and they refer to it as if it were a fully mind-independent thing.

Again the epistemologically most interesting issue is how beliefs like ($k–n$) relate to knowledge and justification. How can such beliefs be justified? In one sense, communal performative beliefs (k) cannot be given an *empirical* justification. That is to say, since communal performative beliefs constitute a reality, they cannot be justified by reference to this reality. The reality lacks the necessary independence of the belief. The justification of (l)-type beliefs is complex. The justification of my belief that I, and we, believe in the institution of money must involve evidence of my own, as well as others', beliefs, intentions, and actions. Here the relevant others are other members of my group. Let us take evidence of these others' beliefs, intentions, and actions first. Such evidence is usually different from the evidence concerning beliefs, intentions, and actions of members of another culture. As members of the same group, we are so familiar with each other that we can confidently predict each other's action by imagining what we would do in similar circumstances. I know what you would do, since I know what one does—one, including myself. The evidence concerning my own beliefs is even more unlike the evidence concerning behaviours in foreign cultures. At least when it comes to familiar social institutions like money or marriage, I know my own beliefs and intentions with a very high degree of certainty. I need not do much checking to feel certain that I believe in the institution of money. Finally, the justification of (m or n)-type beliefs calls for mixed evidence. Some of the evidence must be empirical: I really must have a number of metal discs in my pocket for (m) to come out true.

The Rational Constraint upon Empirical Belief

This and the following section form the heart of my communitarian epistemology of empirical knowledge; it is here that I shall give my answer to the question of how rational constraint on empirical belief is possible. My answer is a version of the 'dialectical theory of justification', but without some of the shortcomings of contextualist renderings. My proposal centres on relations between communal performative and empirical beliefs. I begin with the relation between communal performatives and communal empirical beliefs.

There are two ways in which communal empirical and communal performative beliefs are closely intertwined. The first way is brought to the fore by the observation that the two kinds of beliefs are sometimes hard to tell part. Take a statement concerning a communal belief like (o).

(o) The IAU believes that there are nine major planets in our solar system.

Is (o) a performative, or is it an empirical belief? In other words, should it be read as (p) or as (q)?

(p) The IAU believes (on the basis of experience) that there are nine major planets in our solar system.

(q) The IAU believes (and thereby constitutes a classification which makes it so) that there are nine major planets in our solar system.

The fact that both readings are possible indicates that communal empirical beliefs presuppose and involve performative elements. More precisely, communal empirical beliefs use the classifications constituted by communal performatives. And in using these classifications, communal empirical beliefs reconstitute the communal performative beliefs. Lest my view is being misunderstood, I had better emphasize that the idea proposed here is not a form of idealism. I am not claiming that all empirical beliefs 'really are' performative beliefs. The view advanced here is merely a reformulation—using 'belief-talk'—of the earlier claim according to which natural kinds contain a self-referential component: natural kind terms purport to refer to extra-mental entities, but their referring is made possible by communally constituted paradigms, prototypes, and models.

There is a second way in which communal empirical beliefs presuppose communal performative beliefs. I wrote earlier in this chapter (in the section 'Kinds of Beliefs') that communal beliefs have communities as subjects. I distinguished communities of individuals from mere aggregates of individuals. In the case of the communities the individuals are tied together by commitments and entitlements. Obviously, such communities are themselves social institutions and therefore constituted by communal performative beliefs. Thus communal empirical beliefs have communal performative beliefs as a condition of their possibility. To take (o) as my example, it relies not just on (q) but also on (r):

(r) We (the members of the IAU) believe that we have a system of entitlements and commitments defining us as the IAU, and enabling us to communally adopt empirical beliefs.

In one sense, all communal performative beliefs are 'community-introducing'. They always delimit the community sharing the given belief. We need not assume, however, that every communal performative belief draws a totally new line round a number of individuals. In some cases, the 'we' in question might already have existed as the subject of some other performative or empirical belief. But whatever the prior history, every communal empirical belief needs a communal performative belief—even if the two are formed at one and the same time.

Enough has perhaps been said above to clarify the relationship between communal beliefs of the two kinds. I now turn to discussing links between *individual* empirical beliefs and communal performative beliefs. To get us under way, we can simply register that the two forms of communal performative beliefs also come into play here. Individual beliefs too involve classifications, and they too involve socially constituted subjects. Most (if not all) purely individual beliefs are couched in some terms or other, and such terms are, if not *parts* of received taxonomies, then at least *derived from* received taxonomies. Group-involving individual empirical beliefs ('I, as a member of the IAU, believe that TO66 is not a major planet') are fragments of the communal performative belief that constitutes the classification. As far as the subjects of individual beliefs are concerned, social constitution is central in more than one way. Clearly, one cannot even have the social status of 'being an individual' unless it has been conferred on one by a communal performative belief. The same is true of more particular statuses like 'being an individual worth learning from' or 'being an individual that is a member of our group'. Moreover, typically an individual will only be able to acquire the status 'knower' if she is able to convince others to form with her the communal subject of a belief. This results in the constitution of a new (minimal) community of knowledge, but it also presupposes some prior communities. Without some prior community there would be no rules or norms and other communal beliefs in terms of which the individual could urge acceptance of her new belief. Without some prior community her new belief could not be *justified*.

Let us look a bit more closely at the rules and norms in terms of which empirical beliefs can be justified—and thereby rise to become communal beliefs. In my usage, 'rules' are explicitly formulated standards or prescriptions. 'Norms' are standards or prescriptions that are not stated and that figure implicitly in our practices. We can usually tell when a norm has been violated, but we find it difficult to put the norm into words. Most of our 'epistemic prescriptions' are norms, rather than rules. (If it were otherwise, epistemologists and sociologists of knowledge would be superfluous!) And rules always presuppose norms. How do we know norms, and 'what' do we know in knowing them? My answer is that we know norms in so far as we know communally shared 'exemplars'. These exemplars are cases of actions and beliefs that are taken to fulfil the norms. In other words, the communal performative belief constituting a norm is a belief in the exemplary role of a number of (types of) cases. The general form of a norm-constituting communal performative belief is thus something like (s) or (t):

(s)   We believe that beliefs of type X are justified if they fulfil criteria Y; and the following are exemplary cases in which instances of X do fulfil the criteria Y: [and then follows a list of cases].

(*t*) We believe that beliefs of type X are justified if they are justified in the way in which the following beliefs are justified: [and then follows a list of cases].

This should sound familiar. Thomas Kuhn (1996) has taught us the import-ance of exemplars in science; scientists usually try to convince their peers by assimilating their solution to a recognized paradigmatic solution. Kuhn also showed that implicit norms—that is, exemplars—are vastly more import-ant than explicitly stated rules. All I am doing here is generalizing Kuhn's ideas from science to all different kinds of knowledge. In everyday life too we have our model solutions. How do we justify our beliefs in the times when buses are supposed to arrive? We usually introduce the timetable into the discussion. How do we justify our belief (maybe against the stereotyped social constructivist) that physical objects are real? We hit our fist on the table. How do we justify our belief in a past event that no one else remembers? We cite examples where our memory coincides perfectly with well-known records of the past. And so on.

Let us look at two examples in a bit more detail. Take the bus timetable first. Assume that you and I stand in front of the Playhouse in Edinburgh on 18 December 1999 at 8.10 a.m. and that you ask me for the arrival time of the next no. 17 bus. I tell you that the bus arrives at 8.15 a.m. You ask me why you should believe me. I walk you over to the timetable and point out that 8.15 a.m. figures among the arrival times of the no. 17 bus. Why would that convince you? Why would you accept this justification? It would in general convince you because we think that one important type of justification is justification by appeal to an officially announced intent or plan. We rely on this type of justification when we justify our beliefs in the arrival times of buses, the departure times of aeroplanes, and the starting times of theatre performances. In accepting my justification you accept that the current case (us two at the bus stop, on this date, etc.) is sufficiently similar to a specific group of exemplary past cases; these are the cases in which it was judged correct to justify a belief by appeal to officially announced intent or plan.

Turn now to the debate between the realist and the stereotyped social constructivist (again it is important to think of this as taking place at a specific time and place). Imagine our radical throws doubt over the reality of physical objects by suggesting that physical objects are 'merely social constructs'. The realist is not convinced. The social constructivist challenges him to justify his belief. The realist hits the table with his fist. Why does that convince so many of us? Why are we tempted to accept this justification? It seems convincing to us because when it comes to justifying beliefs in the existence of medium-size physical objects we accept the following principle: the existence of medium-size physical objects can be proved by hitting, bending, or kicking them. In accepting the realist's argument on this occasion, we judge that the pair formed by the currently contested claim (do physical objects exist) and the hitting on the table is relevantly similar to earlier pairs (of claims and acts of hitting) belonging under the same model of justification.

Justifying a belief involves showing that the relationship between the belief and our evidence for it is *similar* or *analogous* to one of the communally endorsed exemplars for types of justification. Each exemplar is a belief–evidence pair. 'Similar' and 'analogous' are the key words. No two situations are ever fully alike, and thus we can never demonstrate identity between an exemplar and a new case. Moreover, since there is no absolute and unique metric for similarity, there cannot be logically deductive arguments in favour of a given assimilation. And that means that every given justification is *in principle* contestable. One can always find respects in which the current case differs from the exemplar. Take the example of an astronomer who claims in 1999 to have discovered a new interplanetary object in the Kuiper Belt called Kusch II. Imagine further that he justifies his observation by claiming that he has followed the exact same procedure (and equipment) used by Jewitt and Luu in 1995 in their recognized discovery of 'Kuiper Belt object 1995 WY2'.[11] Those who are sceptical of the existence of Kusch II will of course question the similarity of the two cases. Was the telescope in good working order in 1999? Was the operator of the telescope sober? Was his name perhaps Martin Kusch? And so on.

The important lesson of the above is a different, and novel, defence of the contextual nature of all justification. If all justification involves judgements of similarity, and if all judgements of similarity are contestable, then no justification can ever be 'once and for all'. Justification is relative not only to

---

[11] David Jewitt (of the University of Hawaii) and Jane Luu (of the University of California, Berkeley) are two leading astronomers investigating objects of the Kuiper Belt who used a 10 m. telescope in their discovery of 1995 WY2.

the exemplars endorsed by a given community, it is also relative to the judgements of similarity that link a given belief–evidence pair to one or more of these exemplars. We can put the lesson differently by saying that justification is never 'algorithmic': we cannot write down, for each type of belief, how it must be justified. Invariantism about justification is wrong because the algorithmic construal of justification is mistaken.

We must also note that the array of recognized exemplars changes over time. Indeed, in some cases the exemplars are simply all of the precedents; thus any new recognized instance of the norm changes the array, and thereby the situation for the next candidate. Justification is not just 'synchronically' relative, it is also 'diachronically' relative. The very meaning of 'justified' can—and does—change for a community as the array of exemplars changes. Noting this possibility of change is of great theoretical significance. For it shows that the norms of justification are as much the *results* of acts of justification as they are the determinants of acts of justification. The communal performative belief constituting a given norm changes—more or less subtly—with each interaction.

The point is perfectly general, not specific to justification. All social institutions display this structure. It is worth restating the general idea in two further ways, one 'Hegelian' and one 'mechanical'. To put it in Hegelian jargon, we can see here how 'I–we' relations and 'I–you' relations mediate one another. Here the 'I–you' relations stand for locally situated interaction, and the 'I–we' relations for the ways in which individuals' choices and decisions are pre-structured for them by their membership in social institutions. Thus, the I–you relations constitute and reconstitute the I–we relations, and the I–we dyad shapes and reshapes the many I–you dyads. Social institutions exist only in this mediation.

My second reformulation will take a bit more space. I want to suggest a simple mechanical model for understanding the 'determining–determined' nature of social institutions and particular interactions. The model can help to highlight the case of norms that exist in groups which are too large for all individuals to be aware of all others' beliefs and justifications. Take a simple aggregate of clocks. Each clock has its own degree of 'individuality', that is, its own characteristic speed of moving its pointers. Of course, as long as the clocks act independently of one another, we have no analogue of social life, and no analogue of social institutions. Social institutions have the function of reducing divergence, and of increasing similarity of output. In the present case we can imagine more than one way in which divergence can be reduced. Suffice it here to mention three. The 'way of the single authority' is to have all clocks linked up to one master clock. And at regular intervals—measured by the master clock itself—the latter resets all other clocks to its time. After that the clocks again diverge. The 'way of the single average' is to have all clocks linked up to one consensus-forming mechanism. At regular intervals (measured by some arbitrarily chosen clock) this mechanism simultaneously calls up information about the current times of all clocks. The mechanism calculates the average of all the readings it receives and resets all the clocks to this value. After that the clocks again diverge. Finally, according to the 'way of the multiple but local consensus', we allow our clocks to move about freely, without being linked to any kind of master device. (Assume the clocks are on wheels.) However, the space in which they can move about is limited, and thus they randomly collide. Whenever two (or more) of them collide, they are able to perform the following operation. They calculate the average of their times, and reset each other to this time. After that they again follow their own speed, and continue to move around until they meet with some other clock(s).

It is of course the third way that is most important for us. The third way models the situation of a social institution in which no member has access to the actions of all, and where conformity coexists with divergence. Indeed, only under very special circumstances will all clocks in the third scenario momentarily show exactly the same time. Moreover, it is the third way that is most significant for understanding how social institutions both determine and are determined by interaction. The time of each clock is adjusted only in one-to-one encounters, and yet it would clearly be wrong to claim that these encounters are primary with respect to each clock's relation to the whole population. For what each clock brings to the one-to-one encounters has been fixed by earlier encounters with clocks of the same population.

It might be objected that the third way of consensus-formation fits badly with my earlier discussion of communal beliefs. The earlier discussion of communal beliefs presupposed that we can all share in the same belief. The clock model, however, precludes that we all have the same belief (i.e. the same time). There is indeed a tension here, but I think it is a fruitful one. First of all, note that although universal coincidence of times will be rare in the third model, frequent random interaction among the clocks guarantees that their times will all move within a certain bandwidth. Clearly communal beliefs have the same feature. Our communal belief that £1 coins are money is a bandwidth-belief. That is to say, each one of us believes (as one of us living in the United Kingdom) that these coins are money—but in a slightly different way. The respective way depends on our expertise in identifying forged coins, on our experience with sudden loss of confidence in money, and on our profession. Second, unless communal beliefs had this bandwidth-nature it would be difficult to understand both how institutions change, and why the monitoring, correcting, and sanctioning of other believers is important.

To sum up: Justificatory norms exist only as communally endorsed exemplars. Such exemplars are belief–evidence pairs. Acts of justification of particular beliefs seek to assimilate the current belief–evidence pair to one of the exemplars. This involves judgements of similarity. Such judgements are always contestable. Acts of justification introduce new precedents of belief–evidence pairs for future acts of justification. In larger groups there need be no unique agreement on one set of exemplars. Frequent interaction guarantees that the exemplars do not drift apart too far. Ergo: Justification is essentially contextual.

The Causal Constraint upon Empirical Belief

All epistemologies of empirical knowledge reviewed above—with the one exception of direct realism—seek to relate rational constraint of empirical belief to causal constraint. In the last 'step', I have explained how communitarianism accounts for rational constraint: rational constraint results from mediation of local interaction and social institution. It remains for me to propose a role for causality. Any dialectical theory of justification must tread carefully in addressing causality. Two dangers loom. On the one hand, we must avoid bringing in causality in a way that reintroduces a view from nowhere, or that privileges our own specific view of the world. I argued above that Michael Williams has fallen in this trap. On the other hand, we had better not deny causality any role if we want to avoid following McDowell into his absolute idealism.

In turning to causality we are forced to change our mode of analysis from the formal to the material mode. That is to say, in analysing the different forms of communal and performative beliefs above, I did not have to commit myself to any specific contents for these beliefs. I merely analysed the relationships between different forms of belief. This changes here. To talk about causal relations is to talk in the material mode. It is to talk about the content of someone's empirical beliefs. Prima facie, this 'someone' might be me, we (as those who share in a common 'folk theory' of knowledge), or some group of scientists. I can formulate my views about how beliefs are caused; I might try to reconstruct our folk theory of knowledge; and I might try to summarize how psychologists see the aetiology of beliefs. I choose the second option. Communitarianism tries to understand the general role of knowledge and justification in human practices. And to do so it must take these practices themselves seriously. After all, these practices are sustained by folk theories of knowledge.[12] Moreover, empirical belief is not a category of cognitive psychology: it is a category of philosophical epistemology. And this philosophical epistemology is largely the product of philosophers' attempts to work out the consequences of their 'folk-epistemological' intuitions. Maybe there are reasons why we eventually might want to change this folk theory of knowledge—perhaps on grounds that derive their rationale from scientific observation. But it is hard to see how we could do so without working our way through the strengths and weaknesses of this theory.

'Empirical belief' obviously is a key category in our thinking about knowledge—even if we perhaps prefer different labels in everyday life: labels like 'beliefs based on perception' or 'beliefs about the world out there'. Moreover, it is an essential feature of empirical beliefs that they have causes in the world outside our mind. Clearly, no culture can be said to have an institution resembling our institution of 'empirical belief' unless it makes this assumption about a central class of beliefs. It is also implicit in our beliefs about empirical beliefs that in simple scenarios the causes of beliefs relate closely to the content of those beliefs. Davidson is of course right about that. One way in which we can put the central role of causality is this. To say 'I have an uncaused but correctly formed empirical belief' is like saying 'I got married but to no one in particular'. For our folk epistemology the question is not whether or not empirical beliefs are caused; the question is how, in

---

[12] We have to start with some culture. I suggest starting with a culture we know.

order for them to be rational and justified, they must be caused, or are allowed to be caused.

It would clearly be a mistake to distribute causality and rational constraint over two distinct regions. We saw how foundationalism and coherentism attempted to do just that: causality for the relationship between experience and the world; rational constraint for the relationship between beliefs (and, as foundationalism has it, for the relationship between experience and beliefs). And we saw that both were unable to avoid sceptical conclusions. We would land ourselves in similar difficulties if we located causality in our relations to the 'external world' and rational constraint in our relations to the 'social world'. Obviously there are all sorts of causal relations between us social creatures. And, as we shall see in a moment, there are rational links imposed upon our causal links to events in the 'extra-mental world'.

Another possible pitfall here is a certain construal of the idea that beliefs are involuntary as far as their coming into being is concerned. This might encourage the thought that the causal route to a belief is one thing, whereas the rational assessment of the belief is a subsequent, and different, thing. But this is clearly wrong. The aetiology of a belief is itself a topic for epistemic evaluation. We might not be able to avoid being caused to believe something, say p, in a given situation, say s, but we might well have the choice of whether or not we enter s in the first place. Depending on the prevailing views of the (type of) belief p, it can be a demand of rationality either to enter, or to avoid entering, s. Exposing myself to the views of Lacanian psychoanalysts might eventually cause me to think like them. If you are a Lacanian yourself, you might think this a good idea; if you are not, you might criticize me for ruining my good sense. Furthermore, there are also cases where we expect people to bring themselves into situations where they will be caused to believe that p if p (is true); and caused to believe $\sim p$ if $\sim p$ (is true). Jerry Fodor calls such cases 'exercises in cognitive self-management' (Fodor 1997). His prime examples are scientific experiments. Thus, in many cases, we evaluate causal routes to beliefs 'prospectively'; at least prospectively with respect to specific instances of types of beliefs. In many other cases, it is true, we assess them only 'retrospectively'.

Not all evaluations of empirical beliefs are evaluations of the beliefs' causal pedigree. And not all justifications of empirical beliefs are justifications of their causal ancestry either. I might justify my belief that TO66 is not a planet by referring you to the verdict of the IAU, or recent theories of the Kuiper Belt. If you accept these theories, you will regard my belief as justified (and share it). The reason for the belief will be, for both of us, the theories about the Kuiper Belt, not the causal story of how I came to know these theories, or how these theories were caused by observations about interplanetary objects. At least this is how common sense judges the issue, and I see no reason why we should contradict common sense here.

But let us concentrate here on cases where the epistemic assessment is indeed focused on the causal route. Here it is again vital to observe how communal constative, individual constative, and communal performative beliefs are intertwined. Take a judgement of the form (*u*), for instance (*v*).

(*u*) The individual belief that *p* is rational since it has been caused in way *q*.
(*v*) She believes that thinking and feeling are intertwined. This is rational for her to believe since her belief was caused by her introspecting her own mental states.

For such judgements to be possible for a community, it needs to have constituted both taxonomies of causal routes, that is, natural (or artificial) kinds, and categories for epistemic assessment, that is, social kinds. For instance, judgements of type (*v*) are possible only in a culture that accepts introspection as a type of causal route to beliefs, and that distinguishes introspection from other types of causal routes; say, seeing, hearing, smelling, and touching. This taxonomy is a taxonomy of natural kind (terms), and constituted by a communal performative belief like (*w*).

(*w*) We believe that causal routes to empirical beliefs can be subdivided into *n* number of types; among them are introspection, seeing, hearing, smelling, and touching.

At the same time, judgement (*v*) also involves the social status 'rational'; it too of course is created by a communal performative. Examples of such communal performatives are (*s*) and (*t*) above, with 'rational' instead of 'justified'. Finally, judgements of type (*u*) presuppose that social statuses (of epistemic evaluation) have been, and are, *imposed upon* natural (or artificial) kinds of causal routes:

(x) We believe that causal routes of type *x* are rational ways of forming beliefs.

Changes in (w) and changes in (x) will go hand in hand, and such changes will be impossible to avoid given that the assessment of epistemic statuses is based on exemplars. On the one hand, new discoveries about introspection as a psychological process might lead us to re-evaluate its epistemic standing. For instance, psychological experiments might show that, at least in some circumstances, introspecting has more in common with fantasizing than with perception. This might lead one to call introspection 'unreliable' and beliefs formed on its basis 'irrational' and 'unjustified'. On the other hand, it is easy to imagine a group of people wishing to defend the claim that introspection is reliable. Faced with the above results, these people will perhaps suggest that it is wrong to speak of introspection in the mentioned circumstances. The message of this should be obvious: taxonomies of causal routes and taxonomies of epistemic worth are both social products. Assessments of causal routes are specific to cultures, and thus not beyond dialectical justification.

Ordering Beliefs, Ordering People

Whatever the strengths of the communitarian theory as developed in the above, it still has (at least!) one important lacuna. Although I have written at some length about the general epistemic significance of communities and institutions, I have said nothing about the 'social order' of such communities, and how they relate to their 'doxastic order' (i.e. order in the realm of beliefs). One might put this point more succinctly by saying that I have yet to address the question of whether, and how, empirical knowledge is political. I shall be brief on this topic. Sociologists of scientific knowledge (including myself) have studied the relationship of social and doxastic orders in many scientific and philosophical disputes, and some of them have formulated more general theories on the matter. I do not want to summarize that literature here. But I want to say enough for it to become clear that my analysis above dovetails with the concerns of that literature; and that I regard the topic as a genuinely epistemological one. The feminist philosopher Miranda Fricker has recently insisted that 'epistemology will not be truly socialised until it has been appropriately politicised'. I fully agree.[13]

In asking whether empirical knowledge is political I am asking whether empirical knowledge is essentially involved in ordering people. By 'ordering people' I mean distributing entitlements and commitments either over different sub-groups of a larger group, or over different individuals within a group. Entitlements and commitments can concern anything from speech-acts to properties.

There are several senses in which knowledge might be claimed to be political. A first sense emerges directly from my proposals in earlier 'steps'. Communitarian epistemology analyses empirical knowledge as communal empirical belief. Communal empirical belief presupposes the constitution of a plural, communal subject, a 'we'. Any such 'we' is a community. Any such 'we' is a way of ordering people in some way. It is to say who is more or less competent in defending the communal belief, whose views matter more or less than others, or who has discretion over whether the belief should be changed or modified, and so on. Ergo: knowledge is political. No ordering of people (and their entitlements and commitments), no communal subject. No communal subject, no communal empirical belief. No communal empirical belief, no empirical knowledge.

Note that this conclusion is the result of an argument that starts from some general observations concerning our intuitions (our folk theory) regarding justification and knowledge. It is not based on the stipulation that knowledge had best been treated as accepted belief. Sociologists of knowledge often make such stipulation, and, for their purposes, rightly so. I am after different game. My aim has been to show that the sociologist need not present this assumption as a mere 'professional commitment' or a 'mere hypothesis'. She can rely on this view because it is supported by the intuitions and the folk theory of knowledge that we all share: traditional epistemologists and sociologists alike. Epistemologists who challenge the sociologists' assumption misconstrue these intuitions.

---

[13] See M. Fricker (1998). My comments on the political nature of empirical knowledge are influenced by my reading not only of the sociology of knowledge but also of feminist epistemology. See e.g. Alcoff and Potter (1993). For an earlier attempt of mine to come to grips with the relationship between power and knowledge, see Kusch (1991).

Second, and closely related to the first point, knowledge might be said to be political since all empirical knowledge presupposes performative beliefs. No knowledge about nature without knowledge about society. No knowledge about nature without knowledge about communally instituted taxonomies, standards, and exemplars. Natural kinds too are social institutions—even though natural kind terms purport to refer to entities that exist independently of our talk. And all social institutions order people. Institutions of empirical knowledge order them into the experts and non-experts, the observers and the observed, the testifiers and the unreliable witnesses, those who treat and those who are treated, the teachers and the students, and so on. Of course, these ways of ordering people exist only in so far as they are believed to exist. (This idea is of course central to my analysis of institutions as performative beliefs.) And thus knowledge of the social order is inseparable from knowledge about the natural world.

Third, I have put much emphasis on the idea that every justification is in principle contestable. Justification involves judgements of similarity and analogy (regarding exemplars), and thus it always leaves room for constructing a challenge. The question of whether A and B are similar is the question of whether or not they are 'similar enough' by some standards or other. Nothing about A and B itself can settle the question of which standards one chooses. This is not to say, however, that standards are necessarily chosen on the basis of political interests or agendas. If this were the case, then we would have a further sense in which all knowledge is political. But to claim that all standards of justification are chosen with an eye to one's political agenda is to exaggerate. I prefer to be more cautious. Almost anything—any further belief or goal—can influence which standards of similarity are chosen. Some of them might be motivated by political interests in improving one's position regarding the distribution of commitments and entitlements. And yet they need not be so motivated. All this is not to deny that justification is indeed essentially political. What makes justification essentially political is not the omnipresence of political interests. What makes it essentially political is the fact that the justifier and her interlocutor bring their respective social power (or powerlessness) to their interaction. It is the social power of one over the other that influences whose views on similarity and analogy (regarding exemplars) prevail.

Fourth, I have, as yet, said little about the truism that empirical beliefs do not come one by one. This is so in particular for empirical beliefs that have the status of knowledge. Communal beliefs are always more or less central members of a group of beliefs, and set apart from (the members of) other groups. Communal beliefs are ordered into groups by relations such as: 'contradict one another', 'have nothing to do with one another', 'belong to different fields', 'one is (should be) modelled on the other', 'one should be used to formulate the other', 'follow from each other', 'if the one must be true, the other must be true as well', or 'you cannot think of the one without thinking of the other'. Such relations are crucial elements of systems of knowledge. And, importantly for us here, they are subject to the very same processes of justification as the beliefs that they relate. The justification of relations between beliefs too is bound to exemplars, based on judgements of analogy and similarity, and thus essentially contestable. This means of course that the boundaries and dependencies between different bodies of knowledge can be constructed in endless different ways. Again, the choice of standards of similarity determines which beliefs will get grouped together, and which dependencies will be asserted. And nothing in or about these beliefs themselves fixes the choice. As case-studies in the sociology of knowledge have shown time and again, the choice between such standards is often determined by the wish of a group to change the prevailing distribution of commitments and entitlements to their advantage.

Finally, empirical beliefs can be said to be political also in so far as they shape their referents. That is to say, empirical beliefs can turn out to have a performative dimension: their 'direction of fit' is twofold. They concern both what is and what ought to be. They fit the world only because they also form the world. Writers on sex and gender have suggested convincingly that such processes are at work in the ways in which our bodies are shaped. We make it so that our empirical beliefs about male and female bodies come out true. Or, theories of what homosexuals think and do became true when some people felt that the category of the homosexual could be useful for their political struggles.[14]

---

[14] I am not of course suggesting that my communitarian epistemology is the only epistemology able to come to grips with such cases.

Knowledge and Social Status Revisited

The above analysis of knowledge and justification has ramifications for the 'ontology of knowledge', that is, regarding the question of how knowledge exists. I have already touched upon this issue in Part I. There I suggested that our folk epistemology of testimony implies that knowledge is a social status, and that 'knowledge' is a social kind term like 'marriage' rather than a natural kind term like 'elephant' or an artificial kind term like 'typewriter'. Having developed a communitarian epistemology of empirical knowledge at least in broad outline, we can now address anew the ontology of knowledge, and without confining the issue to testimony.

Only very few epistemologists of empirical knowledge make their onto-logical views concerning knowledge explicit. In the Anglophone literature I can think of only two authors who are clear on this score: Hilary Kornblith and Karl Popper. Kornblith believes that epistemology studies 'a certain natural phenomenon, namely, knowledge itself' (1999: 161). And he parallels the study of knowledge to that of a natural kind like aluminium. The important upshot of this parallel is that an investigation of the everyday concept of knowledge is not of interest. After all, scientists do not study folk conceptions of aluminium, they study the stuff itself.

Popper clearly thinks of knowledge as a human artefact, albeit as an artefact that humans produce using their natural capacities. Popper speaks of knowledge as 'the third world'. The first world is 'the world of physical objects or of physical states'; the second world is 'the world of states of consciousness, or of mental states, or perhaps of behavioural dispositions to act'; and the third world is 'the world of *objective contents of thought*, especially of scientific and poetic thoughts and of works of art'. In speaking of knowledge as an artefact, Popper explicitly accepts the implication that knowledge can survive even when all humans disappear from the face of the earth. Knowledge remains knowledge, even if unused, just like a 'wasp's nest is a wasp's nest even after it has been deserted; even though it is never again used by a wasp as a nest' (Popper 1972: 106, 112, 115).

Both Kornblith and Popper might draw support for their view from the ways we talk in everyday life—though neither of them will regard such support as necessary. We talk of knowledge as 'natural stuff' when we attribute it to animals and plants ('The dog knows where its bone is hidden';

'The flowers know the path of the sun'). And we imagine knowledge as an artefact when we allow that knowledge is 'produced' or 'created'.

Communitarian epistemology is committed to the view that knowledge is a social status. All of the above analysis points naturally in this direction. 'Knowledge' is a status to which individuals sometimes lay claim for (one of) their beliefs. A belief can gain this status in the eyes of other individuals when these other individuals come to share the belief, come to recognize the rightfulness of the claim, and thereby come to form a minimal epistemic community around the belief. In the process of forming this community, the original belief is no longer held only individually; it comes to be held in a group-involving way by several individuals. The whole process is made possible by communal performative beliefs that constitute the status, exemplars of justification, and epistemic communities. Finally, laying claim to the status 'knowledge' and forming an epistemic community around a belief are local and contextual phenomena. The status exists only in and through individual acts and beliefs that refer to it.

But we do not need all of my argument above in order to see that knowledge is a social kind. First of all, 'knowledge' refers to a bundle of entitlements and commitments. In claiming to know something, we commit ourselves to being able to marshal evidence in support of the claim. We entitle our interlocutors to call on us to present this evidence, and—at least prima facie—we entitle ourselves to the status of someone who is worth consulting and following. Only social kind terms refer directly to systems of entitlements and commitments. Natural kind terms do not.

To this Kornblith and Popper might reply that reference to a system of entitlements and commitments is a mere accidental feature of our concept of knowledge. Here they will draw on the basic reliabilist intuition, to wit, that we can attribute knowledge to people who are themselves unable to marshal justifications. But this is a view that we have already found wanting. It is true that we can *attribute* knowledge without *attributing* (the ability to produce) justification. But this does not mean that we can *attribute* knowledge without *possessing* justification. In calling the information possessed by someone else 'knowledge' we commit ourselves to being able to provide justification both for our knowing that the other knows, and for the other's knowing itself.

It also deserves notice that the social-status analysis of knowledge is not endangered by cases of animal or solitary knowers. After all, we sometimes impose social statuses on humans, animals, and things that are unaware of the status in question. Courts can convict people in their absence; animals and things can be lawful property. We also say that the beta male of a band of chimps will eventually 'inherit' the position of the alpha male, or that a group of lions is having a 'meal'. We do not thereby come to deny that inheritance and meal (as opposed to food) are social kinds.

Treating knowledge as natural stuff makes it impossible to account for its normative properties. The analysis of knowledge as an artefact does not fare much better. Artefacts have functions. We can say what canals, pens, and chairs are for. But to have a function is different from being a bundle of entitlements and commitments. To call something 'a border' is to refer to a bundle of entitlements and commitments (regarding passage, the movement of goods, etc.). To call something a 'pen' is to refer to a function. Calling something a pen often includes the hint that it had better be used one way rather than another; say for writing on paper rather than for stirring a soup. But whatever normativity might be included in function-talk, it is purely prudential. Social kinds are different. Marriage refers to a set of entitlements and commitments between (primarily) two people. Some of these entitlements and commitments are fixed by law, others by custom. Economists might argue that all of these entitlements and commitments can 'ultimately' be explained in terms of prudential considerations by the two parties. But this analysis is not part of how you and I understand the social status of marriage in our daily life. In everyday use, marriage does not refer to a function.

What holds for marriage is also true of knowledge. It is easy to remind people of the fact that attaching the label 'knowledge' to one of their opinions amounts to taking on a certain argumentative burden, and to demanding a certain position of authority. We would not think that someone had understood what knowledge is unless they recognized as much. I doubt, however, that many of us have a clear idea of what might be the general function of knowledge—unless of course we define the function of the word 'knowledge' as signalling a certain bundle of entitlements and commitments. If we accept the latter suggestion, then the view of knowledge as an artefact collapses into the view of knowledge as a social status. Barring this collapse, it is unclear what a general function of knowledge could be. There simply are far too many and varied functions of knowledge ranging from getting us to the train in time, through being able to watch our favourite television programme, to enabling us to fly to the moon.

Again there is no reason to withdraw our analysis in the light of how we speak in ordinary language. It is true that we sometimes speak of knowledge as something that is produced or created. But that is just shorthand for saying that we produce and create whatever the social status is being attached to. No one would think that factories determine which discs count as coins. That is the task of the central bank. And yet we normally would not object if someone remarked that a given factory produces good pound notes or good pound coins. The institution of knowledge-talk does involve the creation of artefacts, and it is dependent on natural processes. Money is too. And yet money, like knowledge, only exists in so far as it is recognized as such in particular contexts. Think of internationally recognized borders between countries. Surely we would think that anyone who studied such borders on the model of natural kinds like aluminium or artificial kinds like canals had missed the mark by a wide margin. If my arguments above are correct, then Kornblith and Popper have done no better regarding knowledge.

Chapter 12

SUMMARY

Part II has covered a lot of ground. It will perhaps be useful to restate the main points. My discussion in this chapter has fallen into two parts: a criticism of other theories of empirical knowledge, and the development of a communitarian alternative. The critical part was structured into three main chapters.

Chapter 8 showed that foundationalism and coherentism fail to give a satisfactory answer to the question of how our empirical beliefs are rationally constrained. Foundationalism claims that our empirical beliefs are rationally constrained by our non-verbal experience. Non-verbal experience is caused by events in the world. Coherentism suggests that empirical beliefs are rationally constrained only by other, further empirical beliefs. And beliefs are caused by sensations and worldly events. Foundationalism and coherentism fail because they seek to solve the problem of rational constraint at the level of the isolated individual. Normativity, however, presupposes a rational standard independent of the individual. And such a standard can be provided only by a community.

Chapter 9 discussed two 'impatient' ways of escaping the see-saw of foundationalism and coherentism: direct realism and reliabilism. The latter two try to overcome the difficulties of the former two by radical means. Direct realism assimilates the world to a system of beliefs. Reliabilism reduces the knower to a reliable instrument for the adoption of beliefs. I argued that neither solution works. Direct realism addresses the question of rational constraint, but it does so by personifying the world in an unacceptable manner. Reliabilism overlooks that reliability is a social status, not a natural fact.

Chapter 10 treated the two main current versions of social epistemology: dualism and duettism. Dualism is based on the abrupt juxtaposition of individual and group; duettism is structured around the idea of I–you interaction. Consensualism and interpretationalism were my two examples of dualism and duettism respectively. I showed that rational constraint of empirical belief cannot be understood on the basis of I–we relations *or* I–you relations *alone*. The task is to understand how the two forms of social relations mediate one another.

In Chapter 11 I turned to communitarian epistemology. I introduced contextualism as an ally of my own epistemology of empirical knowledge. I sided with the conception of dialectical justification and with quietism regarding global justification. But I criticized attempts to combine contextualism with reliabilism. Finally, I sketched the main ingredients of epistemological communitarianism. Central here were the distinctions between kinds of beliefs: communal versus individual, and performative versus empirical. The main results were that an empirical belief can only become knowledge by becoming communal; and that all empirical beliefs presuppose social institutions. In conclusion I maintained that knowledge is political and that knowledge is a social kind.

Part III

Objectivity

Chapter 13

BEYOND
EPISTEMOLOGY

In Parts I and II I sketched a communitarian epistemology of testimony and empirical belief. I sought to motivate this new form of epistemology in two ways: by criticizing received approaches for their individualism, and by outlining communitarian answers to some of the traditional questions in the study of knowledge. In Part III I move beyond the borders of epistemology and discuss some central issues in the philosophy of language and metaphysics. This should not come as a surprise. Although questions about meaning, truth, and reality are not per se epistemological, all epistemological theories presuppose specific answers with respect to these questions. The reason why these answers can usually be left in the background of discussion is that there exists widespread agreement among epistemologists over the *correct* answers to these questions. Thus, most epistemologists share the views that terms have fixed extensions; that the correspondence theory is the correct account of truth; that all descriptions of reality must ultimately be compatible; that we can all be wrong on some given issue; and that epistemological relativism is self-refuting.

For better or worse, I do not share (fully) in this widespread consensus. Lest my position will be misunderstood, or judged to be incoherent, I had therefore better explain where, and why, I differ. This is what I shall try to do here.

I begin, in Chapter 14, with a more detailed defence of one of the most central premisses of my communitarian epistemology, that is, the idea that normative phenomena can exist only within communities. Central in what follows will be a theory of meaning, called 'meaning finitism'. Chapter 15 introduces the basic ideas of meaning finitism by relying on simplified game scenarios before explaining meaning finitism more systematically. Chapter 16 applies meaning finitism to 'true' and 'false' and compares the resulting theory of truth with some of its competitors. Chapter 17 discusses conceptual and ontological relativism, that is, the debate between realism and anti-realism. Chapter 18 discusses two attempts to deal with community-wide error and ignorance. Finally, in Chapter 19 I reply to some often heard objections to epistemological relativism.

It has sometimes been suggested to me—by well-meaning readers—that I should carefully separate the communitarian themes of Parts I and II from the uncompromising finitism and relativism in this Part III. These readers fear that too close a link between epistemological communitarianism and relativism will lead many philosophers to reject the former together with the latter. The worry is undoubtedly justified, but I cannot see ways of driving a wedge between the two projects. My theory of testimony centrally involved the claim that knowledge is a social status, and that content and imposition of a social status depend on local interests and negotiation among social actors. Regarding the normativity of empirical beliefs I argued that the justification of knowledge-claims depends on locally available, contingent paradigms of justification. These views seem to me to call for the kind of position regarding objectivity that I defend in Part III. Needless to say, I would study with great interest proposals on how to defend the ideas of my Parts I and II *without* relying on the ideas in my Part III—but I suspect that such proposals will not be coherent.

Chapter 14

NORMATIVITY
AND COMMUNITY

NORMATIVITY, THE PRIVATE LANGUAGE
ARGUMENT, AND RULE-FOLLOWING

One of the most central premisses of communitarian epistemology is the idea that normative phenomena—rules, norms, conventions, prescriptions, and standards of correctness—can exist only within communities. Put differently, socially isolated individuals are unable to generate normative phenomena. Let me call this idea the 'community thesis'. In what follows, I shall try to defend it.

In contemporary philosophy the community thesis is being discussed primarily in the philosophy of language and mind. More precisely, the community thesis is crucial in arguments against so-called 'private languages'—languages that are used only by a single, socially isolated, individual. Philosophers seeking to demonstrate the impossibility of private languages rely on the link between normativity and community as a premiss in their overall argument. Put in a nutshell, this argument goes as follows:

> For a system of signs to count as a language, actions of sign-use must be classifiable along two related dimensions: the dimension of 'correct versus incorrect', and the dimension of 'seems right versus is right'.
> A phenomenon is normative if it essentially involves the distinctions 'correct versus incorrect' and 'seems right versus is right'.
> Normativity presupposes community.

Ergo: Private languages are impossible.

Often the argument is conducted on a slightly more general level: the question then becomes whether a socially isolated individual would be able to follow rules (regardless of whether or not these rules are rules of a language). In this more general form the argument runs thus:

> One cannot speak of an actor as a rule-follower unless the distinctions 'correct versus incorrect' and 'seems right versus is right' are applicable to the actor.
>
> A phenomenon is normative if it essentially involves the distinctions 'correct versus incorrect' and 'seems right versus is right'.
>
> Normativity presupposes community.
>
> Ergo: Private rule-following is impossible.

Much of the dispute over the possibility of private rule-following is focused on the community thesis. 'Individualists' defend the possibility of private rule-following by denying the thesis; 'communitarians' oppose the possibility of private rule-following by insisting that the thesis is correct. I believe that the communitarians have won the argument, but in order to make this assessment plausible, I shall have to present some key junctures of the dispute.[1]

The debate over the community thesis has two interrelated levels. On one level, philosophers argue for and against the community thesis itself. On another level, and often in the very same paper, philosophers seek to show that Ludwig Wittgenstein is best interpreted as sharing their respective view of the community thesis. The two levels are almost always related to one another not only because the whole issue of private languages was first made salient in Wittgenstein's *Philosophical Investigations* but also because Wittgenstein is—rightly or wrongly—thought of as the ultimate authority in this matter. It seems unimaginable to many philosophers that Wittgenstein could possibly be on the wrong side of this fence. Here I shall nevertheless ignore the question where Wittgenstein himself stood on the issue. Although I happen to believe that he favoured the communitarian side, I shall not attempt to defend this claim in this book.[2]

---

[1] Needless to say, I am not striving for completeness here. Important anthologies on the philosophy of rule-following are Pitcher (1964) and Canfield (1986).

[2] As far as the interpretation of Wittgenstein is concerned, I have learned most from Bloor (1997), Canfield (1996), and Malcolm (1995).

DISTINCTIONS

In order to make the dispute over the community thesis tractable and decidable, it is important to give it a precise content. This is best done by making a number of distinctions.

1. We need to differentiate between two kinds of private language: those that are *essentially* private and those that are merely *accidentally* private. A language is essentially private if the meanings of its expressions are, or depend on, 'epistemically private items' (Craig 1982, 1997). The clearest examples of such items are sensations. You cannot have my sensations, and I cannot have yours. Hence, if our respective sensations are part of the meanings of our respective words, then our respective meanings must differ. Add to this the idea that one can never know someone else's sensations, and we arrive at the claim that all language is essentially private. A language that is merely *accidentally* private does not involve epistemically private items. Someone's language is accidentally private if de facto it is not shared with others—although it could in principle be shared. A secret language that I develop just for my own use would be accidentally private. Sometimes the term 'private language' is reserved for essentially private languages; accidentally private language is often called 'solitary language'. I shall follow this usage here. For my defence of the community thesis I shall only be concerned with solitary languages and solitary rule-following.

2. It is important to distinguish between *physical* and *social isolation* (Bloor 1997: 92; cf. Kripke 1982: 110). Social life is episodic; between our face-to-face encounters we are physically isolated from others. But even when we are physically isolated, we remain socially 'embedded': we are related to others in our thinking, feeling, and acting. We anticipate blame and reward, we make plans that involve others, and we harbour various feelings for them. To be physically but not socially isolated is a frequent experience for most of us. But we are never fully socially isolated. A wolf child (before capture) would be a case of someone who was both physically and socially isolated from other humans. And maybe a severely autistic child can be thought of as being socially but not physically isolated. The case of Defoe's Robinson Crusoe is not so clear. Crusoe grows up in human communities and washes up on the shores of his island only by the time he is already an adult. Subsequently he spends twenty-six years on his own. Was Crusoe socially or

just physically isolated? Intuitions diverge at this point. If we judge him to have been merely physically isolated, we are thinking of his twenty-six lonely years as a (very long) interval between face-to-face encounters. If we opt for social isolation, we are guided by the idea that twenty-six years is too long a period to count as an interval between social interactions.

3. We need to make a number of distinctions regarding rules. One important distinction is that between *rules* and *regularities* (Robinson 1992). Some regularities of human behaviour are 'natural' and innate. Instinctive behaviour fits this bill. Other regularities of behaviour are 'acquired'. Among the latter it is useful to distinguish between those that are acquired voluntarily and those that are acquired involuntarily. Conditioning is a case of the latter, learning a skill a case of the former. Not every regularity of human behaviour is due to a rule, even though the practice of every rule-follower will display some regularity. The natural regularities in an agent's behaviour obviously are never caused by the agent's following of rules. But neither are involuntarily acquired regularities. Rules can be deliberately violated; this precludes the possibility of conditioned behaviour being an instance of rule-following.

4. *Following a rule* differs from merely *acting in accordance with a rule*. Londoners using the Underground know the following rule-governing behaviour on the long escalators: 'stand right, walk left'. They learn the rule by reading the signs. Many tourists in London do not understand English, and hence do not know of this rule; and yet most of them stand right anyway. They act in accordance with the rule but they do not follow it. A rule-follower must, on some level, know both what she *is* doing and what she *is supposed to* do.

5. It is customary to distinguish between the *introduction*—or *stipulation*—and the subsequent *application* of a rule. The introduction stipulates the content of the rule, what is to be done under what circumstances. When we apply rules, we judge whether the given circumstances are those specified by the rule. This distinction feels intuitive and simple, but it is important to recognize how misleading it can be. We cannot draw a sharp dividing line between application and stipulation of the content of a rule, since it is only in and through a series of applications that the rule acquires a clear content. Assume my wife and I introduce the rule that we go running in the morning. Surely, when first introducing the rule, we have not yet foreseen all the varied circumstances that might lead us to modify the rule: visits of relatives, illnesses, sports broadcasts from the Olympics in Australia, lack of time due

to early-morning appointments, hangovers, etc. And yet it seems natural to say that it is only in the process of our facing these varying circumstances of application that the rule itself acquires more and more content. Paradoxical as it might sound, it is only by applying the rule that we stipulate its content.

6. A further important distinction is that between *rule-formulation* and *rule-practice*. Rules can often be formulated in language: 'We should go running every morning', 'Most fish dishes call for white wine', 'Essays have to be handed in at the beginning of January'. But an agent can be said to follow a rule even if he is not thinking of the rule at all. On many mornings my wife and I will go running without even considering our rule. Or think of a baseball player (Searle 1995: 146). He would be greatly impeded in his performance if he had to think of the rules while chasing and throwing the ball. These scenarios are cases where a rule-practice has evolved. A rule-practice is a pattern of actions that the actors regard as being correctly captured by the rule-formulation. The practice persists and develops on the basis of precedent rather than rule-formulation. The actors do 'what we have always done' rather than 'what could be described as falling under the rule-formulation'. This is not to say that the rule-formulation is irrelevant. The possibility of discourse about the practice is what makes it a *rule*-practice rather than an *instinctual* practice. And citing the rule-formulation is an important part of that discourse.

7. The word 'rule' is 'an especially messy cluster concept' (Lewis 1969: 105). We speak of rules in many different contexts. Sometimes 'rule' is used to refer to generalizations or laws of nature, sometimes for maxims or hypothetical imperatives, sometimes for norms and conventions. A detailed analysis of the various uses would be important and helpful, but it has not to date been attempted. Nevertheless, some uses of 'rule' have received closer attention. Interestingly enough, these all tend to be uses that involve communities rather than individuals. In other words, analysts have focused on social rules. The perhaps best-known account was suggested in the early 1960s by the legal theorist H. L. A. Hart; it has recently been amended and improved by the social philosopher Margaret Gilbert. Gilbert offers the following definition of a social rule:

There is a *social rule in a group G* that action A is to be done in circumstances C, if every member of G:

[a] regularly does A in C...

[b] has a 'critical reflective attitude' to the pattern of behavior: doing A in C...

[c] regards doing A in C as a 'standard of criticism' for the behavior of members of G...

[d] regards non-performance of A in C by a member of G as a fault open to criticism...

[e] criticizes any member of G who does not do A in C and puts pressure to conform on members of G who threaten not to do A in C...

[f] believes that every group member *has a claim against* every other group member for the performance of A in C and a consequent *title to exert punitive pressure* on any other group member in favor of doing A in C...

[g] expresses their criticisms and demand using normative language such as 'You *ought* to do A now!' or 'That's wrong'...

[h] feels that members of G are in some sense 'bound' to conform to the pattern: doing A in circumstances C...(Gilbert 2000: 73, 76)

I find this analysis adequate as an account of social rules. The question we will have to ask ourselves below is how much we can give up of this deeply social picture, while retaining the notion of a rule.

8. As we shall see below, all participants in the debate over the community thesis agree that some level of 'multi-subjectivity' is needed for there to be rule-following. In other words, all sides agree on this point: an agent who exists only for one single moment in time could not be said to follow a rule. The disagreement begins after this point and concerns the question whether rule-following presupposes *intersubjectivity* or mere *intrasubjectivity*. Does rule-following presuppose a community of different individuals or will a community of the time-slices (or modules) of one and the same individual do? Needless to say, these two positions will only mark a clear distinction if we ignore multiple personalities, time travel, and people with memory disorders.

9. It is useful to reflect on the kind, or strength, of argument one expects to emerge from the debate over rule-following. Many arguments in the debate are appeals to semantic intuitions concerning the word 'rule'. Communitarians insist that 'rule' really means social rule; individualists are adamant that the category 'rule' is not exhausted by social rules. The difference comes out clearly in disagreement over whether a congenitally isolated individual could invent rules for himself. Communitarians feel that speaking of the social isolate as following rules is stretching the concept of

rule too far. Individualists propose to see the social isolate as analogous to the social group. Communitarians reply that analogy is not good enough. Individualists think this reply begs the question. And so on. Unsurprisingly, not everyone is happy with the expectation that proper concentration on what we *really* mean by 'rule' will decide the issue. More than one philosopher has voiced doubts about the project of a conceptual analysis that involves checking our semantic intuitions in highly unusual circumstances. Leslie Stevenson puts the point as follows:

Why should we expend so much mental effort pursuing the question of the mere logical possibility of these shadowy creatures of myth and philosophical fantasy— Adam before the creation of Eve, a Crusoe isolated from birth, the articulate wolf-child, the solipsist with no concept of other minds? All the evidence goes to show ... their psychological impossibility ... Since actual cases of articulate Crusoes have not come up, we have not had to decide what to say about them. And, on reflection, we can see that there is no reason why our concepts of meaning, knowledge, rule-following, etc., should somehow have built-in guidance for how to apply them to cases never before encountered. (1993: 447)

I sympathize with the general sentiment but I am somewhat less pessimistic. The communitarian viewpoint is strengthened if it can be shown that the individualist's case rests on highly implausible interpretations of artificial scenarios. We should not expect it to be an analytic truth that rule-following is social. But we might come to see that the social nature of rule-following is central to how we think about language, normativity, and ourselves.

10. Finally, the community-dependence of rule-following is not a simple 'yes or no' issue. Community dependence is a matter of degree. A weak degree is acceptable even to the individualist; and communitarianism can be more or less strong. We need then a taxonomy of degrees of community-dependence. Such taxonomy was first suggested by Colin McGinn (1984: 194–9); mine is a further development of his.

(A) *Strongest Present-Tense Community Thesis.* An individual is able to follow a rule only if the individual is currently a participating member of a group in which the very same rule is followed by other members.

(B) *Strong Present-Tense Community Thesis.* An individual is able to follow a rule only if the individual is currently a participating member of a group in which some rules or other—but not necessarily the same rule—is followed by other members.

(C) *Past-Tense Community Thesis*. An individual is able to follow a rule only if the individual *has been, at some point in the past,* a participating member of a group in which the very same rule, or some other rule, was followed by other members.

(D) *Moderate Community Thesis*. An individual follows a rule if and only if the participating members of an existing group judge parts of the individual's behaviour to be *similar to* their behaviour in following the very same rule. The individual in question need not be a member of the group in question.

(E) *Weak Community Thesis*. An individual follows a rule if and only if it is possible to imagine a community in which that rule is followed by participating members.

(F) *Weakest Community Thesis*. An individual follows a rule if and only if the participating members of an existing group judge aspects of the individual's behaviour to be *similar to* aspects of their behaviour in following some rule or other. The individual in question need not be a member of the group in question.

I shall refer to A to E as communitarian views, and to F as the individualist position. Eventually, I shall defend A, a position also advocated in Bloor (1997). C is the most commonly defended communitarian position (e.g. Malcolm 1995; Meredith Williams 1991). D has been put forward by Kripke (1982: 110). E is favoured by Peacocke (1981: 93–4). And F is put forward by, among many others, Baker and Hacker (1984). Most individualist attacks on the community view have been directed (jointly) at A, B, and C. D and E have been scrutinized less often.

AGAINST WEAK AND MODERATE COMMUNITY THESES (D AND E)

Peacocke states the *Weak Community Thesis* E in the following passage:

Nothing in the community view ... excludes the possibility of a permanently isolated desert-islander rule-follower. The community view can count such a person as a genuine rule-follower if he reacts to new examples in the same way as would members of our own community, or of some other conceivable community. The community need not be that (if any) of the rule-follower himself. (1981: 93–4)

The problem with this weak version of the community view is that it places too few constraints on rule-following: 'the subjunctive, together with the requirement of mere *conceivability* of a community, robs the qualification of any restrictive content whatever' (Baker and Hacker 1984: 449; cf. Budd 1984: 319). Moreover, one might ask whether Peacocke's position in this passage actually fits with the view expressed in the rest of his paper. A few pages before the quoted passage Peacocke summarizes Wittgenstein's—and his own—view as follows:

According to Wittgenstein, it is, roughly speaking, the way that others go on in new cases in applying a word, and my conformity with their practice, which determines whether I am following a rule, whether I mean something by an expression or not; and if this is the account; then it is not clear how someone could still mean the same as the other members of the community by some expression and yet try to revise the judgments which, according to Wittgenstein, help to determine its meaning. (1981: 89)

Revising community judgements, conforming to the practice of others—these seem activities that require an actual rather than a merely possible community.

The *Moderate Community Thesis* D is part of the most controversial interpretation of Wittgenstein's later philosophy, Saul Kripke's *Wittgenstein on Rules and Private Language* (1982). In a famous passage of this book Kripke denies that his communitarian interpretation of Wittgenstein makes the latter an opponent of all forms of private rule-following:

if we think of Crusoe as following rules, we are taking him into our community and applying our criteria for rule following to him. The falsity of the private model need not mean that a *physically isolated* individual cannot be said to follow rules; rather that an individual, *considered in isolation* (whether or not he is physically isolated), cannot be said to do so. . . . Our community can assert of any individual that he follows a rule if he passes the tests for rule following applied to any member of the community. (1982: 110)

Kripke's view seems to be that even extreme physical isolation (perhaps even physical isolation from birth) need not give rise to social isolation and thus to the inability to follow rules. Crusoe's social isolation is avoided only if we find ourselves able to attribute to Crusoe the intention to follow one of our rules. For this Crusoe needs to fulfil the criteria for rule-following that we routinely apply to each other in our community.

This strikes me as an incoherent view. It clearly has the consequence that someone might be called a rule-follower even though he never interacts socially with any of us. And that seems to fly in the face of our very criteria for picking out rule-followers among us. When we try to decide whether one of us is following a specific rule, we inevitably engage in social (discursive) interaction. Indeed, the ability to explain oneself is, for us, the central criterion for rule-following. If we stick to our criteria, then Crusoe cannot be regarded as a rule-follower.

A different way of making the same point is to distinguish between Crusoe's and our own categories. For us to be convinced that Crusoe is a rule-follower, *he* must be able to draw a meaningful distinction—'meaningful' by our lights—between 'seems right' and 'is right'. And given our standards for attributing rule-following to an actor, we could not be so convinced unless we were to interact with him discursively. Needless to say, we could of course describe Crusoe's actions in light of *our* distinction between 'seems right' and 'is right'. But the possibility of this description is not enough for Crusoe to pass as a rule-follower; this description merely makes him act in accordance with a rule. (Note that I am not (yet) insisting that Crusoe could not follow rules. I am merely arguing that he could not be said to follow rules if such attribution was dependent on him fulfilling the very same criteria that we in society routinely apply to one another.)

Individualists' criticism of Kripke's moderate community view obviously proceeds differently. Individualists insist—in accordance with F—that we can attribute rule-following to Crusoe even if he does not abide by our rules:

Must Crusoe's rules be the same as ours?... Could he not invent new rules, play new games? To be sure, in order to *grasp* them, we must understand what counts, in Crusoe's *practice*, as following the rules. And that must be evident in Crusoe's *activities*. But that is not the same as checking to see whether his responses agree with ours, let alone a matter of 'taking him into our community'. And our judgment that he is following his rules is quite independent of any judgment about how most members of the English Speaking People would react. (Baker and Hacker 1984: 434)

I find view F unconvincing. But in order to make my case as best I can, I had better first introduce the individualists' arsenal of arguments against stronger community theses A to C.

THE INDIVIDUALISTS' CRITIQUE OF STRONG COMMUNITY THESES (A TO C)

In order to be comprehensive and fair in my treatment of the individualists, I shall introduce all six of their major arguments against A to C. Following this, I shall rebut each of these arguments, often relying on help from other communitarians.

I propose calling the first argument the *Metaphysical Argument*. It appeals to our intuitions of what is conceivable, and hence metaphysically possible. The thought is this. There is nothing inconceivable about a scenario in which God creates a single rule-following individual. And since this scenario is conceivable, it is metaphysically possible. The inventor and champion of this line of thought is Colin McGinn. Here is his formulation:

A vivid way to appreciate the force of what I am calling the natural view is to imagine what it would take to create (in a God-like way) rule-followers or concept-possessors. According to the community view, nothing you can do in the constitution of an individual can justify the assertion that he has concepts or means anything *until* you create other individuals . . . But how could the creation of other individuals wreak such a momentous change in the first created individual? (1984: 191)

The last sentence of the quotation foreshadows the second argument, the *Internalist Argument*. It insists that whether or not an individual is a rule-follower depends solely on facts about that individual's mental states. The point can be made forcefully by imagining catastrophes that have but a single survivor: 'could not the rest of the human race be wiped out while you sleep and yet the next day you awake with your rule-following capacities intact?' (McGinn 1984: 198).

McGinn is also the inventor of the third anti-communitarian line of thought, the *Invention Argument*. He uses it specifically against A but it could also be used against versions of B and C. The idea is simple. If all rule-following had to be communal, then rules could never have a first follower.

But rules must have first followers, or else rules could never be invented. The inventor of a rule is its first follower (McGinn 1984: 195).

A fourth line of reasoning is a parity argument. Since two different parity arguments have been used by individualists, I call the fourth line *Parity Argument 1*. It is an attack on one of the key ideas behind the communitarian position. Communitarians often reason as follows. One can only properly be said to follow a rule if the distinction between 'thinking one is following the rule (correctly)' and 'following the rule correctly' is somehow applicable to the rule-follower. More precisely, for a speaker to use a sign correctly, three conditions have to be met:

(i)   There must be something a speaker, *a*, can do that counts as an instance of 'thinking that he is using a sign correctly';

(ii) There must be something a speaker, *a*, can do that counts as an instance of 'using a sign correctly';

(iii) It must be possible for *a* to do what counts as an instance of 'thinking he is using a sign correctly' without at the same time doing what counts as an instance of 'using a sign correctly'. (Armstrong 1984: 51)

Communitarians insist that (i) to (iii) cannot be met as long as we consider a single speaker (or rule-follower more generally). Only the views of others—views as to how the rule needs to be followed in a given case—can provide a standard by which the individual's aiming for correctness can succeed or fail.

Parity Argument 1 seeks to unsettle this line of thought by insisting on a parity between individual and community. Individual and community are on par: if individuals cannot draw the distinction between 'seems right' and 'is right', then neither can communities as a whole. The individual cannot get access to an 'is right' by referring to his community, for his community can at best offer him a communal 'seems right'. Put differently, Parity Argument 1 poses a challenge to the communitarian: show me how it is possible for a whole community to do what counts as an instance of 'thinking it is using a sign correctly' without at the same time doing what counts as an instance of 'using a sign correctly'. As John McDowell puts the point:

The trouble is that there is a precise parallel between the community's supposed grasp of the patterns that it has communally committed itself to and the individual's supposed grasp of his idiolectic commitments. Whatever applications of an expression secure communal approval, just those applications will seem to the community to conform with its understanding of the expression.... One would like to say: whatever is going to seem right to *us* is right. And that only means that here we can't talk about 'right'. (McDowell 1993: 261)

Parity Argument 2 insists on the parity of individual and group in a different way. The thought is that whatever social *inter*subjective structure the communitarian insists on, the individualist can always point to a similar *intra*subjective structure that can do the same work. For instance, if rule-following presupposes more than a momentary isolated individual, why go all the way to full intersubjectivity? Why not try to capture the necessary 'multi-subjective' check by means of time-slices of the same individual? Parity Argument 2 has been pressed most convincingly by Simon Blackburn:

The members of a community stand to each other as the momentary time-slices of an individual do.... And when the community says 'well, we just see ourselves as agreeing (dignify, compliment ourselves as comprehending the same rule)' the individual just borrows the trick, and compliments himself on his rapport with his previous times. (Blackburn 1984*b*: 294–5)

Parity Argument 2 has been developed further by Paul Gerrans (1998), who attempts to give a more detailed psychological account on how 'intersubjectivity within a single individual' is possible. As Gerrans sees it, we as individuals can form a community within ourselves by running simulations on our own actions. I am to imagine what I would do under given circumstances, and then count each such possible me as a separate individual.

Perhaps the favourite weapon in the individualists' arsenal is the *Similarity Argument*. It is meant to defend the idea that we can easily imagine (congenital) social isolates to behave in ways that leave us with no alternative but to attribute rule-following to them. More concretely, the behaviour of social isolates might lead us to ascribe to them actions of rule-introduction, self-correction in the light of a rule, and awareness of the 'seems right/ is right' distinction. The Similarity Argument supports this idea with various thought-experiments. I shall mention the three most prominent here.

The first example was introduced by Baker and Hacker (1984: 433):

there is no reason why Crusoe should not follow a pattern or paradigm, making occasional mistakes perhaps, and occasionally (but maybe not always) noticing and correcting his mistakes. That he is following a rule will show itself in the manner in which he uses the formulation of the rule as a canon or norm of correctness. Hence, to take a simple example, he might use the pattern—...—... as a rule or pattern to follow in decorating the walls of his house; when he notices four dots in a sequence he manifests annoyance with himself. He carefully goes back and rubs one out, and perhaps checks carefully adjacent marks, comparing them with his 'master-pattern'. And so on. Of course, he is *not* merely following his 'inclinations', but rather following the rule. And it is his behaviour, including his corrective behaviour, which shows both that he is following the rule, and *what he counts as following the rule*.

Several authors attribute the second example to Michael Dummett without, however, giving a page reference (Blackburn 1984b: 297; Gillett 1995: 194; Wright 1986: 214). We are invited to imagine that a social isolate (from birth) finds a Rubik's cube washed up on his island, and learns, on his own, how to solve it. Clearly, solving the Rubik's cube must involve following rules—at least when done repeatedly ('when there is a last corner left to do ...'). Ergo, the social isolate can follow rules. The very fact that he solves the puzzle attests to it.

The third example is that of a social isolate who allegedly learns 'the hard way' that he has broken one of his rules:

Robinson junior... is a child who grows up on a desert island. He develops certain methods of coping with his environment. For instance, he makes pots for himself and has found that the juice of a certain berry, when heated, turns red and remains colour-fast. He uses this to 'label' pots in which he keeps dried fruit and he uses other markers to label other pots. Thus, when he 'wants to eat some dried fruit', he finds a red-dyed pot and gets some. (The quote-marks indicate that so far we have only reported his behaviours and not ascribed to him any contentful thoughts, although it aids description to do so.) Imagine further that one day his brain is altered so that he no longer sees red properly (forgive the naïve neuro-psychology and forget 'qualia'). He now has a new disposition to respond and, being a community of one, has no one to check him. But he can still go wrong and discover that he is wrong. He may, even if he does not notice the change, 'think that he has used all his pots of dried fruit' but find that he has not. He may check upon himself by bleeding an animal and find that the relational techniques by which he copes with his domain have significantly changed. It therefore seems possible that he can unilaterally discern a difference between *seems right* and *is right*. (Gillett 1995: 193)

DEFENDING THE STRONG THESES

I am unconvinced by the individualists' objections. I can be short in my treatment of the first three. Take first the Metaphysical Argument. Clearly the appeal to what is metaphysically possible—what God is able to create—cannot decide the question at issue, since it is precisely the metaphysical possibility over which individualists and communitarians disagree. Individualists believe that socially isolated human rule-followers are metaphysically possible; hence they have no difficulty imagining that God could create a single such creature in isolation. Communitarians regard socially isolated rule-followers as impossible; accordingly they cannot grant that even God could create one. The same must be said about the Internalist Argument. The individualist thinks that at least some normative phenomena are non-relational phenomena of an individual. The communitarian, in contrast, considers all normative phenomena to be relational and social. The Internalist Argument is thus not a real argument: it merely restates the individualist's position. The third argument, the Invention Argument, fails for a different reason. Although it does better than simply restate the individualist's position, it is based on a straightforwardly mistaken assumption. It is simply false that every rule has a first follower, and that this first follower must be the inventor of the rule. Consider the rules of competitive team sports like rugby. Even though the rules of rugby were presumably invented by someone, that someone could not have been following these rules on her own. You cannot follow the rules of rugby on your own, since to follow the rules of rugby is to be following them jointly with others. But once we break the link between inventing and following a rule, the Invention Argument collapses. To invent some rule is not necessarily to be able to follow it on one's own. Only if it were would the individualist have a distinctive argument for his position.

Regarding Parity Argument 1—the parity of group and individual as far as the 'is right/seems right' distinction is concerned—Donna Summerfield has given the appropriate response:

Some will undoubtedly object that the community, as a whole, will be no more able than an individual in isolation to make a distinction between seeming correctness and actual correctness. After all, there will be no distinction between the way in which we all (or most of us) go on and the way in which we all ought to go on.

However, there is an important difference between the individual and the community cases. In the case of an individual in isolation, there will be *no* distinction between seeming correctness and actual correctness. In the case of the community, for *every individual*, there will be a distinction between seeming correctness and actual correctness. (Summerfield 1990: 436)

In a footnote Summerfield adds the speculation that Parity Argument 1 is based on 'treating the community as itself an individual, and supposing that there is one way of going on that seems to this superindividual as though it is correct' (1990: 436). I agree with this speculation. The history of theorizing about individual and group is full of misleading assimilations of the one to the other: either the group is conceptualized as an individual writ large, or the individual is thought of as a community writ small (Kusch 1999: 250–1). It is easy to see how both metaphors can mislead. Take the former metaphor first. Once we routinely think of groups as akin to individuals, we will have few qualms about extending psychological vocabulary to groups in a direct and straightforward way: talk of group minds and collective wills will be hard to avoid. This will make it difficult for us to appreciate that all group phenomena are constituted in and through the *interaction* between individuals. Groups consist of interacting individuals. And once we have lost sight of this idea, we have no way of resisting Parity Argument 1.

Assimilating individuals to groups is no less problematic. I submit that this assimilation underlies Parity Argument 2, that is, the claim that, as far as normativity is concerned, *intra*subjectivity is not principally different from *inter*subjectivity. This thought will seem natural and obvious if we think of the individual mind as a group of interacting voices or time-slices. Indeed, many philosophers will find this thought intuitive—after all, it has informed their theorizing as least since Plato's *Republic*. And yet there are reasons for scepticism regarding this assimilation. Surely, a direct negotiation in the present between myself and my family members differs from a negotiation between myself today, myself yesterday, and myself tomorrow. For instance, my family members might sanction (e.g. browbeat) me if I display intransigence, or fail to cooperate. They might persuade me with unexpected arguments, and they might force me to give in. All this is possible because I have only limited control over the course of the interaction and its termination. A negotiation between my different time-slices is a very different kettle of fish. I have no idea how I can browbeat my previous or future selves, and my present self has full control over the course of the interaction. Does this not show that the two cases are, after all, distinctly different? On this question, I feel compelled to side with Michael Esfeld, who has replied to Blackburn and Gerrans as follows:

In an interaction of two or more persons, there can be a disagreement in the way in which these persons continue a sequence of examples in a shared environment at a time. That disagreement can trigger a process of negotiating by means of sanctions conditions under which there is convergence. By contrast, in the case of one person who is considered as being in isolation throughout her life, there is no possibility of such a process of negotiating a convergence. The present disposition of the person always has a privileged position; for the past self cannot reply and give feedback. It cannot make available for a person a distinction between what she takes to be correct or incorrect and what is correct or incorrect. The same point applies to the simulation of another person: simulation cannot give feedback that makes available for a person an external perspective in the sense of making available for her a distinction between taking something to be correct and something being correct. (2001: 91)

Finally, we have to address the most important argument (or set of arguments) in the individualist's arsenal, the Similarity Argument. Here too I feel that most of the needed rebuttals have already been put forward. A forceful criticism of the example of Crusoe and the Rubik's cube has been presented by Norman Lillegard (1998). Lillegard rejects Blackburn's suggestion according to which it is 'easy to go through the thought experiment of coming across such an individual' (Blackburn 1984a: 84). As Lillegard sees it, this is far from easy. From where, for example, does a congenitally isolated Crusoe get the notion of what counts as a solution, or of anything counting as something?

Crusoe is sitting on the beach. The cube washes up. He picks it up, fools with it. For years perhaps. Then suddenly it pops into his mind: 'perhaps there is a solution to this'. This is ludicrous. Or, nothing pops into his mind (in particular no English sentences) but he simply starts manipulating the cube, making little marks in the sand, looking back at them now and then, and eventually, he has it! What? The solution! I personally can neither imagine, conceive, nor make sense of this. In particular I do not see how anything that Crusoe did could be considered by him to be mistaken or incorrect, except in the sense of failing to get him from A to B in the way that some other 'move' did. But there could not be anything 'correct' about getting to B itself (though doing so might be pleasing, satisfying, conducive to survival, etc.). We can imagine a born Crusoe finding the solution to the Rubik's

Cube only by forgetting who a born Crusoe is, perhaps, by forgetting that he is a *born* Crusoe. (Lillegard 1998, unpaginated)

The important point is that whatever a congenitally isolated Crusoe does, he is too different from the humans we know for us to be entitled—according to our very own current attribution practices—to regard him as a rule-follower oriented towards independent standards of correctness. We cannot regard him as a rule-follower simply on the ground that he manipulates the cube while 'consulting' his marks in the sand. The marks in the sand might cause him to produce a combination of colours on his cube such that we would count the cube as 'correctly solved'. 'Correctly solved', that is, if *we* had done the solving. Compare the current case with ants that leave odour marks in the forest in order to enable them to revisit a food source. We would not normally regard the ants as rule-followers possessing a sense of correct and incorrect—though they may well be guided by something external to themselves (i.e. the odour marks). We would not regard the ants as rule-followers since we have no idea of how ants could acquire concepts like 'correct' and 'incorrect'. We know how we acquire these concepts, and where they figure: in discursive practices of teaching and training, and in justifications and negotiations with others. Put differently, in order for us to think of someone as a rule-follower, we must be able to think of 'correctness' and 'incorrectness' (or their analogues) as concepts that they possess (as actors' categories) (cf. Bloor 1997: 105). There is nothing in the Crusoe-cum-cube story that invites, or allows for, this hypothesis. In this story we find plenty of regularities, and acting in accordance with one of our rules—but we do not find rule-following.[3]

Similar comments are appropriate concerning the pattern (— . . . — . . .) example introduced by Baker and Hacker. Meredith Williams's reply is particularly forceful:

---

[3] This observation blocks Millikan's (1990) attempt to generate normativity out of biological functions. According to Millikan it is evolutionary history that determines the function of organs and actions, and hence also what we ought to do. As Bloor (1997: 105) rightly observes: 'This line of argument does not really allow us to avoid the appeal to society as the basis for normativity. The reason is very simple. The idea of getting a piece of rule following right, or the idea of getting it wrong in particular cases, are *actors' categories*. They are ideas invoked by rule followers, or would-be rule followers, about one another or themselves. Normative ideas cannot be external to the thoughts and actions of a community of rule followers in the way a fact about its historical evolution might be. The actor's own awareness of these norms is constitutive of their very existence as norms . . . '.

given the impoverished world that Robinson Crusoe inhabits, there is no way that we can distinguish corrective behavior from a modification of the rules or from the termination of one game for another or from the introduction of an exception permitted by the rule. Perhaps the 'and so on' implicit in the master-pattern warrants systematically altering the pattern inscribed, so that the four dots Crusoe put down initially were the correct continuation, and Crusoe's gesture that we took as a sign of annoyance was rather a sign of rebelling, his examination of the master-pattern and his subsequent behavior a rejection of that master-pattern for another. Other stories could be told that change the interpretation of his behavior and the rule he is purported to follow. That his behavior is seen as corrective depends upon how *we*, as a matter of course, would take the master-pattern.... But what about Robinson Crusoe himself? Would he count his behavior as corrective, that is, as constrained by something other than his own whim or amusement in drawing the pattern of dots and dashes? From his point of view, he engages in a repetitive behavior derived from a series of dots and dashes initially drawn on the wall, 'derived' in the sense that he reproduces the same series of dots and dashes as produced in the original sequence. Nothing more can be said of his behavior and its relations to the so-called 'master-pattern' without reintroducing the notion of his engaging in an act of interpreting the pattern, and that, of course, has already been rejected as an account of rule-following. (Williams 1991: 111)

This leaves us with Gillett's 'Robinson junior', who put his dried fruits into red pots before losing his ability to pick out red from other colours. Allegedly, the isolated Robinson junior is able to arrive at the distinctions 'right versus wrong' and 'is right versus seems right' on the basis of his disappointment and surprise when noticing that all his dried fruits are gone. I fail to see why this disappointment should give rise to an understanding of correctness. Simply the disappointment of not finding the dried fruits where expected is not enough. Nor is it clear to me why Robinson junior should grasp the difference between 'seems right' and 'is right' upon bleeding an animal. Assume that Robinson's changed eyesight makes him see red things as green things, and green things as red things. Gillett seems to think that upon bleeding an animal Robinson reasons as follows: 'Ah, the pots with dried fruits seemed to have disappeared, but now I realize that it is only their apparent colour that has changed. The cause of their appearance changing must lie within me—in my deficient colour vision—for the colour of the animals' blood has always been the same as the colour of pots with dried fruits.' I am unconvinced. Anyone who can reason in such a complicated fashion must surely already have the concept of correctness; he does not need to acquire the concept on the basis of this reasoning!

STRONG (B AND C) OR STRONGEST (A) COMMUNITY THESIS?

Above I have defended the strong theses of community dependence (A, B, C) against individualistic criticism. It remains for me to explain why I favour A, the strongest thesis, over the weaker ('strong') theses B and C. Most communitarians regarding rule-following are advocates of C. This is clear from the fact that almost always it is the *congenitally* isolated individual that is the central focus of discussion. Advocates of the Past-Tense Community Thesis C are relying on the following thought. A congenitally isolated individual cannot acquire the conceptual distinction between 'seems right' and 'is right'. However, once an individual has learned to make this distinction in and through interaction with others, the distinction remains permanently available to the individual—even if he finds himself in long periods of physical isolation, or even if he decides to introduce a new rule for himself. Advocates of the Strong Present-Tense Community Thesis B are proposing a synchronic version of the same general idea. If only the distinction between 'seems right' and 'is right' is generally available in a community, and if an individual has learned the distinction from others, then the individual can apply it to his own rule-following, never mind whether the rule is shared with others in the same community.

I disagree with these lines of thinking. When we ask whether an individual A can follow rule R *now*, we are asking whether A can *now* meaningfully distinguish between 'seems right' and 'is right' with respect to actions governed by R. And for this it is not enough to point to A's ability to distinguish 'seems right' from 'is right' with respect to some other rule, or to A's *past* ability to distinguish 'seems right' from 'is right' with respect to R. Consider again the distinction between rule-stipulation and rule-application. I suggested earlier that this distinction is not clear-cut. Paradoxically put, in applying a rule, we stipulate its content. In deciding how to apply my rule 'go running in the morning' I decide which rule it is I am actually following. Clearly, as long as I do so on my own, I am not encountering any friction; however I choose to apply it my rule is correct, since it is only my decision regarding application that fixes (momentarily) the rule's content. In other words, whatever seems right to me is right. And this means that the distinction between 'seems right' and 'is right' does not have a foothold in my practice. It can apply to me only if a gap can open up between what I decide to allow as correct and what others are willing to accept as correct *with respect to my rule of going running*. The problem of generating a distinction between 'seems right' and 'is right' for this rule is not solved by having the distinction available for some other rule. My family might have a rule to go out for dinner on Sundays, and, given that we interact and correct each other in applying this dinner-rule, I have access to the distinction between 'seems right' and 'is right' for this rule. But again, having the distinction available here does not make it accessible to me if then I try to follow the running-rule on my own.

But can I not solve the Rubik's cube on my own today—even though everyone else has long since moved on to more exciting computer and board games? Can I not distinguish between what seems like the correct solution and what is the correct solution? Maybe the cube rests on the table, and maybe the three visible faces are each of a single colour. But when I turn the cube round, I realize that some faces of the cube are not of one colour. What *seemed* like the right solution *is not* the right solution. Moreover, I certainly know what solving the Rubik's cube consists in. Here then, it seems, there is a clear-cut separation of rule-stipulation and rule-application even for the solitary rule-follower—provided only he is in general able to understand the distinction between 'seems right' and 'is right'.

Closer inspection shows that things are not as they seem. In fact, the case of the Rubik's cube does not differ at all from the case of the morning run. To tell myself 'try to end up with a single colour on each face' is like telling myself 'go running in the morning'. The content of the latter rule is determined (temporarily) only as I make further decisions about how to follow the rule in different circumstances. In the case of the Rubik's cube these include the following: Do I wish to end up with a single colour on each face of the Rubik's cube? Or do I wish to end up with a particular pattern of different colours on one or several of the faces? Do I have to achieve a given pattern in a particular number of moves? Less than a hundred? No more than sixty-five? Do I have to achieve a particular distribution of colours within a specific time period? Am I allowed to consult literature with advice on how to solve the cube? Am I allowed to try out a sequence of moves and then take them back if they do not result in a useful position? Does my solution have to be the result of planning or are trial and error and chance allowed as proper routes? Am I allowed (at any stage) to disassemble the cube with a screwdriver and then put it back together such that each of the faces is of a single colour? The list of such questions is of course endless.

SUMMARY

In this chapter I have tried to show that normativity can only exist for interacting individuals. The various individualistic responses to the communitarian position regarding rule-following fail without exception. Moreover, of the three main communitarian views—the Past-Tense Strong Thesis, Strong Present-Tense Thesis, and the Strongest Present-Tense Thesis—the last is the most plausible and defensible. It is this thesis that ultimately supports the communitarian epistemology proposed in this book. It is also the thesis which informs the views of language, truth, and objectivity that connect with this epistemology, and that I will explain in what follows.

Chapter 15

MEANING FINITISM

TWO GAMES

Meaning finitism runs counter to many of our deepest intuitions about language, truth, and reality. This makes the position difficult to understand, and even more difficult to accept. I shall therefore explain it twice. In this section I shall introduce meaning finitism and its opposite—meaning determinism—in a playful and radically simplified manner. My central simplification will be to model the two different views of meaning on two simple game scenarios. I call these games Risto and Seppo.[1]

Imagine the following game, called Risto. (Don't try this at home!) In order to play the game one needs a room filled with various objects, two players (A and B) and a stamp (along with an ink pad). During the first stage of the game, player A stays outside the room. While A is out, B takes the stamp, walks around the room and stamps various objects. Some of the stamp-patterns will be openly visible, others will be on surfaces that are blocked from sight or covered. All of the stamp-patterns are identical in shape and colour. After some time A is allowed back inside the room. His task is to identify all those objects that have the stamp-pattern; such objects are called 'ristos'.[2]

Our second game, Seppo, needs the same kind of room as does Risto. But Seppo requires three players (A, B, and C). No stamp or ink pad is needed.

---

[1] I have chosen two Finnish male names in order to make sure that most readers will not associate a meaning with these terms.

[2] Although it is not important for my argument, we might imagine that A and B play competitively. The more ristos A identifies in a given amount of time, the more points he gets, and then the roles are reversed.

While A again is out of the room, B and C agree among themselves to call three objects 'seppo'. They must choose three objects that they regard as similar. Let us call these objects 'object$_1$', 'object$_2$', and 'object$_3$,' and their collection the 'seppo-array'. Then A is allowed to return to the room. A is told which three objects are called 'seppo'. Subsequently, A must go round the room, suggest further 'seppos', and justify his choice to B and C. That is to say, he must find further objects that in his opinion are arguably similar to one or more of the three objects originally picked by B and C. Whether A's choice is correct or not depends on the judgements of all three players. When A's suggestion concerning a new seppo is accepted by majority rule (A, B, and C all vote), then the new object is entered as object$_4$ into the seppo-array. At the same time object$_1$ is dropped from the array. The game then continues relative to the new, changed seppo-array. After a given number of rounds, B (and later C) continues in A's role, but no new array is chosen at that time.

Risto and Seppo obviously differ in a number of respects. First, while ristos are identified on the basis of perception alone, seppos are determined on the basis of perception *and negotiation*. As a consequence, no player could identify seppos on his own. Second, in Risto we have a fixed set of objects that fall under the concept 'risto'; 'risto' thus has a 'fixed extension'. The same does not hold for Seppo. 'Seppo' does not have a fixed extension. After all, at any given time no more than three objects are definitely seppos. And which three objects fall under 'seppo' changes over time—as a new object is entered into the array, the eldest one is dropped from the array. Note also that no object falls under 'seppo' prior to the vote taken by A, B, and C. It would be incorrect to say things like 'many objects in the room really are seppo, it just so happens that the players haven't found them yet'. To make such a claim would be to overlook the essential openness of similarity judgements. It might well be the case that at one stage in the game, and relative to one array, some object is collectively judged to be a seppo; while at another stage in the game, and relative to a different array, the very same object is judged not to be a seppo. In Risto similarity judgements are less central; indeed, we might even say that all ristos are (type-)identical in so far as they all bear the mark of the stamp. Finally, and following from the above, it makes sense in Risto to say that a successful player makes progress towards identifying all of the ristos. But in Seppo this is not the case.

Although the array drifts over time, it does not drift towards 'the final set of all seppos'.

We can also use our games to get a feel for how truth figures in meaning finitism and meaning determinism. We can bring in truth in two ways. On the one hand, we can ask what makes statements 'object$_n$ is a risto' or 'object$_n$ is a seppo' true. On the other hand, we can inquire what happens to truth if 'risto' or 'seppo' turned out to be fancy stand-ins for the word 'true'. I shall take up the two options in turn.

What makes statements 'object$_n$ is a risto' or 'object$_n$ is a seppo' true? The answer is not hard to find. 'Object$_n$ is a risto' is true if and only if object$_n$ bears the mark of the stamp. This truth is 'recognition-transcendent'; it holds whether or not we or player A recognize it. Moreover, there are a specific number of true statements of the form 'object$_n$ is a risto'. And that number of statements does not change. And thus it makes sense to say that a successful A discovers more and more truths. Again, the situation with Seppo is different. 'Object$_n$ is a seppo' is true if and only if object$_n$ is judged (by the community) to be similar to the three elements of the current seppo-array. Although the communal similarity judgement is sensitive to empirical properties of encountered objects, the truth of 'object$_n$ is a seppo' is not recognition-independent; it only holds if the players recognize it as such. Truth is determined and fixed only *at a time* but one and the same object can be judged to be a seppo at one time, and, at a later time, when the array has changed, it might be judged not to be a seppo. There is no fixed number of statements with the form 'object$_n$ is a seppo' that is true over time. A successful A cannot be said to discover more and more truths. And talk of getting ever closer to the truth does not make sense.

What happens to truth if 'risto' or 'seppo' turned out to be fancy stand-ins for the word 'true'? To make sense of this scenario we have to slightly change our games. Imagine that the two games were not played with respect to normal physical objects but with respect to sentences. Imagine these sentences written on pieces of paper and distributed over the room. In Risto B stamps some of the pieces of paper; in Seppo B and C select three sentences as 'seppo'. The consequences should be obvious. In Risto it again makes sense to say that truth is recognition-transcendent; that 'true' has a fixed extension; and that a successful A gets closer to identifying *the* truth. A successful A 'tells the truth'. In Seppo truth is not recognition-independent;

'true' does not have a fixed extension; only a statement that is similar to the array-statements is true; and a successful A does not get closer to identifying *the* truth. A successful A does not 'tell the truth'. There simply is no truth there waiting to be told!

Needless to say, these games are remote from theories about meaning and reality that have been proposed by philosophers.[3] And yet, I do feel that they capture the gist of meaning finitism and other theories of meaning. Meaning finitism is committed to thinking about meaning on the model of Seppo; other theories of meaning tend to commit themselves to construing meaning on the model of Risto. Who then is right? What makes meaning finitism compelling? This is the question that I shall try to answer in the next chapter.

SYSTEMATIC EXPOSITION

One way to motivate meaning finitism is to recall a medieval and early-modern distinction between two views of creation: the 'deistic' and the 'continued-creation' views. According to the first conception, after the world has been created by God, it runs its predetermined course without any further divine intervention. After the initial creation the creator is a *Deus otiosus* (an idle God). According to the continued-creation view, however, creation and preservation of the created order are one and the same process; creation is moment-by-moment creation. God is never idle.[4]

In analogous fashion we can distinguish between deistic and continued-creation views of meaning. For simplicity's sake, let me focus on general terms. Philosophers of language in the deistic camp take meanings as given. These philosophers act as if meanings—and the terms with which meanings

---

[3] In order to bring our two games closer to real life (i.e. real theories), we would of course have to make a whole number of changes to them. Here are the most important ones. In both games we would have to allow for many classificatory words, rather than just one. In Risto there would be no turn-taking among the players; player A would be science; and player B (the 'stamper') would be God or evolution. In Seppo we would have to drop the stipulation according to which the array can never have more than three elements. We should also allow that the elements of the array are 'exemplary cases', or 'paradigms', rather than just any classified elements. And we have to change the rules for dropping elements out of the array: which elements are dropped is itself something that must be negotiated among the players.

[4] I am grateful to Stephen Snobelen for helpful information regarding this distinction.

are associated—had always already been created in the past, and created once and for all. Put differently, the creation or constitution of meaning is treated as a resource rather than as a topic of philosophical reflection. The topic of philosophical-semantic reflection lies elsewhere: its aim is to understand how the previously constituted meaning *determines* an extension, and how the term is *true of* this extension. It is this determination and this relationship of truth that deistic philosophy of language seeks to conceptualize. Most of mainstream philosophy of language falls within the deistic or 'meaning-determinist' camp.

The continued-creation view in the philosophy of language sees meanings as developing over time as terms are applied. Since meanings are continuously made (and remade) by language-users, meanings are never sufficiently stable and fixed for them to be able to determine extensions. Nor does it make sense to assume that terms are true of their extension. Accordingly, the continued-creation view rejects central ingredients of the dominant conception: the idea of semantic determination, the notion of fixed, unchanging extensions, and the central role of truth in semantics. Meaning finitism is to date the best-developed version of the continued-creation view.

'Meaning finitism' has been developed by the two leading theorists in the sociology of knowledge, Barry Barnes and David Bloor.[5] It is a theory about what is involved in the mastery of a language. For purposes of exposition Barnes and Bloor focus specifically on the mastery of an empirical classification, and on how such a classification is learned. However, meaning finitism is a general theory of meaning; it is not just a view of how we acquire empirical concepts.

As far as learning an empirical classification is concerned, meaning finitism emphasizes the importance of *ostension*. For instance, children often learn the meanings of words for medium-size objects in their environment by paying attention to where their parents and teachers point. For example, adults usually teach children the word 'cat' by pointing to instances of what the adults regard as cats. Adults typically indicate both paradigmatic and borderline cases. Borderline cases might be 'big cats' like lions and tigers. To stress the importance of ostension is not to deny that sometimes

---

[5] The best general accounts are Barnes *et al.* (1996, ch. 3), and Bloor (1997). See also Barnes (1992).

children learn new words on the basis of verbal definitions. A parent might, for instance, introduce the child to the word 'tiger' by describing a tiger as a 'very big cat'. Nevertheless, ostension is crucial and basic since all verbal definitions rest on, or are necessarily supported by, ostensive definitions.[6]

During their linguistic training children encounter only a finite number of instances of a given category. And for different children the array of instances is different. Unless you grew up in 'my neck of the woods', and around the same time, you will have learned to identify cats on the basis of a different learning set from mine. Moreover, a child living in the centre of London is likely to encounter cats less often than a child living in the countryside; and the cats encountered in the two places might well differ in weight, colour, and behaviour.[7]

Not all encountered examples of a given category have the same status; there are, as already mentioned, more or less central cases. I shall call the central cases 'exemplars'. These are examples where the adult will have been especially certain and emphatic in her identification. Exemplars are paradigmatic cases; cases that the child is expected to treat as particularly important. Thus, as the result of her training, the child acquires an 'array of exemplars'.[8]

---

[6] Recent work on word-learning emphasizes that children learn relatively few words through ostension, that the frequency of ostensive labelling varies with culture, and that language-learning children are active participants in interaction rather than passive recipients of adults' knowledge. See especially Bloom (2000) and, more generally, Corsaro (1997). It might be thought that finitists' emphasis on ostensive learning conflicts with this empirical work. But it does not, and for two reasons. On the one hand, the empirical studies are primarily concerned to refute the claim that ostensive labelling is all-pervasive; they are not denying that ostensive labelling is one important source of language-learning, among others. On the other hand, finitism is not tied to any assumptions about the frequency of ostensive labelling. Finitism insists that, in deciding how to apply a word, the speaker must judge the similarity between learned exemplars and newly encountered entities. Here it does not matter whether the exemplars have been learned via ostensive labelling or via some other mechanism. Nevertheless, in the main text I shall follow Barnes and Bloor and focus on ostensive labelling.

[7] Matthew Ratcliffe has pointed out to me that all cats in Malaysia have stumps for tails. Note here that the finitist is not committed to denying that different cultures might have the same exemplars for a given word. The finitist is happy with such contingent cultural universals.

[8] This does not commit finitism to the view that the meaning of each word is represented (in the mind of the speaker–hearer) by a simple list of concrete examples or exemplars. The array of exemplars might well be represented in a more abstract and summary fashion. One such summary might be the weightings in a neural net.

Linguistic training creates linguistic *dispositions*. A child who has been trained in the use of the word 'cat' has developed a complex disposition to use that word in certain circumstances and not in others. If the teaching has been successful, the child will often utter the word 'cat' when an animal called 'cat' by the adults is salient in the child's environment. Later on the child will also be able to use the word in the absence of cats; say, when the child desires the company of a cat, or if the child tries to convey his or her fear of cats.

The child's application of the word 'cat' to a newly encountered entity involves, or can be reconstructed as, a judgement concerning *similarity*. The child has to determine whether the newly encountered entity is sufficiently similar to an exemplar in her 'cat'-array for it to merit being called 'cat'. Three points are worth making with regard to similarity here. First, the meaning finitist does not maintain that judgements of similarity are completely subjective and contextual. Most of the time we have no difficulty in agreeing that two cats are more similar to each other than are a cat and a bulldozer. Second, the reason why we tend to agree on these matters lies partly in our common physiology, and partly in our common linguistic training. Our physiology makes it difficult, if not impossible, for us to 'see' certain entities as similar. And our linguistic training has both re-enforced such natural dispositions and created new ones. It is probably a result of such training that we identify cats even in abstract—say, highly stylized— pictorial representations of cats.[9] Third, however strong the influence of physiology and education, there always remains room for difference. Our judgements of similarity do not always coincide. And they tend to diverge in particular when we have different interests (goals and aims).

It is not just physiology and linguistic training that incline us to favour one judgement of similarity over another. Whether or not a child judges a newly encountered entity—say a stuffed toy cat—to be relevantly similar to her exemplars (of real cats) might depend on whether the child is interested in watching an animal chase after a ball, or whether the child is eager to caress the furry body of a cat-size creature. If the latter interest looms large, then the perceived similarity between the stuffed toy and live cats will be

---

[9] For an intriguing study on how children learn how to name representations, see Bloom (2000: 171–90).

higher than if the former goal is more salient. To that extent, similarity is in the eye of the beholder.

The array of exemplars for a given category changes over time. The child builds up an array over time by adding new exemplars to older ones. Later on some exemplars will be dropped and replaced. Moreover, it is not just via training that new exemplars are added. Children add their own exemplars on the basis of their own similarity judgements.

Meaning is a normative phenomenon. That is to say, in general we expect uses of language to be open to evaluations along the axis 'correct' and 'incorrect'. (I write 'in general' in order to leave room for the phenomenon of 'poetic licence'.) In language-learning this is obvious enough. The adult does more than just alert the child to salient exemplars of a given category. The adult also monitors the child's own attempts to use the category, praises correct applications, and sanctions incorrect ones. The applicability of 'correct' and 'incorrect' is not only an issue of language-learning, however. The problem of normativity runs deeper. The deeper issue comes into view once we ask the 'Second-order Question about Linguistic Correctness' (in analogy to the 'Second-order Questions about Rationality' in Part II): why is it that the dichotomy 'correct versus incorrect' can be applied to uses of language?

Meaning finitism holds that a plausible answer to this question must invoke the *consensus* of a *community* of language-users. What makes an application of a word correct rather than incorrect is that one's interlocutors let one get away with, or perhaps even praise, the way in which one has judged the similarity between a shared exemplar and a newly encountered entity. Only others' agreement can constitute correctness. This is not to deny that we are responsive to things in our environment; it is to deny that this responsiveness constitutes correctness. The environment does have a causal influence on what we come to believe, but it does not determine how we must use our terms.

But why should we think it impossible for an isolated individual to do the following: introduce a new category by picking an array of exemplars; apply the category to new cases on the basis of similarity judgements relative to the array; and monitor her own performance for correctness in the light of the exemplars? Would not the exemplars provide the isolated individual with an independent standard? Would not the exemplars enable her to distinguish between 'is correct' (i.e. is indeed highly similar to an exemplar) and 'only seems correct' (i.e. only seems similar to an exemplar for a while)?

The envisaged scenario is undermined by two considerations: similarity is not identity; and arrays 'drift'. That is to say, the imagined situation would be a plausible one if the application to new cases involved judgements of identity rather than judgements of similarity, and if the judgements referred back to a fixed and unchanging array of exemplars. In such a scenario there would be a clear 'fact of the matter' as to whether a given application is correct or incorrect, and such a fact of the matter would not involve a community. However, similarity and drift are central and not eliminable. And since they are not eliminable, the individual does not have the resources to monitor her own performances in light of an *independent standard*. All the isolated individual can go on are her own performances and her own dispositions. But this 'standard' does not stand still. It is changed by whatever the individual decides to do. And thus it is no independent standard at all. It cannot sustain a distinction between 'correct' and 'seems correct'. We get an independent standard only if we bring in continuous interaction among individuals, that is, if we bring in the community. Interaction with others does not just determine exemplars during the process of language-learning; it is also needed to confirm, or deny, that the 'drift' in an individual's array of exemplars goes into the 'right' direction, and usher in 'correct' *judgements*.[10]

At this point it is important to bring in the theory of social institutions that has already been central in Parts I and II. Recall three features of social institutions in particular. First, institution-creating and -re-creating talk (and belief) is ultimately self-referring. It is the talk about money that creates money as the referent for such talk.[11] Second, social institutions are themselves subject to the 'logic' of finitism: they are performed and their paths are not predetermined by rules and norms. (Rules and norms are themselves social institutions.) Social actors have to make decisions

[10] Note that this does not mean that 'identity' is beyond the 'logic' of finitism. The individualist would have to give a theory on what is involved in making a judgement of identity.

At this point the aficionados will of course expect me to say something about the important debates around Saul Kripke's 'sceptical paradox' concerning rule-following (Kripke 1982). See Appendix 15.2.

[11] This is not to deny that the physical environment is a precondition of any such talk taking place.

regarding metal discs and other objects: is this a situation in which it is appropriate to use metal discs for exchange? Is this a metal disc similar to those we have used as money before? And third, many social institutions have the character of my 'model of local consensus'. To reiterate, assume that clocks move about in a confined space, and that each one of them regularly collides with one or more of the others. Whenever such collisions happen, the colliding clocks 'collectively' calculate the average of their times, reset themselves to that time, and then separate—each one now again displaying its unique way of running at some given speed—before in turn colliding with other clocks. In this scenario all consensus is local and temporary, and none of the clocks can 'know' what the 'collective consensus'—that is, the bandwidth of all times—of all clocks would be.

Meaning finitism contends that meanings are social institutions, and that being an exemplar for correct usage is a social status. Meanings have existence only in practices in which uses are judged, invoked, ascribed, corrected, challenged, and conveyed. 'Correct use', or 'use in accordance with the meaning of the word', is a social status that we attach to some linguistic behaviours and not to others. No individual on her own can constitute such status. Moreover, an individual can know 'the meaning' of word only on the basis of its (chance) encounters with other speakers of the language. No individual has full access to the 'bandwidth' aspect of meaning: only the historian of a language can capture this aspect of meaning, and she can do so only for a past period.

Note also that since meaning is the product of social interaction, it is not just *individual* interests that guide the application of terms to newly encountered entities. *Shared interests* are much more powerful determinants of judgements of similarity. They make a bigger difference because they enter in many more acts of judgements and because they lead to collective actions.

Barnes, Bloor, and Henry summarize meaning finitism in five theses. The first thesis is that 'the future applications of terms are open-ended' (Barnes *et al.* 1996: 55). This thesis amounts to the claim that the future correct application of a term is never entirely fixed in advance; what counts as a correct application depends on judgements at the time. The second thesis says that 'no act of classification is ever indefeasibly correct' (1996: 56). This captures the idea that all classification must happen on the basis of similarity and analogy rather than identity. The third thesis states that 'all acts of classification are revisable' (1996: 57). This introduces a perspective that I have not yet made explicit in the above. The thought is that judgements found correct at an earlier time might be reclassified as incorrect at a later time (and vice versa). One reason for this might be a drift in the array of exemplars. Another reason might be a change in interests. Such reclassification is of course a ubiquitous phenomenon in the sciences. Barnes, Bloor, and Henry mention the following example:

The terms 'dead' and 'alive' may be successfully applied on the basis of simple empirical examination, and indeed dead persons are routinely discriminated from living persons on this basis. But medical practitioners who make this distinction as a matter of course in their day-to-day activity may at the same time reflect back upon their own practice, whether in particular cases or in general, and find it wanting. They may conclude . . . that some bodies with the appearance of being alive and routinely treated as 'living' in existing practice, are 'really' dead and better treated as such. In concluding thus, practitioners typically hold that bodies of the kind in question are not merely being incorrectly identified now, but have been in the past. The conclusion is taken to have implications for earlier practice and for the way that instances were assimilated to similarity relations in that earlier practice. (1996: 57)

The fourth thesis claims that 'successive applications of a kind term are not independent' (1996: 57). I have sought to capture this idea above by saying that successive applications of a word change the array of exemplars and thus influence subsequent acts of classification. Finally, the fifth thesis alerts us again to a phenomenon that I have not yet stressed. This is the claim that 'the applications of different kind terms are not independent of each other'. Take, for instance, the relation between the terms 'duck' and 'goose'. Our developing dispositions to call certain birds 'ducks' are, by the same token, dispositions to call certain birds 'ducks' rather than 'geese' (1996: 58–9).

Perhaps the single most important ingredient of meaning finitism is the rejection of fixed extensions. Standard philosophical semantics distinguishes between the 'intension' and the 'extension' of terms. The intension is the meaning and the extension is the class of all things to which the term is correctly applied. Thus the extension of 'cat' is the class of all cats, and the extension of 'table' is the class of all tables. The meaning is taken to 'fix' or 'determine' the extension. For the meaning finitist, such extensions do not exist. As Bloor puts the central point:

There is no class of things existing in advance of the application of a label. Here and now, there is no determinate class of things which will, or could, truly be called swans. The content of that class depends on decisions which have yet to be taken, and so does not yet exist.... [Extensions] are simply fictions generated by a philosophical theory. (Bloor 1997: 24)[12]

It is tempting but incorrect to summarize the finitist theory of meaning as 'all concepts are vague'. The distinction between vague and non-vague stands orthogonal to the distinction between meaning as 'finite' and meaning as 'fixed by extensions'. Take a concept like 'bald', the prototype of a vague predicate. What makes 'bald' vague is not that its application is based on exemplars and judgements of similarity. Instead, 'bald' is vague because we are collectively willing to accept both 'X is bald' and 'X is not bald' as assertible of the same X and at the same time. Regarding non-vague terms (like '1 metre long') no such tolerance is generally displayed. More formally, a concept C is vague if the communal practices of evaluation allow for different speakers to apply both C and $\sim$C to a given entity. A concept C is non-vague if the communal practices of evaluation do not allow for different speakers to apply both C and $\sim$C to a given entity. Put differently, all acts of concept-application are underdetermined by past practice. But this does not make the concepts vague. 'Vague' and 'precise' are two social statuses that communities attach to concepts.[13]

Finally, it would be a misplaced objection to allege that meaning finitism conflates words and things. According to this objection, the finitist cannot explain why, in order to classify correctly some animals as 'cats', we should engage in biological inquiry rather than in a semantic study of our linguistic community. To the objector it sounds as if meaning finitism is saying something like 'the community can make anything a cat by calling it "cat"'. Hence the only way to find out whether anything is a cat is to see whether the community is calling it so. But this is too quick. The sentence 'the community can make anything a cat by calling it "cat"' is itself based on a conflation: the 'make' is ambiguous between creation and categorization. Communities cannot (physically) create cats by labelling certain furry animals 'cats'. But they can of course group together certain animals by

---

[12] Giving up talking about extensions as classes does not of course forbid us from talking about 'arrays' as collections of objects to which the term has been applied up to the present.

[13] My comments on vagueness are indebted to Lynch (1998: 61).

using the label 'cat'. For me (as a member of an English-speaking community), to find out whether a given furry animal is a cat is to attend primarily to the animal; to feel its fur; to listen to the sounds it produces; and to see whether it chases mice. In all this I can keep questions of (communally established) exemplars in the background. This is because I know it to be unlikely that I am out of harmony with my fellows' categorizations of cats. And yet, every act of categorization is a stab into the semantic dark; it involves an evaluation of similarity between exemplars and the new case. And it might always turn out that my fellow speakers do evaluate this similarity differently from me. Thus there is no guarantee that my act of categorization is right until the others have agreed with it. Put differently, it is true that the meaning finitist cannot make a sharp distinction between questions of empirical truth and questions of semantic correctness. But to deny that these two types of question can be sharply separated is not of course to be guilty of collapsing the former into the latter.

Appendix 15.2
MEANING SCEPTICISM

The debates around Kripke's meaning scepticism (Kripke 1982) have already been discussed from a finitist perspective (Bloor 1997). I shall address here only one point. This is the point whether a communitarian (consensus-based) view of rule-following can provide a defence against meaning scepticism.

Imagine yourself calculating '57 + 68', and assume that you have never done this particular calculation before (although you have done many others). Presumably you will come up with the answer '125'. At this stage Kripke imagines the following challenge coming from a position that is sceptical of the possibility of rule-following. The sceptic asks as follows (my formulation, not Kripke's):

What fact about you determines that the answer is '125' and not something else? Why could the correct answer not be '5'? Perhaps in using '+' the rule you have been following has been this: $x + y =$ *the sum of x and y; except when x = 57 and y = 68, in which case the answer for 57 + 68 is 5.* (Let us say that this rule defines quaddition.) Which fact about you determines that in using '+' you have always been practising addition rather than quaddition? What fact about you determines that you were following the 'straight rule' (i.e. addition) rather than the 'bent rule' (quaddition)?

Kripke discusses a number of possible answers, showing in each case that the answer is insufficient. It will not do, for example, to insist that in using '+' you always *intended* to add. On the one hand, it is unlikely that you ever formed such intention. On the other hand, the sceptical problem will immediately reappear. The sceptic can continue by asking 'What fact determines that by using the word "always" you mean "without any exception" rather than "without exception, except when the numbers 57 and 68 are concerned"?' Nor will it do to invoke the disposition (to add) that I have acquired when being confronted with the sign '+'. This response is unhelpful since dispositions lack normativity: having the disposition to react to '+' in one way rather than another does not capture the fact that I *ought to* react in one way rather than another. For Kripke the moral of the story is that meaning-attributions ('By "+" he means addition') are not stating facts; instead they signal whether the speaker regards the attributee as a member of his community (of calculators). Ultimately, Kripke seems to suggest, what makes your answer '125' correct and the answer '5' incorrect is that others in your community agree with your result.

In a difficult but important paper Simon Blackburn has challenged Kripke's community-based answer to the sceptic (Blackburn 1984*b*). Blackburn insists that, when faced with the sceptical challenge, the community is no better off than the individual. Assume that we have a community with three members, A, B, and C. Prior to time *t* A, B, and C have added many numbers, and they have always agreed with one another on the result. Again, however, they have never yet calculated '57 + 68'. At time *t* A is faced with '57 + 68', and concludes that the answer is '125'. Is A's answer correct? Is the past agreement of A, B, and C the fact that secures '125' as the correct answer? Surely, Blackburn argues, the reply must be no. A cannot rely on the others' agreeing with his past calculations, since among these past calculations '57 + 68' never occurred. And thus, for all A knows, there is no fact about either him or his community that determines that by '+' the community means addition rather than quaddition. Nor is there any guarantee that the society does not consist of divergent calculators. That is to say, maybe A, B, and C have all seemed like adders prior to t but at t B turns out to have meant, all along, quaddition when using '+', and C turns out to have meant, all along, 'skaddition' when using '+' (skaddition is like quaddition, except that the $57 + 68$ equals 12). Ergo, Blackburn concludes, Kripke has failed to establish that bringing in the community makes a difference.

I beg to differ. There is a difference between the individual and the community, or rather, between the isolated individual and the individual within a community. At time t, when challenged to provide a suitable fact, the isolated individual can only point to its own past performance and suggest some link between that past performance and the present case. Kripke shows that this is too slim a basis. However, the individual within a community can *also* point to the actions and assessments of *other* individuals at t; he can point to others' letting him get away with '125', or he can point to others' coming to the same result. He can even bring in negotiation and debate as a mechanism that creates agreement. Indeed, this might be crucial in the case where A, B, and C really do answer '125', '5', and '12' respectively. If A, B, and C form a community, then they will be able to negotiate whether it is best to continue their past practices with '+' by giving '125', '5', or '12' as the collectively agreed 'correct' answer to '57 + 68'. Their ability to agree on this result will of course depend on their sharing goals and interests that make such agreement desirable and achievable. In other words, interacting individuals can constitute and monitor standards at t—standards in the light of which the actions of any one of these individuals can be assessed and corrected. No isolated individual can do this without erasing the borderline between 'is right' and 'seems right'.

Chapter 16

TRUTH

MEANING FINITISM AND TRUTH

Meaning finitism does not apply just to terms like 'cat' and 'red', but also to expressions like 'true' or 'false'. A few examples will suffice to bring this out. Think of how we learn to use 'true' and 'false' correctly. We get shown (or explained) a number of situations where we can predicate 'true' or 'false' of (1) people, (2) materials and events, and (3) statements:

(1) He is a true friend. He is false friend. He is a true villain. He is a true Spaniard.

(2) This is true gold. These are my false teeth. This was a false alarm.

(3) It is true that Mary is the head of the physics department. It is false that Harvard is the best university in the world.

On the basis of such learning situations we develop dispositions to use the word 'true' in some circumstances but not in others. We do so ultimately on the basis of—explicit or tacit—judgements of similarity and dissimilarity with earlier situations where we used 'true' correctly. Whether our judgements are acceptable, whether we can, as it were, 'get away with making them', depends on the judgements of others. Think of the following types of exchange:

(1′) 'Is this piece of gold like the piece of true and pure gold that John showed me yesterday?' 'Yes.' 'Well, I guess it's a piece of true gold then.'

(2′) 'Does John behave towards me as Mary does?' 'Pretty similarly, he too helped me write this paper.' 'Well, I guess John is a true friend too then.'

(3′) 'Does the statement "Mary is the head of the physics department" fit with what I know about the physics department, as the statement "Otto is the head of the philosophy department" fits with what I know about the philosophy department?' 'Yes.' 'Well, I guess the statement about Mary is true then.'

In all of these cases we can of course imagine negotiations over the application of 'true'. Peter might deny that John's behaviour towards me is sufficiently similar to Mary's, and Peter might have some social interest in doing so. Or Fred might wish to challenge the assumption that a statement like 'Mary is the head of the physics department' relates to the world in the same way as a statement like 'The cat is on the mat'. Fred might therefore deny that a statement like 'Mary is the head of the physics department' is true.

Thus meaning finitism applies to 'true' and 'false' as much as it applies to any other words. Among such 'other words' are the terms that have played a role in characterizing and defining the meaning of 'true'. I am thinking of words like 'correspondence', 'coherence', 'copying', 'fact', and so on. They too are learned on the basis of a finite number of examples, and they too can be used correctly and incorrectly only against the backdrop of a linguistic community. Moreover, and perhaps most importantly, if, or since, 'true' and 'false' are subject to the same finitist 'logic' as are 'chair' and 'cat', they too come without a fixed extension. 'True statement' does not have as an extension the class of all those statements that might have been, or might be, correctly classified as true. Which statements will be so classified depends on how the community 'decides' to extend the analogy from the past into the present and future—and back.

Meaning finitism in general, and 'truth finitism' in particular, are relativistic doctrines. Barnes, Bloor, and Henry are card-carrying cognitive relativists. And sometimes they use finitism in order to justify their relativism. However, they never apply finitism to truth. Indeed, occasionally they even formulate finitism in a way that seems to exempt truth. For example, Barnes, Bloor, and Henry write that 'no statement of belief is ever indefeasibly true or false' and in so writing they make a point about concepts used in beliefs, not a point about true and false (Barnes *et al.* 1996: 71). They also propose that truth-values change when the exemplars of our terms change.

But they do not say that 'true' and 'false' too have drifting arrays of exemplars. A meaning finitism that includes 'true' leads to a more coherent relativism than a relativism that tacitly excludes 'true'.[1]

It is not difficult to see why 'truth finitism' is relativistic. After all, according to my account, the exemplars for 'true' are selected under contingent social conditions. There is no absolutely right or wrong way for picking exemplars for 'true' and for judging the similarity between exemplars and newly encountered statements (beliefs, sentences, etc.). And thus there are no 'facts of meaning' that determine the application of 'true'. Different possible or real communities may develop their arrays of exemplars—say, of 'true friends' or 'true statements'—in many different ways, and there is no vantage point from which communities can be judged right or wrong; no vantage point, that is, other than the local and contingent vantage point of some other community.

Note here that my form of truth relativism should not be glossed as 'truth is consensual belief'; or as implying an imperative like 'one ought to believe whatever one's community decides'. To equate 'truth' with 'consensual belief' would be adequate only if in our community the exemplars for these two concepts coincided. They do not. Although consensus is essential for certifying uses of the term 'true' as 'correct', consensus is not part of the meaning of 'true'. No native speaker of English would accept 'consensually believed' as a definition of 'true'.

Treating truth as consensual belief might also lead one to accept a mistaken form of 'collective voluntarism': as if a group could collectively make something true by willing it to be true. Nor would it be correct to construct community consensus concerning 'true' on the model of a voting system. My third model of consensus allows neither for the unified will nor for the voting system. As a member of a group one tends to take certain statements for true, and this tendency or disposition is shaped and formed by the interactions with others of the same group. 'We decide collectively' should almost always be understood in terms of something like my model of the randomly meeting clocks. In other words, collective decisions are never made once and for all; they are processes, not products. We do not 'consult' our collective's decisions to see whether we have applied terms correctly—

---

[1] Needless to say, I would not have been able to formulate finitism regarding truth had it been for Barnes's and Bloor's example.

there is nothing stable and unchanging to consult here. What keeps us in line with others is local encounters with others.

Philosophical audiences have many difficulties with truth finitism. I sympathize. Here are two objections that are often made. According to the first objection, truth finitism conflates the property of being true with knowing the meaning of the word 'true'. 'Surely', the objection goes, 'the property of being true is something which is independent of however we choose to use the word "true". Even if truth finitism were right about the linguistic facts, it would not be right about truth as such.'

In reply, the finitist can point out that to talk of a 'property of truth' is to replace tacitly a drifting array of exemplars with a fixed extension of instances. The idea of a 'property of truth' is intelligible only on the tacit assumption that 'true' has a fixed extension; that is, an extension that exists independently of how we decide on similarities between past and present uses. Only if the extension is independent of such decisions does it make sense to oppose the property of truth to knowing how to use the word 'true'. In other words, the objection comes down to a relapse into the very idea that finitism dismantles with its observations on the learning and mastery of language. This is not to deny, of course, that in everyday life we distinguish between knowing the meaning of 'true' and knowing truths. In daily life we assume that someone knows the meaning of 'true' if she can competently participate in negotiations over the 'truth status' of friends, materials, or statements. One can be a competent participant in such negotiations without knowing more than just the standard truth exemplars. And obviously one does not need to know all that will, or could, be judged similar to these exemplars.

This brings me to the second objection. It laments that truth finitism blurs the distinction between 'true' and 'taken for true'. Surely, it is one thing what a community takes to be true. But what *is* true in fact is something different altogether. Is there not a community- and language-transcending 'true' (*simpliciter*) in addition to the community-sponsored 'true for us'?

Two comments need to be made in reply. On the one hand, the objection might in turn be criticized for making sense only against the background of fixed extensions. On the other hand, it is worth insisting that the distinction between 'merely believed to be true' and 'true' is an important distinction *internal to* our very practice of truth-talk. A society that did not employ something like this distinction would not be regarded as having anything like a concept of truth. At the same time, the very distinction is itself subject to the 'logic' of finitism. The contrast between 'true' and 'merely taken to be true' is learned and applied on the basis of exemplars. And this makes it a contrast that is defined by collective and contingent processes.

FINITISM AND PRAGMATISM

In the remainder of this chapter I shall briefly explore the relationship between truth finitism and some other theories of truth. My aims are to bring out the distinctiveness of the finitist position, to develop it further through confrontation, and to 'save the phenomena'. That is to say, the finitist theory of truth had better be able to explain what other theories got right, and where they went wrong. My goal here is not, however, to provide a comprehensive survey of past and contemporary work on truth. Fortunately such detailed surveys already exist.[2] Instead, I shall be highly selective and move at a relatively low level of resolution. I begin with William James's pragmatism.

James does not have a concisely formulated and comprehensive theory of truth. Nevertheless, it is easy to identify a number of recurring themes to do with truth in his writings. The most famous theme is the equation of the true with the expedient or useful, clearly expressed in the following often cited passage: ' "The true", to put it briefly, is only the expedient in the way of our thinking, just as "the right" is only the expedient in the way of our behaving' (James 1975: 106). This idea has never found favour with James's critics. They have not found it difficult to come up with cases where the true does not coincide with the useful. For instance, it might be useful for me to believe now (in January 2001) that I will be able to finish this book soon. Having this belief might increase the probability that I will. And yet, this hardly makes it true. Bertrand Russell insisted that finding out whether a belief is true is quite distinct from finding out whether it is useful to believe. It is one thing to find out whether popes are infallible; it is another thing to

---

[2] The best such critical survey is Kirkham (1992). Kirkham's book has been an invaluable help in writing the following sections.

discover whether it is useful to believe in the infallibility of popes (Russell 1999: 69–82).

James does not deny, however, that agreement with reality is an important ingredient in, or perhaps prerequisite of, truth. Indeed, he stressed that expediency presupposed such agreement: 'That . . . ideas should be true in advance of and apart from their utility, that, in other words, their objects should be really there, is the very condition of their having that kind of utility' . . . (1975: 278).

Let this be the second theme of James's reflections on truth: truth involves agreement with reality. Perhaps we can combine the two themes into the thesis that it is expedient to believe ideas that fit reality. James's theory would then not be a radical alternative to the correspondence theory of truth; it would be a way of extending it. Nevertheless, the implausibility of the expediency formula would not have gone away. One might still wonder whether true beliefs really are—always and everywhere—expedient.

Sometimes James writes as if he believed reality to be fully mind-dependent: 'An experience, perceptual or conceptual, must conform to reality in order to be true. By "reality" [pragmatism] . . . means nothing more than the other conceptual or perceptual experiences with which a given present experience may find itself in point of fact mixed up' (1975: 225).

The evidence is not clear-cut, however. Thus, in a footnote to the just quoted passage James adds that he merely means to 'exclude reality of an "unknowable" sort, of which no account in either perceptual or conceptual terms can be given'. Reality includes 'any amount of empirical reality independent of the knower'. Moreover, James is resolute that 'pragmatism is thus "epistemologically" realistic in its account' (1975: 225). Perhaps James's view comes to this. Although reality is mind-dependent in some sense, it is not under our voluntary control. We cannot but constitute a world of a certain kind. In experiencing the mind-dependent world we are passive rather than active.

A third important theme is the indefinability of concepts like 'conforming to reality', 'agreeing with reality', 'satisfaction', and 'expediency'. The meaning of these terms is said to vary with context. Definitions are impossible since there are too many ways 'in which these requirements can practically be worked out'. 'Ordinary epistemology contents itself with the vague statement that the ideas must "correspond" or "agree"; the pragmatist insists on being more concrete, and asks what such "agreement" may mean in detail' (1975: 270).

James claims that mainstream philosophy works with a concept of correspondence that is abstract and 'saltatory', relying on the notion that the gap between mind and world can be bridged by a unique one-to-one correspondence between mental and worldly items. In relying on this conception, philosophers neglect the infinite variety of correspondences (in the plural) that serve us in different local circumstances. Correspondence is a many-to-many relationship. To recognize this is to move from a 'salta-tory' to an 'ambulatory' concept of truth; it is to adopt the pragmatist view.[3]

James is a relativist about truth. This is the fourth theme. He allows that 'truth may vary with the standpoint of the man who holds it' (1975: 301). This relativism coheres with the idea that expediency and correspondence can only be judged 'locally'. Interestingly enough, James is happy to apply relativism even to the truth of pragmatism.

Finally, a fifth theme is that 'truth is made': 'Truth is simply a collective name for verification-processes, just as health, wealth, strength, etc., are names for other processes connected with life, and also pursued because it pays to pursue them. Truth is *made*, just as health, wealth and strength are made, in the course of experience' (1975: 104). Again, this thesis is supported by other ideas already mentioned. Truth is made in so far as it is us who lay down local criteria of expediency and correspondence.

There is much in James's remarks on truth that fits with truth finitism. To begin with, James is right to insist on the importance of the expedient. After all, the expedient is what serves our interests. And interests, individual and collective, are crucially involved in decisions over how we should apply our terms to new cases. Interests guide our judgements of similarity. No considerations of expediency, no application of 'true' to newly encountered beliefs. Moreover, truth finitism vindicates James's suggestion according to which we 'make' or 'create' truths: in the end it is us who decide which exemplars and which similarities are 'truth-makers'.

Furthermore, James is not incoherent in combining correspondence with expediency. I have just given a finitist defence of expediency. Of course the correspondence intuition can be defended as well. We do speak of true beliefs

---

[3] A recent defence of James's 'ambulatory' conception of truth is Latour (1999).

fitting the facts, or corresponding to the facts. But we must beware not to turn these innocent paraphrases into the saltatory conception of truth. 'Fit' and 'correspond' have many and diverse exemplars and do not pick out a unique one-to-one relationship between language (mind) and world. It must also be remembered that 'true' has exemplars that do not appear in the array for 'fits' or 'corresponds'. Mathematical truths provide examples. Finally, James's relativism regarding truth also agrees with finitism. In both cases relativism results from seeing truth as, in good part, a human product—created under local contingencies.

For all that, I cannot go with James all the way. He errs in supposing that 'true' can be defined in terms of expediency. It is one thing to say that considerations of expediency figure centrally in the selection of exemplars and in judging similarity. It is another to conclude that 'the true' means or is (at least in part) 'the expedient'. No native speakers would recognize the formula 'the true is the expedient' as a correct definition. Put differently, expediency is a precondition for all categorization; but there is no special link between expediency and truth.

More fundamentally, it is impossible to overlook that James remained an individualist at heart. He did not appreciate that the processes of truth-making are *collective* processes, and that whatever objectivity truth possesses is owed to the collective. Put differently, James did not grasp the normative—indeed, moral—quality of truth. This was pointed out, against the pragmatist movement as a whole, by no less than the father of modern sociology, Émile Durkheim. Durkheim insisted, rightly, that it is a condition of adequacy of a satisfactory theory of truth that it can explain the following three key features of truth:

1. A *moral obligation*. Truth cannot be separated from a certain moral character. In every age, men have felt that they *were obliged* to seek truth. In truth, there is something which commands respect, and a moral power to which the mind feels properly *bound* to assent;

2. A *de facto necessitating power*. . . . The true idea *imposes itself* on us. . . . When man perceives it, he is sometimes obliged to change his whole way of thinking. . . .

3. Truth has a third character . . . *impersonality*. (Durkheim 1983: 73–4)

Durkheim held that only a social theory of truth and collective representations can do justice to these characteristics:

representation is a collective achievement . . . This is what explains the impression of resistance, the sense of something greater than the individual, which we experience in the presence of truth, and which provides the indispensable basis of objectivity. (1983: 85)

James's pragmatism does not have the resources to fit Durkheim's bill. James almost always focuses on the individual and her beliefs. And he lacks notions of the collective, of collective decisions, and of consensus.

Finitism is in a more favourable position. The theory of social institutions (running through this book) is able to do justice to the objectivity of truth in precisely the way Durkheim suggests. The objectivity of truth is the objectivity of a social institution. Truth is objective because the exemplars of truth are collectively taken to be the exemplars of truth.

TRUTH AS IDEALIZED CONSENSUS

The consensus theory proposed by the pragmatist Charles Sanders Peirce is not as individualistic as is James's theory. Peirce speaks of 'my social theory of reality, namely, that the real is the idea in which the community ultimately settles down' (Peirce 1931–58: vi. 610). This passage speaks of reality rather than truth, but for Peirce truth and reality are but two sides of the same coin. Thus he would not have objected to speaking of his 'social theory of truth, namely, that the true is the idea in which the community ultimately settles down'. Other passages in Peirce support this reading:

The opinion which is fated to be ultimately agreed to by all who investigate is what was meant by truth. (1931–58: v. 407)

Truth is that concordance of an abstract statement with the ideal limit towards which endless investigation would tend to bring scientific belief . . . (1931–58: v. 565)

If a general belief . . . can in any way be produced, though it be by the faggot and the rack, to talk of error in such belief is utterly absurd. (1931–58: viii. 16)

The last quotation shows that Peirce thinks of 'universal agreement' as providing the definition of truth. The first two quotations add a further element: that it needs scientific methods in order to arrive at the truth.

In believing that 'endless investigation' would lead towards universal agreement on a single theory of everything, Peirce proves himself to be an extreme 'epistemic optimist'. He justifies his optimism by pointing out that all scientific inquirers investigate the same one world, the same reality. As scientific representations of this reality get more and more accurate, they must also increasingly converge. Accordingly, Peirce is happy to equate 'the true' with what 'accurately reflects objective reality' (1931–58: v. 564).

This is not convincing. As Kirkham is right to lament, at this point Peirce's ideal-consensus theory relies on the correspondence theory as a condition of its plausibility (Kirkham 1992: 83). Moreover, Peirce cannot have it both ways: he cannot make reality both the *cause* and the *outcome* of universal agreement. He does the latter where he writes: 'Reality is independent, not necessarily of thought in general, but only of what you or I or any finite number of men may think about it. . . . On the other hand, though the object of the final opinion depends on what that opinion is, yet what that opinion is does not depend on what you or I or any man thinks' (1931–58: v. 408).

From the viewpoint of truth finitism Peirce is on the right track only in so far as he recognizes the importance of consensus in our truth-talk. But he is wrong to *define* 'the true' or 'the real' as what will be agreed upon after endless investigation. In doing so, he treats as a definition of 'true' what is merely a condition of the possibility of correctness in the application of 'true'. There cannot be a correct application of the word 'true' unless there is a society that collectively constitutes exemplars. But these exemplars do not guide us in the application of the expression 'what is agreed among us' or 'what we all ideally should agree with'. They guide us in the application of the expression 'true'.

There is also a deep problem in the Peircean assumption that progress of inquiry will take us closer and closer towards the truth. Such assumption makes sense only if we assume that 'true' has a fixed extension. In other words, talk of such progress assumes that there is a set of propositions that form the extension of 'true propositions'. Progress then consists in our getting our hands (or minds) on an ever increasing number of such propositions. Alas, this whole picture is based on reifying the drifting array of exemplars into a fixed extension. There is no way of knowing which statements or propositions will be judged as relevantly similar to the drifting array of exemplars of the present and the future. These relevant similarity judgements have not yet been made. And thus there is no way of telling whether we, or some future science, would count the agreed-upon statements of the future as true or false.

Peirce and other ideal-consensus theorists seek to do justice to two important intuitions: that truth is in some important ways social, and that truth cannot be made by a single collective voluntary act. Ideal-consensus theorists can conceive of only one way of putting these two intuitions together. They project the truth-constituting consensus into an ideal future. Truth finitism suggests a different way of explaining the two intuitions. The key is a different idea of consensus, that is, the model of randomly meeting clocks. Truth is social in so far as we need each other in order to constitute exemplars for, and judgements about, correct applications of 'true'. And yet all such consensus is local only. It is impossible to predict the ways in which the dispositions of all community members will develop over time (in and through innumerable interactions). Whatever we agree upon as true today might tomorrow be judged false in the light of others' and our own evolving exemplars and interests.

DEFLATIONISM

Deflationist theories of truth are the fashion of the day. Their common credo is that there is less to truth than we (philosophers) have previously thought. Truth is not a property—or at least not a 'substantive' property. To say of a sentence (or belief, or proposition, etc.) that it is true is not to say that the sentence possesses the property of truth. It is saying something much more modest, and indeed, something altogether different in kind. Different deflationist theories disagree, however, over what this 'something more modest', or 'something altogether different' actually is. Here I shall mention four versions of deflationism.

Peter Strawson suggested in the late 1940s that to call a proposition 'true' is simply to endorse it. Thus to utter 'It is true that the plane landed at 12.30' is not tantamount to saying 'The proposition "it is true that the plane landed at 12.30" has the property of being true'. Instead the first utterance means 'I strongly endorse the proposition that the plane landed at 12.30'. As Strawson would have us believe, 'true' functions as an essential part of 'performative utterances'; that is, acts of doing rather than acts of describing. Strawson realized himself that not all uses of 'true' fit the endorsement thesis. We are not endorsing anything when we ask 'Is it true that the plane landed at 12.30?'

In addition to endorsement, 'true' can also express doubt, surprise, and disbelief (Strawson 1949, 1999).

W. V. O. Quine's version of deflationism interprets 'true' as 'a device of disquotation' (Quine 1999). Start from the idea that the 'disquotational scheme' DS states the essential feature of our 'true'-talk:

(DS) 'X' is true if and only if p.

For instance,

'Snow is white' is true if and only if snow is white.

In such a biconditional 'snow is white' appears twice; once *in*, and once *without*, quotation marks. The quotation marks around the first occurrence of 'snow is white' signal that we are not actually *using* the words to talk about snow and its being white. We are merely *mentioning* the sentence. This is more obvious if we think of examples where we talk *about* the sentence 'snow is white'. Take, for instance, the sentences

'Snow is white' consists of three words.
'Snow is white' is a sentence of English.
'Snow is white' can be translated into Finnish as 'lumi on valkoinen'.

In every case the expression in quotation marks is *mentioned* rather than *used*. We might also say that 'Snow is white' (in quotation marks) is the *name* of the sentence 'Snow is white' (when it appears outside quotation marks).

Quine's point, that truth is disquotation, comes to this. When we combine such quoted expressions (i.e. the name of such a sentence) with 'is true', then we 'cancel' the effect of the quotation marks and return to using, rather than mentioning, the words 'snow', 'is', and 'white' to talk about the whiteness of snow. So for Quine, too, predicating 'true' is not to predicate a property, it is (merely) to cancel the effect of quotation marks.

Another, more recent, theory—advocated by Dorothy Grover, Joseph Camp, Nuel Belnap, and Robert Brandom—is the 'prosentence theory'.[4] The authors observe that language has many 'proforms'; these are linguistic expressions that acquire their content from antecedent expressions. The

---

[4] Important papers on prosententialism are collected in Grover (1992). See also Brandom (1994, ch. 5).

best-known cases of proforms are of course pronouns (1), but there are also 'proforms' for verbs ('proverbs', (2)) and 'proforms for sentences' ('prosentences' (3)):

(1) Mary loved John, and *he* loved *her*, too.
(2) Mary loved John, and so *did* Jane.
(3) Peter: 'Mary loved John'. Jack: 'If *that is so*, then why didn't she go out with him?'

Prosentence theorists ('prosententialists') maintain that 'that is true' is a prosentence, and that 'true' has meaning only as part of this expression. 'That is true' can function syntactically like 'that is so' in (3). Prosentence theorists hold that all other occurrences of 'true' can be 'analysed away'. That is to say, for every sentence in which 'true' occurs outside the formula 'that is true' we can find another sentence that meets two conditions: it captures the content of the first sentence, and it contains 'true' only as a part of the formula 'that is true'.[5] For instance, 'It is true that France is a member of the United Nations' can be paraphrased as: 'France is a member of the United Nations, and that is true'. Prosentence theorists assume that the deep structure of our languages only knows of 'that is true' *qua* prosentence; it does not feature 'true' as a predicate.

Finally, Paul Horwich suggests that although 'is true' expresses a predicate, the predicate in question is not 'substantive'.[6] Truth is not a property about which scientific and philosophical inquiry should expect to make any discoveries. All that there is to truth is captured in the equivalence scheme ES:

(ES) The proposition that *p* is true if and only if *p*.[7]

The 'theory of truth' consists of the infinite list of instances of ES:

The proposition that snow is white is true if and only if snow is white.

---

[5] Or its modal and temporal variants: 'that was true', 'that will be true', 'that would be true', etc.

[6] Horwich (1990). Several critical discussions of Horwich's work are collected in Blackburn and Simmons (1999). Close to Horwich is Michael Williams (1986).

[7] Note the difference between DS and ES. DS talks about sentences, whereas ES talks about propositions. Horwich favours ES since DS cannot easily handle indexical expressions like (*).

(*) 'I am drunk' is true if and only if I am drunk

(*) is not true; for when *you* say 'I am drunk' my being drunk is not a truth-condition.

The proposition that grass is green is true if and only if grass is green. The proposition that the sky is blue is true if and only if the sky is blue. And so on for all propositions...

Horwich suggests that 'true' serves 'a certain logical need':

On occasion we wish to adopt some attitude towards a proposition—for example, believing it, assuming it for the sake of argument, or desiring it to be the case—but find ourselves thwarted by ignorance of what exactly the proposition is. ... In such situations the concept of truth is invaluable. For it enables the construction of another proposition, intimately related to the one we can't identify, which is perfectly appropriate as the alternative object of our attitude. (1990: 2–3)

For example, I might trust you enough to believe whatever you said last night at 9.50 p.m.—and yet not know what exactly you did say. In such a situation I can express my belief about your statement by saying 'What you said at 9.50 p.m. is true'. And if I later find out that what you said was 'The plane arrives at 5 a.m.', then I can infer that the plane arrives at 5 a.m.

How do these proposals relate to truth finitism? As far as Strawson's performative theory is concerned, it does identify an important feature of our use of 'true'. We often use 'true' in order to endorse statements. Such acts of endorsement are of course subject to finitistic constraint: in deciding whether to endorse a given statement I am judging the similarity between it and accepted endorsement-worthy statements. And my peers might well judge my endorsement to be incorrect. At the same time it is clear that the endorsement thesis in itself does not rule out other theories of truth. For instance, Goldman defends a correspondence theory of truth according to which calling a sentence true is to endorse it as 'descriptively successful' (1999, ch. 2).

Do Quine's or Horwich's proposals pose a threat to finitism? If DS and ES capture all there is to know about 'true', what space is there for indeterminacy, for exemplars, and for decisions concerning similarity? Are not DS and ES trivially easily applied?

The objection poses no problem for finitism. ES is unacceptable because it talks about propositions. Propositions are the determinate meaning entities, abstract entities that can be expressed by declarative sentences. That is, the very notion of a proposition is tied to the model of fixed extensions. DS is more of a challenge. It is indeed trivial. But this triviality does not undermine finitism. This is because DS does not decide for us to which sentences it ought to be applied. DS does not apply straightforwardly in cases of vagueness and to Liar paradox sentences.[8] If 'tall' is a vague predicate, then the truth-value of 'Jim is tall' is indeterminate. And hence 'Jim is tall' does not imply ' "Jim is tall" is true'. Or assume that we are dealing with a sentence L with the content 'L is false'. Applying DS to L we get:

(*a*) 'L is false' is true if and only if L is false.

Since L is the sentence 'L is false', we can replace the last 'L' in (*a*) with 'L is false'. And since double negation equals affirmation we get the unacceptable result:

(*b*) 'L is false' is true if and only if L is true.

The moral should be transparent: we must decide case by case whether or not a given sentence is such that we regard DS as applicable. And this involves us in collective decisions over which predicates we wish to regard as vague, and which sentences we regard as paradox-prone.

The prosentence theory does not threaten finitism either. The use of proforms is governed by exemplars as much as are any other elements of language. In the case of proforms the exemplars are syntactic structures. A finitistic theory of meaning has difficulties with the prosententialist methodology, however. The claim that 'true' has meaning only as part of 'that is true' runs counter to native speakers' intuitions. What the prosententialists have shown is that we can construct an artificial language in which 'true' does not appear independently. But it is sheer dogmatism to then go on and claim that this artificial language 'must be' the deep structure of our natural language.

CORRESPONDENCE THEORIES AND MINIMALISM

The history of the correspondence theory in analytic philosophy has been one of retreat. Early on in the twentieth-century Bertrand Russell proposed that a belief is true if its content corresponds to a fact.[9] Indeed, it was Russell who made the very expression 'correspondence theory' popular. By 'correspondence' Russell meant isomorphism. The underlying assumption

---

[8] See e.g. Sainsbury (1998: 105–8).

[9] Russell's version of the correspondence theory is explained well in Russell (1912).

was that a true belief and the corresponding fact relate to one another like the two remaining pieces of a torn-apart piece of paper.

By mid-century, the assumption of such isomorphism had become dubious. In 1950 J. L. Austin insisted that 'there is no need whatsoever for the words used in making a true statement to "mirror" in any way, however indirect, any feature whatsoever of the situation or event'.[10] In defence of this view, Austin pointed out that a fact like the cat's being on the mat need not be described with the seemingly isomorphic statement 'the cat is on the mat'.[11] We can imagine a language in which the same fact is picked out by a single-word sentence. Austin therefore proposed a new correspondence theory in which the relationship between a true statement and the corresponding fact is purely conventional. In George Pitcher's useful taxonomy, Austin treats correspondence as 'correlation' and not, like Russell, as 'congruence' (Pitcher 1964: 10). The basic idea can perhaps best be explained by means of a simplified analogy.

Assume that we had introduced linguistic conventions such that '1' picks out one *type* of fact, '2' picks out another type of fact, '3' a further type of fact, and so on. Imagine further that we had introduced the convention that, by uttering a number and simultaneously pointing to a spatio-temporal region, we pick out a *particular* fact. We can then say that a given particular act of uttering a number and pointing is true if and only if the following conditions are met: the pointing picks out a particular fact, say f; the number picks out a type of fact, say F; and f is a member of F.

Austin's proposal was famously criticized by Strawson. Most influential was Strawson's attack on Austin's assumption that true statements are statements *about* facts. Take a statement like 'the cat is on the mat'. Strawson is adamant that what the statement states (i.e. the proposition) is *about* the cat and the mat only; it is not additionally *about* the fact that the cat is on the mat. Strawson also rejects the whole idea according to which facts are part of the world's furniture. If facts were part of the world, then it should be possible to locate them in space and time (1999: 166–7). But while it is correct to say (1), it is incorrect to say (2):

---

[10] Austin's classical paper is 'Truth' (1999); here p. 155.

[11] The fact and the statement might be regarded as isomorphic since the fact consists of two individuals (the cat, the mat) and a relation (is on), and the statement of two nouns ('the cat', 'the mat') and a verb plus proposition ('is on').

(1) It is a fact that I was in Madrid on 1 January 2000.

(2) The fact took place in Madrid on 1 January 2000.

Some philosophers are unconvinced (Searle 1998). They argue that facts are part of the world on the ground that facts can be causes. Consider (3) for example:

(3) The fact that Napoleon recognized the danger to his left flank caused him to move his troops forward.

It seems that the fact here is the cause of the troop movement. Strawson has a reply to this argument (1998). (3) shows only that facts can be *causally explanatory*; it does not show that facts *act causally*. Events act causally; facts do not. This becomes clear once the linguistically awkward (3) is replaced by the more normal (4). (4) talks about the relationship between two events.

(4) Napoleon moved his troops forward because he recognized the danger to his left flank.

Strawson claims that far from being worldly items, facts are 'what true statements state'. That is to say, whenever a given statement *p* is true, it is correct to say that *p* 'is a fact'. Put differently, the relationship between true statement and fact is 'internal': it is as close as the relationship between 'playing' and 'engaging in a game or play'. Whenever it is correct to say that someone plays, then it is also correct to say that they are engaged in a game or play. After we have decided on the playing, there is nothing *further* to do in order to determine whether we have identified a game or play.

Strawson's criticism of the correspondence theory led to further retreats. Now they concerned 'facts' as much as they concerned 'correspondence'. Alfred Tarski's work on truth in formal languages was helpful here. Correspondence theorists found a new way of speaking of the correspondence between sentence and world, a way that did not use facts. Take again 'the cat is on the mat'. The sentence is now analysed (very roughly) as having two components: 'cat' and 'X is on the mat'. 'Cat' refers to the set of all cats, and 'X is on the mat' refers to the set of all things that are on mats. 'The cat is on the mat' is true if the individual talked about is a member of both sets. Some correspondence theorists hope that 'reference' will one day be replaced by a causal theory on how language links up to the world.

Other correspondence theorists have been less eager to use Tarski's work on formal languages as a tool for reformulating the correspondence theory. One reason has been the observation that *formal* languages might not be a good model for understanding *natural* (i.e. changing!) languages. These correspondence theorists try to avoid talk of facts as parts of the world. Either they try to get rid of fact-talk altogether, or they employ a very 'thin' notion of fact. For John Searle, for instance, 'fact' is simply the covering term for the right-hand side of all instances of DS (Searle 1998). And Goldman writes: 'An item X (a proposition, a sentence, a belief, etc.) is true if and only if X is descriptively successful, that is, X purports to describe reality and its content fits reality' (1999: 59).

Finally, some authors go still further in their retreat. Theirs is a correspondence theory without facts and without correspondence! The core of this position, sometimes called 'minimalism',[12] is expressed by William P. Alston as follows: 'A statement (proposition, belief...) is true if and only if what the statement says to be the case actually is the case' (1996: 5).

This brief sketch of developments in the correspondence theory suffices for my purposes here. I now turn to some observations on the correspondence theory from the perspectives of the present study.

First of all, it is interesting to note that most correspondence theorists conceive of truth as a natural property; 'truth' is a natural kind term in the sense in which I have introduced the term earlier. In order to determine whether a given sentence (a proposition, or belief...) is true we must investigate empirically detectable features of that sentence and of the world. There is no in-principle difference between this kind of investigation and an inquiry into whether or not a newly discovered comet is smaller or larger than our moon. Thus, according to Russell we determine the truth or falsity of beliefs by searching for the presence of an isomorphism between belief and fact; according to Austin we figure out the truth and falsity of statements by studying the empirical links between acts of pointing, conventions, signs, and facts; and according to the Tarskians we separate out truths from falsehoods by tracing the relations between the members of different sets. (Needless to say, Tarski's view of language is completely at odds with finitism.)

---

[12] Alston (1996) also speaks of 'alethic realism'. Minimalism in this sense must not be conflated with Horwich's 'deflationary' minimalism.

The interesting thing to note here is that correspondence theorists have despaired of finding an empirically detectable feature that might work. Throughout the twentieth century the candidates for such features have become ever thinner, and increasingly more difficult to detect. For instance, Goldman's 'fitting reality' is both thinner than 'isomorphism between belief and fact', and more difficult to detect. Indeed, it is hopelessly vague. How much reality, and which reality, are we supposed to check? And what does it take to 'fit' a reality? Is a loose fit enough? Or do we need a tight fit? And how do we tell the one from the other? Alston marks the end point of this development. If we want to study truth as a natural property, then we are not helped by the formula that true statements tell us what is the case. The link between 'x is true' and 'x is the case' is as internal as is the relation between 'x is true' and 'x is a fact'.

Second, as I have emphasized in earlier chapters, natural kind terms are partly self-referential. They are self-referential in so far as standards and exemplars for a given natural kind are conventional. (Something is a standard for us because we have collectively taken it to be such a standard.) Applying this analysis of natural kind terms to truth leads to the following remark. Even if truth were a natural kind in the way conceived of by the correspondence theorist, it would still be importantly social. 'Correspondence', 'fit', 'congruence', or 'isomorphism' can be understood and applied only on the basis of a finite array of accepted exemplars. Moreover, deciding whether a newly encountered pair (a statement, a fact) constitutes a case of 'correspondence' (etc.) is a judgement of similarity rather than identity. It is a judgement informed by interests and salience. And such a judgement is correct only if it is acceptable to one's peers.

Third, we need to answer these questions: Is truth a natural kind in the first place? And are we obliged to think of truth as a natural kind once we acknowledge that expressions like 'fitting the facts' or 'corresponds' occur frequently in our truth-talk? One thing is clear: if the notion of truth as a natural kind involves the thought of fixed extensions, then the finitist will have to protest. However, as the last paragraph suggested, the advocate of truth as a natural kind (also known as the correspondence theorist) can regroup. She can accept the communitarian analysis of natural kind terms, and propose that 'true' is like 'cat' or 'tree': successive applications of the term are underdetermined by past practice, and yet they are in part responsive to detectable empirical features. Alas, in going down this route, the correspondence theory is changed beyond recognition. First, truth is no longer 'recognition-transcendent' in the traditional sense: whether something is true or false is up to us in so far as it is us who decide on the application of 'true' in new cases. Second, the revised correspondence theory incorporates a strong element of consensus and expediency. Consensus is the standard of correct application, and interests guide *judgements* of similarity. Third, the revised theory had better heed James's insight according to which the meaning of 'fit' or 'correspondence'—and thus also of 'true'—is highly context-dependent. Reconstructed in finitist terms, this amounts to saying that the exemplars of 'fit' and 'correspondence' are many and varied, and perhaps even in tension with one another. Compared with more ordinary 'empirical terms' like 'cat' or 'tree', the underdetermination of the similarity *judgement* by received exemplars is therefore considerably increased. Local contingencies of interests and consensus will thus be even more important here than in the case of 'ordinary empirical terms'. And fourth, and finally, 'correspondence' or 'fit' can no longer be conceived of as 'correspondence' or 'fit' with a completely mind-independent reality (as the next chapter will argue). It is hard to imagine that any correspondence theorist would recognize this revised theory as her own.

SUMMARY

In this chapter I have outlined truth finitism and related it to other, better-known theories of truth. It should be clear by now that truth finitism stands orthogonal to other theories of truth. It does not, for instance, propose a direct alternative to the correspondence theory or to disquotationalism. That is to say, truth finitism does not start from a definition of 'true', or from a study of its semantic or syntactic functions. Nevertheless, truth finitism works as a filter of acceptability for other theories of truth. Most important in this respect is the insistence that there are no fixed extensions or intensions, and that the application of 'true' is guided by exemplars, interests, and consensus. Peirce's theory of truth as ideal consensus, the coherence theory, and the correspondence theory did not pass muster by these criteria. A correspondence theory modified so as to survive finitistic criticism is no longer a correspondence theory at all. On the other hand, truth finitism accords well with central elements of James's pragmatism and Strawson's and Quine's deflationism.

Chapter 17

REALITY

In this chapter I turn from truth to reality. The two topics are often run together; for instance, it is sometimes thought that the correspondence theory of truth commits one to the view that reality is mind-independent. This is incorrect. There is no reason why the 'facts' that correspond to true beliefs might not themselves be beliefs or ideas. While I follow those philosophers who separate the two issues of truth and reality, I nevertheless see those issues as connected in at least one important respect: finitism is a constraint both on theories of truth, and on theories of reality.

Theories of reality are usefully divided into 'forms of realism' and 'forms of anti-realism' (or 'realisms' and 'anti-realisms'). Most of such theories make global claims about the nature of reality, and how it relates to our concepts and representations. They present us with claims about 'all objects', 'all descriptions of the world', 'all facts', and 'all possible referents'. Finitism rejects all such claims as meaningless. What counts, say, as an object, a description of the world, a fact, and a referent depends on decisions not yet taken. None of these expressions has a fixed extension. And thus they cannot be used in the way intended by the realist or the anti-realist. Finitism thereby leads to a view *beyond* realism and anti-realism.

REALISMS

Among recent statements and defences of realism, those provided by Susan Haack and John Searle stand out for their clarity. I shall therefore concentrate on them here. I begin with a summary of their views.

Haack calls her position 'innocent realism'.[1] Its core is the thesis that 'the world—the one, real, world—is largely independent of us' (1998: 156). The restriction 'largely' is necessary since we humans both intervene in the world and are part of it. The second thesis of innocent realism contends that our descriptions of the world are true if (and only if) they accord with the way the world is. The truth or falsity of our descriptions is thus settled by the world; whether any given 'description is true or false does not depend on how you or I or anybody *thinks* the world is' (1998: 157).

The third thesis concerns the relationship between different descriptions of the world. There can be more than one true description, but different true descriptions must all be compatible. Compatible descriptions can all be combined into one long conjunctive description. It thus makes sense to say that there is only 'one true description of the world' (1998: 160). However, Haack does not assume that this one true description will be (or could be) provided by a single science or a single theory. Innocent realism allows that the ultimate true description of the world be 'heterogeneous':

A heterogeneous true description of the world is no less true for its heterogeneity; any more than a map which superimposes a depiction of the roads on a depiction of the contours of the relevant terrain, or a map which inserts a large-scale depiction of a major city in a corner of a small-scale depiction of a state, is less accurate for *its* heterogeneity. (1998: 160)

Innocent realism rejects the claim that the world is 'the totality of mind-independent objects'. We might call this the fourth thesis of innocent realism. Haack regards 'object' or 'thing' as 'the most hospitable notions' (1998: 157–8). We can count a pack of cards as one object, as four, or as fifty-two objects. And thus the notion of there being one totality of objects does not make sense.

Haack's fifth thesis is that many true descriptions of the world make no reference to human existence. For instance, it is true to say that there are stones in the world. And these stones would have been there even if humans had never evolved. Finally (sixth thesis), innocent realism insists that we can make 'direct' contact with the world. This happens in perception. Haack is happy to concede that perception involves conceptualization. But conceptualization does not make our contact with the world 'indirect'. Despite

---

[1] Haack explains her 'innocent realism' in Haack (1998).

concepts, 'in perception we are in contact with something real, independent of our interpretations, of how anyone thinks it to be'. Support for this view comes from the 'potential for surprise'. Haack quotes Peirce in support: 'A man cannot startle himself by jumping up with an exclamation of "Boo"!' (1998: 162–3).

Searle calls his realism 'external' and sums it up in the sentence 'the world (or alternatively, reality or the universe) exists independently of our representations of it'. 'Independence' here means that, even if no humans had ever existed, 'the word would still have existed and would have been exactly the same as it is now' (1998: 152–3). Searle is particularly eager to separate his external realism from a number of further doctrines.

To begin with, he insists that external realism does not commit one to the correspondence theory of truth—a view of truth that Searle is committed to on separate grounds. Theories of truth are semantic theories; they tell us the meaning of the word 'true'. But external realism (and its opponents) are ontological, or metaphysical, views; they do not concern what things mean, they concern 'what there is'. Moreover, Searle warns against conflating external realism with epistemological views. He rejects Hilary Putnam's claim according to which realism is related to a 'God's Eye View'. Putnam writes that 'the whole content of Realism lies in the claim that it makes sense to think of a God's Eye View (or better a view from nowhere)' (1990: 23). Searle chastizes this claim as a conflation of epistemology with ontology. The language of 'views' belongs to the former, not to the latter (1995: 154).

Searle is adamant that external realism need not assume the existence of one privileged vocabulary for describing the world. He is happy with the notion that different aspects of reality can be described with different 'and even incommensurable' vocabularies (1995: 155). He also insists that 'every representation has an aspectual shape'; that it is produced from a 'point of view' (1995: 175–6). Here it is unclear whether Searle's position differs from Haack's. Is Searle rejecting the conception of one true description of the world (never mind whether it is homogeneous or heterogeneous) or is he merely rejecting the idea of *one homogeneous true* description of the world? Alas, he does not tell us.

Searle defends his external realism in two ways: he attacks arguments for anti-realism, and he gives a 'transcendental argument' in defence of realism (1995: 177–97). I shall turn to his criticism of anti-realist arguments further below. His 'transcendental argument' is meant to establish that the assumption of an independent world is a condition of the intelligibility of our ordinary talk and action. We usually assume that the sentences of our shared language can be understood by speaker and hearer in the same way. Take, for example, sentences like 'My dog has fleas' or 'Hydrogen atoms each contain one electron'. Searle comments:

Normal understanding requires sameness of understanding by both speaker and hearer, and sameness of understanding in these cases requires that utterances of the referring expressions purport to make reference to a *publicly* accessible reality, to a reality that is ontologically objective. But the condition on public accessibility to the sorts of phenomena in these examples is that the way that things are does not depend on your or my representations. (1995: 186)

Haack's and Searle's highly similar versions of realism are, as we shall see, far *too strong* for some anti-realists (including the finitist anti-realist). And yet, their versions are *weaker* than some other forms of realism. These latter, *stronger*, forms must be mentioned here however briefly, for they are the main target of many anti-realist attacks.

Bernard Williams offers a very strong form of realism. Like Haack and Searle, Williams insists that the world is independent of our representations, and that our representations are true or false of this reality. But he goes further. He also holds that scientific inquiry converges on the one true 'absolute conception of the world'. Williams summarizes his views as follows:

In reflecting on the world as it is *anyway*, independent of our experience, we must concentrate not in the first instance on what our beliefs are about, but on how they represent what they are about. We can select among our beliefs and features of our world pictures some that we can reasonably claim to represent the world in a way to the maximum degree independent of our perspective and its peculiarities. The resultant picture of things, if we can carry through this task, can be called the 'absolute conception' of the world. In terms of that conception, we may hope to explain the possibility of attaining the conception itself, and also the possibility of other, perspectival conceptions. . . . the absolute conception will . . . be a conception of the world that might be arrived at by any investigators, even if they are very different from us . . . The aim is to outline the possibility of a convergence characteristic of science, one that could meaningfully be said to be a convergence on how things (anyway) are. (1985: 138–9)

Williams's realism is stronger than Haack's and Searle's in so far as he adds three new ideas: first, that there is one single, homogeneous, true description of the world; second, that science converges on this true description; and third, that all cognizers (even those with different forms of cognition) converge on it.

A closely related, if not identical, form of realism is 'metaphysical realism'. It was formulated by Hilary Putnam in the late 1970s to act as a foil for his own 'internal realism'. (I shall treat internal realism as a form of anti-realism.) Putnam characterizes 'metaphysical realism' as follows (the numbering is mine):

On this perspective, [1] the world consists of some fixed totality of mind-independent objects. [2] There is exactly one true and complete description of 'the way the world is'. [3] Truth involves some sort of correspondence relation between words or thought-signs and external things and sets of things. I shall call this perspective the *externalist* perspective, because its favorite point of view is a God's Eye point of view. (Putnam 1981: 49)

Metaphysical realism seems fully compatible with Williams's 'absolutism', but incompatible with Haack's innocent and Searle's external realism. Neither Haack nor Searle commit themselves to (1) or (2). Their emphasis on heterogeneity and even incommensurability does not fit with the metaphysical realist's dream of one true and complete description.

ANTI-REALISMS

Like realism so also 'anti-realism' comes in a number of different forms. I shall here concentrate on three: Nelson Goodman's 'irrealism', Hilary Putnam's 'internal realism', and Michael Lynch's 'pluralism'.[2]

Goodman's position is the most radical. Goodman's starting point is the innocent observation that we can have different descriptions of the world. Consider, for instance, the following line (call it '#'):

   x x x

How many objects (xs) are on line (#)? Two possible answers might be the following:

---

[2] Goodman (1978, 1989); Putnam (1981, 1983, 1989, 1992, 1994); Lynch (1998).

(1) There are three objects on line (#).

(2) There are seven objects on line (#).

The first answer hardly needs an explanation. It is the correct answer given our everyday understanding of what we mean by 'objects'. The second answer would be given by a mereologist. In mereology, for every two particulars there is an object that is their sum. Adding subscript numbers to the three objects for ease of exposition, we can identify the mereologist's seven objects as follows:

$$x_1$$
$$x_2$$
$$x_3$$
$$x_2 = x_1 + x_2$$
$$x_5 = x_1 + x_3$$
$$x_6 = x_2 + x_3$$
$$x_7 = x_1 + x_2 + x_3$$

The idea of different, equally true, descriptions of the world (or a 'mini-world' like (#)) does not as such threaten realism. The realist regards (1) and (2) as compatible descriptions of the same world. She may say, for instance, that (1) and (2) are two elements of the one true *heterogeneous* description of the world. But are (1) and (2) compatible? The obvious reasoning behind a positive answer is that (1) and (2) can be replaced by (3) and (4):

(3) According to the conventions of our everyday ontology there are three objects in line (#).

(4) According to the conventions of mereologist ontology there are seven objects in line (#).

(3) and (4) do not contradict one another. They relativize the contradictory pair (1) and (2) to different ontologies. As the realist sees it, this reformulation brings out that everyday ontology and mereology simply mean different things by 'objects'. And thus (1) and (2) are compatible.

Goodman is not impressed with the realist's manoeuvre. He points out that whereas in using statements like (1) and (2) we *commit* ourselves to a specific number of objects in (#), we do not take on any such commitment in (3) or (4). To re-establish a commitment regarding (3) and (4), we must prefix them with a claim like 'this ontology is the right one'. So modified, (3) and (4) are again incompatible (1978: 114–15).

Moreover, Goodman challenges the realist to explain what the allegedly compatible descriptions are *descriptions of*: 'What, then, is the neutral fact or thing described in these different terms?' It cannot be the fact that there are three objects; or the fact that there are seven objects; or the fact that there are either seven or three objects. Or, put differently, if, as the realist alleges, the two ways of counting are compatible in so far as they are 'purely conventional', what is the non-conventional substratum? 'When we strip off as layers of convention all differences among ways of describing *it*, what is left? The onion is peeled down to its empty core' (1978: 118).

To many interpreters it has seemed that Goodman draws the conclusion that there is *nothing* below conventions—that there are no facts at all. But this impression is wrong. Goodman's point is a different one. He believes that it is the realist's relativizing moves (3) and (4) that cause the trouble. If we do not turn our conflicting claims (1) and (2) into mere conventions, then we are not in danger of losing our grip on our *worlds*.

Goodman really means worlds (plural) not just world (singular). He reasons as follows. (1) and (2) are both truth. (1) and (2) are incompatible. A single world does not allow for incompatible facts (as correlates of truths). Hence, (1) and (2) are true of different actual (!) worlds. Who made these worlds? We. We literally *made* them by developing our different ontologies (1978: 119).

Here one might object that we actually have again lost the possibility of conflict between (1) and (2). If (1) is true in one world, and (2) is true in another world, then how can (1) and (2) conflict? Note that if they did not conflict, then the realist would have won the day after all. There would still be but one true description—albeit one true description of many worlds rather than one world. To maintain the conflict between (1) and (2), Goodman therefore has to insist that whole worlds can be in conflict and that the world of which (1) is true is in conflict with the world of which (2) is true. (But what is it that these worlds are disagreeing over?)

Hilary Putnam's 'internal realism' sympathizes with elements of Goodman's 'irrealism'. The sympathy comes out most clearly in Putnam's famous claim that 'the mind and the world jointly make up the mind and the world' (1981, p. xi). And yet Putnam rejects the idea of multiple actual worlds. As Putnam sees it, what the above example really shows is that metaphysical realism is wrong. It is wrong to assume that there is one fixed totality of mind-independent objects, and it is incorrect to presume one true and complete description of the 'way the world is'. The above example brings this home since (1) and (2) are both true descriptions of (#). And they are both true despite the fact that they are based upon different uses of the word 'object', and different assumptions about the 'intrinsic properties' of objects (here, their number). In Putnam's own words:

> If there isn't one single privileged sense of the word 'object' and one privileged totality of 'intrinsic properties', but there is only an inherently extendable notion of 'object' and various properties that may be seen as 'intrinsic' in different inquiries, then the very notion of a totality of all objects and of the *one* description that captures *the* intrinsic properties of those objects should be seen to be nonsense from the start. (1994: 304–5)

The thesis that (1) and (2) are incompatible but true descriptions of the same world not only threatens metaphysical realism, it also endangers innocent realism's assumption of one heterogeneous true description. For while a 'heterogeneous description' allows for a variety of different, and perhaps even incommensurable, partial descriptions, it does not permit incompatible partial descriptions.

Putnam rejects Goodman's arguments in favour of many worlds; for Putnam the needed plurality is one of 'conceptual schemes', not of worlds. And he takes up Goodman's challenge to explain just what (1) and (2) are *both* descriptions *of*. (1) and (2) are 'very different sentences' that 'describe the same state of affairs'. Putnam believes he can refuse the challenge to say more; he feels it is sufficient to point out that there is a pre-theoretical notion of 'state of affairs' that we all understand as making sense of the situation at hand (1992: 122).

Putnam is also hostile to the idea that a defence of the 'one-world' assumption presupposes a defence of 'direct access' to the world of thought and language. Such defence is not needed if realism simply means the idea 'that thought and language can represent parts of the world which are not parts of thought and language' (1994: 299).

Moreover, Putnam thinks that we need to be careful in regarding (1) and (2) as incompatible. To assume that they are incompatible is to presuppose that *the same sentence*, say (2), has the *same* meaning in everyday parlance and among mereologists. It is unclear that it does. At the same time, Putnam is not suggesting that 'object' means *different* things in the two language games. His point is rather 'that the notion of "meaning", and the ordinary practices of translation and paraphrase to which it is linked, crumble when confronted with such cases' (1992: 119).

Another aspect of Putnam's internal realism is the idea that although each conceptual scheme is a system of conventions, decisions taken within, or according to, a conceptual scheme are not conventional:

> *given* a version, the question 'How many objects are there?' has an answer, namely, 'three' in the case of the first version ... and 'seven' in the case of the second version ... Once we make clear how we are using 'object' ... the question 'How many objects exist?' has an answer that is not at all a matter of 'convention'. That is why I say that this sort of example does not support cultural relativism. (1989: 175)

Finally, it is worth pointing out that Putnam's position has developed considerably over time. Most important for our present concerns is his shift from a Peircean epistemic conception of truth as acceptability under ideal conditions, to a version of correspondence theory. Putnam now takes it to be obvious that 'the ubiquity of conceptual relativity does not require us to deny that truth genuinely depends on the behaviour of things distant from the speaker' (1994: 309).

In combining conceptual relativity with a realist theory of truth, 'the most recent Putnam' concurs with Michael Lynch. Lynch sees his own 'pluralism' as an improvement over Putnam's 'internal realism' (1998: 28). The alleged improvement is precisely the replacement of truth as ideal acceptability with realist truth (*à la* Alston above). In addition to 'pluralism', Lynch also uses the label 'relativistic Kantianism' for his and Putnam's position (1998: 4). And indeed, 'relativistic Kantianism' does capture the view very well.

For instance, relativistic Kantianism fits with Lynch's insistence—against Goodman—that there is but one 'noumenal world'. Lynch not only finds this idea of many worlds 'anti-intuitive in the extreme'; he also objects to it on moral grounds: 'If we live in different worlds, why should I care what happens to yours? Why should I have a concern for a world that I can never inhabit?' (1998: 95).

In Lynch's pluralism, propositions as well as facts are relative to conceptual schemes. One cannot explain any proposition without stating to which conceptual scheme it belongs; and one cannot pick out a fact without specifying its scheme. 'Facts are *internal* to conceptual schemes, or ways of dividing the world into objects' (1998: 22).

Lynch does more work (than Putnam) in trying to explain how (1) and (2) can be different propositions, incompatible with one another, and both true. The first condition is met in so far as (1) implies not-(2), and (2) implies not-(1). It is more difficult to show how (1) and (2) can express incompatible propositions. (1) and (2) can only be incompatible if they do not involve completely different concepts of object. But what do the concepts of object in the two frameworks share? Lynch suggests that mereologists and non-mereologists share the same 'minimal concept of an object'. According to Lynch, many concepts have, as it were, two layers. Think, for instance, of the concept of 'mind' and the two claims (5) and (6):

(5) The mind is independent of the body.
(6) The mind is the brain.

How can the spiritualist and the materialist disagree over the mind? Do they not simply mean different things by 'mind'? And if they do simply mean different things, why do they take themselves to be disagreeing with one another? Lynch thinks the disagreement can be preserved. Spiritualist and materialist share the same 'minimal concept' of mind. The minimal concept of 'mind' is of something that thinks, solves problems, and develops. This concept is shared between the spiritualist and the materialist. And thus they do genuinely express incompatible propositions in (5) and (6). What (5) and (6) show is that spiritualist and materialist extend the *same* minimal concept in different ways (1998: 66–72).

And what holds for 'mind' also applies to 'object'. Mereologist and non-mereologist share the same minimal concept of 'object'—say, as something that can play a role in counting, and as something that has one of its paradigm cases in 'middle-sized dry goods'. Nevertheless, mereologist and non-mereologist extend these paradigms in incompatible ways. And thus (1) and (2) are themselves incompatible. Lynch specifies what incompatibility means here: 'if these propositions were relative to the same scheme, they would be inconsistent' (1998: 93).

THE REALISTS' RESPONSE

Here I shall only briefly mention how Haack and Searle deal with the mini-world case. Searle is adamant that the example has no implications concerning the alleged mind-dependence of the world:

a realist who was a convinced conceptual relativist would say that there really are three objects, as the criterion for counting objects has been set in the first system of classification, really seven as the criterion has been set in the second. . . . But the real world does not care how we describe it and it remains the same under the various different descriptions we give of it. (1995: 163)

Moreover, Searle argues that the mini-world example presupposes realism. The example cannot even be explained without referring the reader to something; be it the three xs, or the ink on the page. Finally, Searle has no difficulty with humans choosing whatever vocabularies they like. But he insists that

once we have fixed the meaning of [the] terms in our vocabulary by arbitrary definition, it is no longer a matter of any kind of relativism or arbitrariness whether representation-independent features of the world satisfy those definitions, because the features of the world that satisfy or fail to satisfy the definitions exist independently of those or any other definitions. (1995: 166)

Haack's comments on the mini-world case differ from Searle's. To begin with, she asks how Putnam can say both that (1) and (2) are incompatible but true statements *and* that our concept of meaning leaves it underdetermined whether (1) or (2) have the same concept of object.

Furthermore, according to Haack, (1) and (2) are fully compatible. 'Object' in (1) means 'ordinary physical object' and 'object' in (2) means 'mereological object'. Hence there is no contradiction is making the two claims (1) and (2). As if this were not enough, Haack also criticizes the mereological concept of object as 'well, peculiar, to put it mildly'. She therefore suggests a distinction between 'natural' and 'artificial object terms', putting the objects of (1) and (2) in the first and the second category respectively (1998: 159).

Finally, Haack maintains that (#) has but one true description:

Though there are different true descriptions of Putnam's imagined situation ('there are three regular physical objects', 'there are seven mereological objects'), it doesn't follow, and neither is it true, that there is no one true description ('there are three regular physical objects, but seven mereological objects'; or, better, 'there are seven mereological objects, *of which* three are regular physical objects'). (1998: 159)

FINITISM AND REALITY

Perhaps enough has been said in order to convey a sense of the contemporary realism debate. I now turn to assessing the above positions in the light of finitism.

1. To repeat a point I have already stressed often, the finitist must reject the idea of one true description of the world—never mind whether this one true description is heterogeneous or homogeneous. A set of all true descriptive sentences does not make sense in a finitist theory of meaning. For the idea of such a set presupposes that the extensions of all terms are fixed once and for all. And this is, according to finitism, an incoherent idea. Terms are applied step by step to new cases; the application is guided by interests; no exemplars are sacrosanct; and the correctness of the application is determined by interactions within a community. On this picture, language is too fluid, too contextual, and too social for the conception of a 'final' true description to make much sense. Thus communitarian epistemology cannot side with Haack and Searle.

2. Haack goes to some length to distinguish her position from metaphysical realism. In particular she insists that her 'innocent realist' is not committed to the idea of a fixed totality of objects. And she agrees with Putnam that 'object' can be understood in many different ways. Note, however, that although Haack might be able to avoid commitment to a fixed totality of *objects*, she does not avoid commitment to a fixed totality of *facts*. Presumably a true description consists of sentences or propositions. And surely these sentences or propositions must correspond to facts—after all, innocent realism is committed to truth as correspondence. Ergo, the innocent realist must believe in a fixed totality of facts. Again, this is a view ruled out by finitism: if there is no fixed extension for 'true sentence or statement', there is no fixed extension for 'fact'. Or, put differently, the idea of *the world* as the *sum*, or *totality*, of *facts* is incoherent.

3. The finitist must also discard central assumptions and arguments of anti-realism. In particular, communitarianism must reject the idea that

relativity and underdetermination play a role only in the choice *between* different conceptual schemes, but not regarding choices *within* conceptual schemes. Putnam in particular seems to think of conceptual schemes as axiomatic systems, and as semantic structures that determine the use of terms precisely and uniquely. Once we adopt the mereological system we *must* say that there are seven objects; if we stick to the everyday conception of object, we *must* say that there are but three objects. All this is unacceptable to the finitist. If finitism is the correct view of meaning, then indeterminacy must rule supreme *within* as well as *between* conceptual schemes. And indeterminacy must rule supreme even if we conceive of conceptual schemes as being like axiomatic systems (an assumption which is dubious on other grounds). We learn the concept of mereological object by being shown a number of examples by our teachers; we apply the concept in new circumstances on the basis of *judgements* of similarity; and we take our peers' agreement as a sign that we have got things right. And over time the exemplars might shift and drift. Historians eventually tell us that they did.

4. It is easy to see why Putnam feels inclined to favour the axiomatic and 'meaning-determinist' line. Only if conceptual schemes are like axiomatic systems can relativism be blocked and community-based epistemology be kept at bay. Truth is still fully determined by something *other than* human interaction and agreement. In ignoring the role of the community, Putnam does not stand alone; almost all participants in the realism debate do likewise. Take, for instance, Lynch's otherwise insightful comments on how a 'minimal concept' can be correctly 'extended' in different directions by different speakers. Surely whether such extensions are correct and acceptable or not is something that must be negotiated and agreed upon in interaction with others. Or consider Goodman's different worlds. Goodman never feels inclined to ponder the question of how worlds are built collectively. And yet surely the worlds of science and art are collectively constructed worlds.

5. Once we reject the idea that conceptual schemes are like timeless axiomatic systems, it becomes more difficult to speak of their (once-and-for-all) incompatibility. That is to say, if a conceptual scheme develops over time, if it can drift and shift, then its relation to other conceptual schemes must be subject to change. Indeed, such a change might even enable formerly 'alien' cultures to understand one another. More importantly, it

always takes a third conceptual scheme to judge that two conceptual schemes are incompatible. The problem is this. According to the conceptual relativist, two conceptual schemes are incompatible if, and only if, they license incompatible descriptions of the same facts. But the conceptual relativist also insists that facts are relative to conceptual schemes. And thus conceptual relativism collapses. We can avoid this problem by making the *judgements* of incompatibility scheme-dependent. Users of a conceptual scheme CS_1 are able to judge that CS_2 and CS_3 are incompatible provided that *the facts* (of which CS_2 and CS_3 produce incompatible descriptions) are identified on the basis of CS_1. There is then no community-independent fact of the matter as to whether two conceptual schemes are incompatible. CS_2 and CS_3 might be judged incompatible using the standards of CS_1, and regarded as compatible on the basis of the standards of CS_4. Perhaps there is also a sense in which the phenomenon of incompatibility is, at least in part, *constituted* by actors' *judgements* (that is, by *judgements* of members of CS_1, CS_2, or both). Take a case where advocates of CS_1 are agreed among themselves that CS_1 and CS_2 are incompatible. Such agreement is as much a prescription as it is a description. For it amounts to the agreement that advocates of CS_1 need not make an effort *to make* CS_1 and CS_2 compatible—thereby changing and developing CS_1.

6. To reject conceptual schemes as monolithic and determinate systems of meanings is not of course to give up conceptual relativity (and thus anti-realism). Instead it is to urge a different form of conceptual relativity. This form of conceptual relativity puts the emphasis on the fact that present use of any classifications is always determined by contingent local interests and goals, and that the future path of any classification is open.

7. Communitarian epistemology in general, and finitism in particular, are not forms of idealism or anti-realism in general. General statements of idealism or anti-realism (e.g. 'all facts are ideas') are just as meaningless as are general statements of realism (e.g. 'the world is largely representation-independent'). Far from endorsing either realism or anti-realism, finitism leads to a rejection of both. If finitism is correct, then neither view can be stated in a meaningful way. Realism and anti-realism are trying to speak about everything out there (facts, objects) and how it relates to everything in here (all representations). And this is something that finitistic reflection rules out as incoherent. Of course, we can talk about this or that object being

correctly represented, or this or that entity being independent of our representation. But all such talk is meaningful only locally, and contingently. It cannot be the starting point for a generalization.

8. The twin diseases of realism and anti-realism are best cured with Wittgenstein's medicine. The task must be to remind ourselves how terms like 'real', 'reality', and 'world' are actually used in everyday life. To take 'reality' first, it is worth noting that everyday speech easily accommodates a plurality of realities—largely following the many and varied uses to which we put the word 'real'. There are 'real lies', 'real dreams', 'real objects', 'real fictions', and there are the realities of life, of love, and of science. The distinctly philosophical use of the term (reality is what is out there) probably derives from the way in which we appeal to 'reality' in criticism: 'Stop dreaming, and start facing reality'. Here reality is invoked as something beyond control. But it is not *one thing or fact*, or *the sum of all things or facts*. On one occasion it might be the reality of a job, on another occasion it might be a relationship. Goodman has nicely commented on this relativity of reality:

The physicist takes his world to be the real one ... The phenomenalist regards the perceptual world as fundamental. ... For the man-in-the-street, most versions from science, art and perception depart in some ways from the familiar serviceable world he has jerry-built from fragments of scientific and artistic tradition and from his own struggle for survival. The world, indeed, is the one most often taken as real; for reality in a world, like realism in a picture, is largely a matter of habit. Ironically, then ... not only motion, derivation, weighting, order, but even reality is relative. (1978: 20)

'The one world' is not much clearer. Ordinary language talks happily of worlds in the plural, from the world of show business and the art world, to the world of crime and the world of politics. Any configurations of objects and ideas can be a world. Contrary to what Goodman alleges, not much 'making' is needed to produce a world. The realist's singular, 'the *one* world', owes its initial intelligibility to religion and the dream of physical reductionism. For the member of the Judaeo-Christian tradition, the unity of the world is a unity of creation. And for the physicalist, ontological variety can be reduced to physical entities. But it is of course sheer dogmatism to go from the plausible view that all events can be described in physical terms to the radical claim that all events receive their true description in physics. It is also important to register the many ways in which the appearance of 'the one single uniform physical world' is a 'construction'. Note only the work that goes into guaranteeing the ubiquity of the principal physical constants. We spent three times the amount directly involved in science and technology on this effort (Hunter 1980). 'The one physical world' does not come cheap!

9. Finally, at one point Goodman writes that the debate between pluralists and monists (regarding worlds) 'evaporates under analysis ... The one world may be taken as many, or the many worlds taken as one: whether one or many depends on the way of taking' (1978: 2). Strangely, though, he later goes back on this pronouncement and opts for plurality of worlds rather than interest-relativity of the whole issue. Finitism takes the latter view: whether we talk of one world or many is not a deep philosophical issue; different purposes may be served by shifting from the one to the other. Moral purposes may sometimes be served by speaking of 'the one world', as Lynch suggests; but they may also sometimes suggest switching to the plural, when perhaps we are urging tolerance. Science, art, politics, and everyday life do not need a fixed unique and given world. They all do fine talking about electrons, genetic codes, novels, acts of parliament, and child care; none of them needs anything as tall as 'the world'.

Chapter 18

OBJECTIVITY

For many philosophers, to deal adequately with the nature of truth and reality is *eo ipso* to deal adequately with the nature of objectivity. That is why I could write about truth and reality under the heading 'objectivity'. Some philosophers, however, construe 'the problem of objectivity' in a more narrow fashion. For these latter philosophers, to solve 'the problem of objectivity' is to provide a certain type of explanation for *how we (collectively) could all be wrong in our beliefs*. Here by 'certain type of explanation' I am referring to constraints on which factors can legitimately be invoked in an answer to the question. For the philosophers I have in mind here, these constraints are that reality or truth may not be brought in as something 'given', and that the (at least) partial role of intersubjectivity in the constitution of objectivity must be respected.

I shall discuss two such explanations, offered by Robert Brandom and John Haugeland respectively. I am giving these views considerable space here because they constitute an important recent new opening in debates over objectivity in general. At the same time, I do not believe that either account of objectivity (*qua* possibility of communal error or ignorance) works. Brandom and Haugeland want objectivity to be more than, and independent of, consensus. And that is a mistake. What objectivity there is exists only as, and dependent upon, agreement. There is no better argument for the latter view than to study where Brandom and Haugeland go wrong. This will lead us to the following insight. The accepted beliefs of a community cannot be false if by 'being false' we mean something like 'false independently of what anyone says or thinks'. This view of community-wide error relies again on the idea of a fixed set of truths—a fixed set of truths that the community in question reaches only in part. Alas, there is no such set. There is, however, a different sense in which communities can be wrong or ignorant: their views can be classified as 'wrong' or 'ignorant' by the lights of some *other* community (or a later time-slice of the same community).

OBJECTIVITY AND I—THOU SOCIAL RELATIONS

Robert Brandom proposes a theory of how 'objectivity... precipitate[s] out of the social soup' (1994: 54). He explicitly rejects all notions of objectivity that ground objectivity exclusively in intersubjectivity, or—as he prefers to say—in a 'we'. What is wrong with all such proposals, we are told, is that they make it impossible for the whole community to be lacking in objectivity, that is, for the whole community to be in error. The intuition that we need to do justice to, Brandom insists, is that whereas a whole community cannot be in error about social institutions like greetings, it can be in error about which concepts correctly capture the facts:

Whatever the Kwakiutl treat as the appropriate greeting gesture for their tribe ... is one ... The question is whether *conceptual* norms ought to be understood as being of this type. There is good reason to think that they ought not. It is a fundamental feature of our understanding of our concepts that they incorporate *objective* commitments. Thus, our use of the term 'mass' is such that the facts settle whether the mass of the universe is large enough that it will eventually suffer gravitational collapse, independently of what we, even all of us and forever, take those facts to be. We could all be wrong in our assessment of this claim, could all be treating as a correct application of the concepts involved what is objectively an incorrect application of them. (1994: 53)

In order to be able to assess Brandom's own proposal, we need to get clear on some of the central ideas of his philosophy. Two ideas form the cornerstones of his work: the meaning of an expression is the material inferences in which the expression can figure; and truth, knowledge, and objectivity must be understood on the basis of their role in social discursive practices. By 'material inferences' Brandom means inferences that depend for their correctness on the *contents* of premisses and conclusions (1994: 97). Material inferences thus contrast with formal inferences in which the correctness only depends on the *form* of premisses and conclusions. For instance, (1) is a material inference, (2) is a formal inference. (Every inference with the form of (2) is correct: p & q, ergo p.)

(1) Today is Monday. Ergo, tomorrow will be Tuesday.
(2) Today is Monday and my birthday. Ergo, today is Monday.

What gives an expression its meaning are the material inferences in which it can figure. We learn what a given word means by noticing what difference its occurrence in a sentence makes to material inferences. We know the meaning of 'dog' to the extent that we recognize as correct inferences like the following:

(3) I hear barking. There must be a dog somewhere close by.
(4) Filo is a dog. He can't fly. He can't run faster than 30 miles per hour. He can't swim under water for very long. He can't defeat a lion.
(5) The cat is running away. It's probable that the dog is chasing it.

Different speakers of the same language coincide in many of the material inferences that they find correct for a given expression. But in so far as different speakers have different beliefs about the referents of their expressions, their inferences might well disagree (1994: 636). Thus a vet is able to draw inferences from the quality of a dog's fur to the health of the animal; most of the rest of us are unable to do this. Brandom emphasizes that his 'meaning inferentialism' is 'strong' (1994: 131). By this he means that concepts are inferentially related not only to other concepts, but also to circumstances and consequences. Circumstances are given in perception; consequences materialize in actions. Thus the perception of red things entitles me to infer the presence of coloured things; and a belief in a healthy diet entitles me to proceed to the action of going to a health food shop.

Brandom's second key idea is that concepts have a life only in social discursive practices. To be a user of concepts is to be subject to norms concerning how these concepts ought to be used. And norms exist only in social practices. Most norms are implicit—that is, unformulated—in practices; only some are explicitly formulated. Moreover, the core of social discursive practice is 'the game of giving and asking for reasons'. The game is played by collecting 'commitments' and 'entitlements' to propositional contents; by 'score-keeping', that is, by keeping track of the commitments and entitlements of one's interlocutors; and by inferring further commitments and entitlements both for oneself and for the other players (1994: 141–2). For instance, imagine yourself in the following dialogue with a bus-driver at the Cambridge train station (Cambridge, England, that is):

(6) *You.* I am going to the centre of Cambridge.
(7) *She.* You have to take the no. 10 bus. It leaves every ten minutes. The last one left three minutes ago.
(8) *You.* So the next one is due in seven minutes.
(9) *She.* Correct.

In (6) you commit yourself to the propositional content that you are on your way to the centre of Cambridge. This entitles the bus-driver to draw various inferences: that you are not going to Cambridge, Massachusetts; that you want information about how to get to the centre by bus; that you have not got a taxi waiting for you already; or that you are not playing a silly game. In (7) the bus-driver takes your commitment for granted and in turn commits herself to a number of propositional contents; to wit, that the no. 10 bus is the right bus for you; that it leaves every ten minutes; and that the last one left three minutes ago. In (8) you take the bus-driver's commitments as an entitlement to draw an inference concerning the arrival of the next bus. And in (9) the bus-driver acknowledges both her own earlier commitment, and your entitlement. Commitments and entitlements can be undertaken, attributed, acknowledged, and unacknowledged: from (6) onwards the bus-driver attributes to you the commitment to the propositional content of (6); and in uttering (6) you have undertaken the same commitment. The bus-driver acknowledges her commitment to knowing the correct time of the next departure by uttering 'correct' in line (9).

The ideas of concepts as 'inferentially articulated' and of the above 'game' are interrelated. It is precisely the inferential articulation of concepts that allows us to infer *new* commitments and entitlements from earlier ones: 'The commitments one is disposed to avow are *acknowledged* commitments. But in virtue of their inferentially articulated conceptual contents, assertional commitments have consequences.... These *consequential* commitments may not be acknowledged.... They are commitments nonetheless' (1994: 194).

Brandom uses the machinery of entitlements and commitments to analyse knowledge attributions (1994: 201–4). Say you attribute to your bus-driver the knowledge that it is the no. 10 bus that will take you to the centre of town. In doing so, you *attribute* to your bus-driver the *commitment* to the claim that the no. 10 bus will take you to the centre of town (call this the first element); you *attribute* to her an *entitlement* to that *commitment* (second element); and you yourself *acknowledge commitment* to that very same propositional content, that is, that the no. 10 bus will take you to the centre of town (third element). The three elements can be related to the classical formula of knowledge as justified true belief. The first element corresponds to the belief part; the second element to the justification part; and the third element to the truth part. It is particularly important to see the point of the reconstruction of the truth-condition in terms of an acknowledged commitment by the attributer. In attributing knowledge rather than belief to your bus-driver you commit yourself to the very same propositional content that forms the content of her knowledge.

I have already mentioned that Brandom advocates the prosentential theory of truth. The details of his proposal need not detain us here. But it is important to add that he rejects talk of 'facts' as anything more than 'true claims'. Facts do not 'make claims true'; facts 'simply *are* true claims' (1994: 327). The importance of this view in the present context is in how Brandom seeks to rebut an objection to this view. According to this objection, the thesis that facts are true claims is an expression of an 'idealism of linguistic practice'. Brandom seeks to avoid this accusation by insisting that 'our discursive practice is empirically and practically *constrained*':

It is not up to us which claims are true. . . . discursive *practices* . . . do not stand apart from the rest of the world . . . our discursive practices could not be what they are if the nonlinguistic facts were different. . . . Discursive practices essentially involve to-ing and fro-ing with environing objects in perception and action. . . . Discursive practices incorporate actual things. They are solid—as one might say, corporeal . . . What determinate practices a community has depends on what the facts are and on what objects they are actually practically involved with, to begin with, through perception and action. The way the world is constrains proprieties of inferential, doxastic, and practical commitment in a straightforward way from *within* those practices. (1994: 331)

This claim concerning the manner in which discursive practices are embedded in the world is not Brandom's master argument for objectivity, however.

This latter argument is part of his theory of representation and belief-attribution.

The key element in his analysis here is a traditional distinction between two ways of attributing beliefs (and other propositional attitudes) to others. Take the following two belief attributions that you might carry out regarding your bus-driver:

(10) She believes that the no. 10 bus goes to the city centre.

(11) Of the no. 10 bus she believes that it goes to the city centre.

In (10) all elements of the bus-driver's belief are within the that-clause. Thus they all are 'within the scope' of the word 'believes'; that is, within the scope of the 'belief-operator'. In (11) 'the no. 10 bus' has been pulled out of the that-clause, and thereby moved out of the scope of the 'belief-operator'. In order to maintain the grammaticality of the resulting sentence, we have to insert a pronoun, 'it', at the original position of 'the no. 10 bus'. (10) is an example of a '*de dicto* attribution', while (11) is a case of a '*de re* attribution' (1994: 505).[1]

Analysed in Brandom's theory of entitlements and commitments, in (10) you attribute to the bus-driver a commitment (to the propositional content that the bus goes to the city centre); and you undertake a different commitment yourself (that you are willing to acknowledge whatever can be inferred from the bus-driver having the belief in question). But in (11) you undertake a further commitment: by lifting the no. 10 bus out of the that-clause, you commit yourself to the existence of the no. 10 bus. Brandom calls this further commitment a 'substitutional commitment'—and distinguishes it from the earlier mentioned 'doxastic' commitments. You are substituting an element of your own belief system for an element of the bus-driver's belief system: the no. 10 bus as you know it, for the no. 10 bus as known to the bus-driver. Or, to take one of Brandom's own examples, consider the difference between (12) and (13):

(12) The shaman believes *that* drinking the liquor distilled from the bark of that kind of tree will prevent malaria.

---

[1] In a *de dicto* attribution the attributer places the whole *dictum* (the whole proposition) within the scope of the propositional attitude, e.g. belief. In a *de re* attribution the attributer focuses on the *res* (the entity) that the propositional attitude is about.

(13) He believes *of* quinine (= of quinine he believes) that malaria can be prevented by drinking *it*.

In moving from the *de dicto* attribution (12) to the *de re* attribution (13), the attributer (say, we) substitutes 'the bark of that kind of tree' with 'quinine'. In doing so, we bring in a concept, 'quinine', that has inferential connections to other concepts we know (1994: 514).

Brandom makes two main claims concerning this analysis of content attribution. The first is that it constitutes a reconstruction of 'the representational dimension of discourse'. We talk *about* the same things in so far as we are shifting from *de dicto* to *de re* attributions. The latter pick out what we are—albeit from radically different perspectives—talking about (1994: 529).

The second main claim is that *de re* attributions provide the key to objectivity, and thus the key to the possibility that whole communities could be wrong. The initial crucial step is to see that in making a *de re* attribution, the attributer specifies the conditions under which the attributed belief would be, by his lights, true. The shaman's belief concerning the liquor is true if quinine has the ability to prevent malaria. The bus-driver's belief concerning the no. 10 bus is true if what you know about the no. 10 bus licenses the belief that it goes to the city centre. In each of the cases we have—from the standpoint of the attributer–interpreter—a distinction between what *is true* and what *is taken to be true*. The shaman *takes it to be true* that the liquor prevents malaria; our knowledge about quinine specifies for us whether this *is true*. The bus-driver *takes it to be true* that the no. 10 bus goes to the city centre; your knowledge about the no. 10 bus determines for you whether this *is true*.

As Brandom sees it, it is the existence of this gap that secures objectivity. Concepts are always perspectival in so far as their contents are different for different individuals; different individuals have different inferential articulations for the same concepts. But objects are 'non-perspectival in a strong sense'. In deciding whether the shaman is correct in calling the liquor 'malaria-preventing' we are invoking the object called 'quinine'. We are not treating what we know about this object as merely 'true for us'. We are treating what we know about quinine as what quinine is *in fact*. Assume that I come to the conclusion that quinine does not have the claimed malaria-preventing properties, and that thus the shaman's belief is false. It would then not help him if all other shamans agreed with him. I would judge the whole community wrong; and I would do so relying on simple and central elements of our social and discursive practices. This shows, Brandom claims, that objectivity does not derive from intersubjectivity; it derives from the ways in which individuals interpret the beliefs of other individuals. Or, to use Brandom's jargon, it shows that 'I–thou' social relations are more basic than 'I–we' social relations:

> *I–we* accounts mistakenly postulate the existence of a *privileged* perspective—that of the 'we', or community. The identification of objectivity with intersubjectivity so understood is defective in that it cannot find room for the possibility of error regarding that privileged perspective; what the community *takes* to be correct *is* correct.... The alternative is to reconstrue objectivity as consisting in a kind of perspectival *form*, rather than in a non-perspectival or cross-perspectival *content*. What is shared by all discursive perspectives is *that* there is a difference between what is objectively correct in the way of concept application and what is merely taken to be so, not *what* it is—the structure, not the content. (1994: 600)

A CRITICISM OF BRANDOM ON OBJECTIVITY

Brandom's work is an important source of inspiration and insight for any social theory of language, knowledge, and objectivity. But despite my admiration for his general project, I am unable to agree with Brandom's 'I–thou' account of objectivity. To bring out my dissatisfaction, I shall comment on four key ideas: the claim that concepts have 'objectively true applications'; the notion that discursive practices are defined by their dependence on specific discourse-external facts and objects; the view that concepts, but not objects, are perspectival; and the contention that only an 'I–thou' construal of objectivity can explain how whole communities could be in error.

It is important for Brandom that concepts can have 'objectively incorrect applications'. Here 'objectively' means 'determined by the facts' rather than 'determined by the consensus of a community'. For it could be that the whole community applies a concept 'objectively incorrectly'. The intuitive idea is clear enough: given the way I have learned the word 'cat', it would be 'objectively incorrect' for me to use 'cat' in order to refer to a greyhound. And it would likewise be incorrect if my whole community called the greyhound 'cat'.

But here we had better tread carefully. Why would it be incorrect for me to call a given greyhound a 'cat?' It would be incorrect because our array of exemplars of entities to which the word 'cat' can be applied correctly does not contain anything that would strongly resemble a greyhound. The lack of similarity between cats and greyhounds is obvious. In other words, what makes the use of 'objectively' in the phrase 'objectively incorrect' natural in this case is the relative absence of similarity between a greyhound and a cat. It therefore seems to us that no community *judgement* is needed to establish the verdict 'incorrect'. It seems as if the verdict is secured by the facts alone. Alas, this impression is wrong. No facts can themselves determine how they must be categorized; no entities can determine our *judgement*s of similarity concerning them. Are not greyhounds similar to big cats like cheetahs? And are not domestic cats similar in behaviour to small domestic dogs, like poodles? And what if we came to base *judgement*s of similarity concerning cats and dogs on their genetic structure? What would we say if the respective genetic structures turned out to be very similar by some well-entrenched standard of similarity? What is right and wrong about the similarity between cats and dogs is not settled by our concepts; it must be settled by community consensus. The notion that the whole community could be wrong in calling the greyhound 'cat' is based on two assumptions: that the array of exemplars is fixed and unchanging, and that the exemplars are able to determine *one single way* of using the classification. I have been urging that both assumptions are wrong.

It should be obvious that what applies to 'cat' and 'dog' also applies to 'mass'. We know what 'mass' means on the basis of a finite number of situations in which the term was used both in empirical settings and in theoretical considerations or calculations. Part of what defines the meaning of the term for us is the belief that the universe has a mass, and that this mass is such that eventual gravitational collapse is inevitable. However, like 'cat' and 'dog' so also the concept of mass drifts and shifts—as even a superficial glance at the historical literature should make obvious enough. The current exemplars for identifying the mass of a body are far from sacrosanct; as physicists move to the study of new phenomena they will change their exemplars for 'mass' again and again. Thus it might eventually no longer be acceptable to insist that 'the universe has a mass'. But is it not objectively incorrect *now* to deny that the universe will suffer gravitational collapse? It is, but here the objectivity is only one of intersubjectivity. It is incorrect now because of the way in which we train ourselves and our physicists. Training gives us the sense of similarity that protects the statement from refutation.

I also find it hard to agree with Brandom's treatment of how discursive practices relate to 'the rest of the world'. In particular I am puzzled by the claims that 'our discursive practices could not be what they are if the nonlinguistic facts were different'; and 'what determinate practices a community has depends on what the facts are and on what objects they are actually practically involved with'. To begin with, talk of 'nonlinguistic facts' sounds odd coming from an author who insists that facts are simply true claims. Moreover, we do not get much advice on how we are to understand the 'dependence' of practices on facts and objects. Do the facts and objects of a given environment determine one unique discursive practice? Or do they merely deselect certain discursive practices from the realm of physical (or social?) possibility? Brandom does not tell us. For what it is worth, the evidence of anthropology and history suggests that many different discursive practices can flourish among 'the facts and objects' of this world. Are they all equally objective?

Contrary to what Brandom alleges, he has not shown that objects are 'non-perspectival in a strong sense' (1994: 594). What he has shown is that the attributer of a *de re* belief-attitude does not *treat* the object as perspectival. When we attribute to the shaman the belief 'of quinine he believes that it prevents malaria', we are not treating quinine as perspectival. We are dropping any reference to 'our perspective', we are taking our beliefs about quinine as the truth. True enough. But this only shows that *de re* attributers neglect the perspectival character of their beliefs about the object; it does not show that the beliefs and the objects are not perspectival. Of course they are perspectival; their perspectival nature is made visible the moment we attribute beliefs about these objects to the *de re* attributers themselves. The absence of perspective is thus itself only perspectival. Perspective is not absent in any 'strong sense' at all.

Note, moreover, that Brandom is also open to a criticism that I directed earlier at Davidson's duettism. To evaluate another's beliefs as right or wrong, correct or incorrect, is itself an activity that can be carried out correctly or incorrectly, rightly or wrongly. And there is no right and wrong outside social institutions. Social institutions in turn presuppose intersubjectivity and consensus. They presuppose a 'we'. In other words, Brandom's attempt to make 'I–thou' primary with respect to 'I–we' has not succeeded.

Brandom's general criticism of community-based views of objectivity does not cover all such approaches. He claims that they turn the community into a super-subject—'as somehow having attitudes and producing performances of the sort more properly associated with individuals'—and that they privilege the community 'globally'. Recall once more my three models of consensus. Only for the first model (where the times of all individual clocks answer to one 'master clock') does it make sense to speak of a global privilege. According to the third model (the model of the randomly meeting clocks) there is no community subject with 'clocky' attributes. The 'community of clocks' does not show a time, it does not have a determinate time, and it cannot be consulted by any individual clock. And yet, in so far as the individual clocks interact, there is a configuration of times that is more than, and different from, the individual times. Consensus on time is created locally, but these local interactions have global effects. Transfer this model to our discursive practices. We update our linguistic intuitions in local encounters with small groups of interlocutors. As we move around in social space, we adjust our use of concepts to fit with the needs and demands of many other speakers. The result is that our concepts are usually relatively stable, and yet always open to change. What 'objective correctness' there is to our use of concepts derives from the coincidences of our *judgements* of similarity with those of others—those others that we encounter face to face, in the media, in the churches, in schools, and in the lecture halls.

I am not saying that we could not be collectively in error. What I am saying is that the *judgement* according to which a whole community is, or was, wrong can only come from within another community (or a later time-slice of the same community). And such *judgement* will have to be based on the exemplars and the consensus in that other community.

OBJECTIVITY AND ILLEGALITY

John Haugeland (1998) insists that there are two distinct kinds of norms governing our representations of the empirical world. The first kind of norm is fixed by community consensus. This type of norm is 'instituted' by the community, and to follow such a norm correctly is nothing but *to be taken to* follow it correctly by one's peers. The community could not be wrong in interpreting and applying this norm. If the community says that a given action is correct, then it is correct in fact. The second kind of norm, however, is not fixed by community consensus. Whether or not this norm has been followed is an 'objective' issue. Collectively thinking that it has been followed correctly has nothing to do with the question of whether or not it has indeed been so followed.

Take, for instance, the activity of 'telling' in the sense of 'identifying and discriminating: telling what (who, when, where, whether . . .) something is, telling things apart, telling the differences between them, and so on' (1998: 313). Some aspects of telling are subject to the first, consensus-based, norms. Thus, in order for an action to qualify for the label 'telling', it might have to employ an accepted method or vocabulary. And it is for the community to say whether or not the vocabulary or the method is used correctly. The socially instituted rules governing the activity—as far as vocabulary or method are concerned—have a 'rule-to-world direction of fit'. The world—that is, the individual act of telling as a worldly event—has to fit the rules. In the case of a misfit between rule and world, it is the individual act of telling that is to blame. These socially instituted aspects of telling are similar to social institutions like dances, greetings, or games. The proper way to dance is the way in which (almost) everyone dances; the proper manner of greeting is the way in which (almost) everyone greets; and the proper way to play a game is the way in which (almost) everyone plays the game (1998: 314).

There is, however, an important difference between telling and dancing. In the case of dancing the normativity of the activity is, as it were, 'exhausted' by the collective stipulation. Not so in the case of telling. This brings us to the second type of normativity. This type of normativity is not 'instituted' by stipulation; it must be 'constituted' through recognition. Acts of telling are not just properly or improperly carried out; they can be true or false. That is to say, acts of telling also involve a 'world-to-telling direction of fit'. If the telling does not fit with the world, then it is the telling, not the world, that is to blame. This objective normativity is not dependent upon community consensus. Even though the community can make a given act of telling 'proper' by regarding it so, it cannot make the given act of telling 'correct' or 'true' (1998: 315).

Having distinguished the two kinds of normativity, Haugeland goes on to explain how 'objective normativity' is possible. His aim is to avoid defining objectivity in terms of a totally independent reality 'out there'. Instead, he seeks to show how objectivity can emerge from within a practice.

Start with the distinction between 'regulative' and 'constitutive' rules (1998: 318). Regulative rules 'regulate' activities that exist prior to the introduction of the rule; constitutive rules 'constitute' the activity that they are about. Thus 'think before you talk' is regulative, and 'chess bishops move diagonally' is constitutive. Talking existed before the rule about thinking was introduced; chess bishops are defined by the rule about their movements.

Haugeland suggests that the category of constitutive rule(-following) needs to be developed into a fourfold distinction. The first type of constitutive rules is 'constitutive regulations'. These are the rules that tell humans what to do in order to carry out the activity in question. An example of such a rule in chess might be 'move the bishops diagonally' (1998: 319).

The second type of constitutive rules is 'constitutive standards' (1998: 320). Constitutive standards define what can, and what cannot, happen within a given activity. In the game of chess the constitutive standards define which moves are possible for different pieces, what type of board is needed, or what configurations of pieces count as checkmate. Constitutive standards do not refer to human actions; they have the form 'the bishop moves diagonally' rather than 'move the bishop diagonally'.

The third type of constitutive rules is 'constitutive skills' (1998: 322). Haugeland defines 'constitutive skill' as 'a resilient ability to tell whether the phenomena governed by some constitutive standard are, in fact, in accord with that standard'. Resilience is important since the exercise of this ability must be conscientious, serious, and persistent in the face of difficulty. In the game of chess constitutive skills are the abilities to tell whether a given move is 'legal', whether a given board qualifies as a chessboard, or whether a given configuration of pieces constitutes checkmate. Constitutive skills tell whether the rules of the game have been followed. Constitutive skills also follow rules, however. These are the rules of determining whether, say, a given move is correct. These meta-rules concern the rules the following of which is being monitored. But the two levels of rules are not identical. This is especially clear if we think of the two levels as distributed over, say, a player and a referee. The player might follow a rule like 'move the bishops diagonally'; the referee might follow the rule 'in order to check whether the bishops have moved legally, check the record of the game, and determine whether they have always been moved diagonally'. Constitutive skills are not the only skills important in rule-governed activities. Equally important are 'mundane skills'. Mundane skills in the game of chess are simply the resilient 'ability to engage in play'. This includes the abilities to identify pieces and their positions, to move and capture pieces, to keep track of whose move it is, and so on. Obviously, mundane skills and constitutive skills presuppose one another: constitutive skills evaluate the performances of mundane skills, and mundane skills are presupposed in the exercise of constitutive skills.

Finally, the fourth kind of constitutive rule(-following) is 'constitutive commitment' (1998: 341). A constitutive commitment is 'a dedicated or even a devoted way of living . . . a resilient and resolute first-personal *stance*'. It is a commitment not to other people but to 'an ongoing, concrete game, project, or life . . . a way, a style, a mode of playing, working or living'. The authority behind such a norm is no other than the individual who is so committed. In the game of chess this is the determination to be responsive to the rules and situations on the board, the determination to correct performances of one's mundane and constitutive skills, and even the determination to change these skills themselves.

Having introduced Haugeland's four types of constitutive rule, we can turn to three further key concepts of his proposal: 'the excluded zone', 'precarious equilibrium', and 'constitution'. Moves in chess can be either legal or illegal. As Haugeland points out, there is something paradoxical about the category of 'illegal' moves. Strictly speaking there should be no such moves at all. And yet illegal moves—say a rook moving diagonally— are obviously conceivable. Moreover, an illegal move is clearly different from a non-move: moving the rook diagonally is different from hiding it under the table. The identification of a move as 'illegal' involves an interplay of constitutive and mundane chess skills. (Hiding a piece under the table does not involve mundane chess skills—though other kinds of skill might well be involved.) Take the example of the rook that is moved diagonally and thus illegally. Moving the rook correctly involves three mundane chess skills: (1) the ability to know which types of movement define each chess piece; (2) the ability to discriminate between different chess figurines; and (3) the ability to link types of movement to chess figurines. The player who moves the piece incorrectly must have exercised at least one of these three skills incorrectly. What enables players or referees to notice the illegality of the move is constitutive skills. In making this *judgement* constitutive skills point to 'incompatibilities': incompatibilities between the current move and other moves (by the same player on other occasions, by other players), incompatibilities between the performances of the same skills on different occasions, and incompatibilities between the outputs of the different inter-acting skills. Haugeland calls the set of illegal moves 'the excluded zone' (1998: 333). The moves within it are 'conceivable' but not 'possible'. Only legal moves are possible. Keeping the excluded zone empty is a non-trivial achievement; it demands the continuous interplay of mundane and consti-tutive skills.

In order to see what Haugeland means by 'precarious equilibrium' we had better focus momentarily on a special case of chess-playing (1998: 333). Imagine someone who knows the rules of chess only vaguely. Let that person be shipwrecked on an island, alone with his chessboard and figurines. This novice might notice that exercising his various mundane skills for moving pieces leads to positions that his constitutive skills tell him are illegal; say, two pieces end up on the same square. In this situation the novice might decide to 'test' his mundane skills systematically. He might play many games against himself, write them down, and then check for incompatibil-ities. Having collected plenty of the latter, he might then try to reduce them by either changing some of his mundane skills or modifying his constitutive skills. He does the latter if he comes to accept that two pieces can be on one square; he does the former if he modifies, say, his ability to tell rooks from bishops. No one can tell him how he should go about emptying what he encounters as his excluded zone. And he might have to go through several rounds of adjustments of both mundane and constitutive skills before he reaches a position where his constitutive skills do not detect incompatibil-ities. When this situation has been reached, the novice has reached 'precar-ious equilibrium'.

Having made so much of constitutive rules, Haugeland owes us a defini-tion of constitution. He insists that 'constitution' means neither 'creation' nor 'counting as'. To constitute a tree is neither to create a tree, nor to count something as a tree. To think of constitution as creation leads to idealism; to construe it as counting-as leads to a regress (how do we constitute the 'something'?). The correct definition of constitution is 'letting be':

Constituting objects is letting them be by finding and showing that they make sense in some determinate way, and can consistently be told and otherwise coped with as such. This is . . . true for ordinary . . . chess pieces. Letting them be the objects that they are, namely chess pieces, is nothing other than making sense of them as chess pieces by playing chess with them. (1998: 329)

Similarly, we constitute trees by 'finding them' from within our practices. In both cases, such 'finding' depends on mundane and constitutive skills, constitutive standards, and regulations. To speak of trees or chess pieces independently of the exercise of such skills makes no sense.

Haugeland wants us to shift away from thinking of games as the paradigms of normativity. But rather than simply throwing the game metaphor overboard, he prefers to modify the chess example step by step so as to bring chess close to empirical inquiry. Consider first 'normal chess' (1998: 329). Haugeland points out that even normal chess has 'empirical content'. The game can only properly take place if the board can support the figurines, if the figurines are not blown away by the wind, if the size of the board fits the size of the figurines, and so on. The importance of this empirical content to normal chess can be brought out by considering a different game, 'esoteric chess' (1998: 327). Esoteric chess has the same rules as ordinary chess, but it does not come with the familiar figurines and boards. In esoteric chess the players have to go out and find—not make—a medium that can be used for playing chess. This will only be possible if such a medium (clouds perhaps?) shares some important empirical properties with ordinary chess. The pieces, as defined by the rules, must be distinguishable; moves must be visible, and turn-taking must be achievable.

A different departure from normal chess is 'semi-automatic chess' (1998: 321). In semi-automatic chess 'random legal moves are automatically inserted between the moves made by the players'. One step further from semi-automatic chess we get 'automatic chess'. Automatic chess has three distinctive characteristics: First, the moves made by the pieces on their own are qualitatively different from moves made by the players (they move the pieces differently). Second, only a small number of moves are made by the players. And third, players need not compete; they are allowed to cooperate. The important thing to note about automatic chess is that it is still governed by constitutive *standards* but that constitutive *regulations* are only of minor importance. Finally, 'empirical chess' combines the key elements of esoteric and automatic chess. The human players cooperate rather than compete with one another; and the game must be 'found'. Empirical chess is 'playing chess with nature' (1998: 329–31).

In order to understand empirical chess (or empirical science!) properly, we must bring the concepts introduced earlier to bear on its case. In empirical chess the players–investigators seek to find a set of phenomena that can be captured in a system of constitutive standards (i.e. laws of nature). The attempt to find this system involves the exercise of mundane and constitutive skills, an excluded zone, and a precarious equilibrium. Mundane skills are here the skills involved in, say, measuring, observing, theorizing the phenomena; constitutive skills are the skills that monitor for incompatibilities. In other words, constitutive skills monitor whether the excluded zone is indeed empty. If the excluded zone is non-empty, then this is good indication that phenomena and standards (or mundane and constitutive skills) are out of their 'precarious equilibrium'. This observation in turn calls for readjustments.

This is the point at which we can understand Haugeland's notion of normativity as objectivity—rather than consensus. In his committed attempt to find, and work out, a system of constitutive standards, the investigator might encounter 'illegal phenomena': phenomena (constituted by her mundane skills) that do not pass muster as far as constitutive skills are concerned (1998: 338). Of course, such phenomena must be in a minority, or else the whole distinction between 'legal' and 'illegal' would have no application; there would be no system of standards at all. The committed investigator encounters these incompatible phenomena as 'objective': they cannot be made to go away by a collective decision of any sort. And any community who would attempt to do so would be in error. Haugeland sums up his position in the following passage:

Constitution, making sense of objects, is not free. It depends on an equilibrium among a number of constitutive and mundane skills—an equilibrium which, since it excludes the bulk of what it renders conceivable (testable), is empirically precarious. But at the same time, and for as long as it lasts, it is also an empirical achievement. The constituted objects [i.e. objective phenomena] participate in this achievement, deriving determinacy and normative status from it. But they also have an ability to resist that transcends that participation, because it is they, and they alone, upon which the equilibrium itself rests; by not cooperating, they have the power to bring it down. Even though in so doing they must annihilate themselves as what they are, nevertheless they can.... scientific observations, theories, and explanations, like those in everyday life, are objective precisely because and to the extent that *objects* (objective phenomena) stand as accessible independent criteria for their correctness—*truth*—as made possible by an independent structure of constitutive and mundane *rule-following*. (1998: 353–4)

A CRITICISM OF HAUGELAND ON OBJECTIVITY

Turning from explication to evaluation, there is undoubtedly some important truth in Haugeland's distinction between two kinds of normativity. Clearly, for instance, the normativity of linguistic use is different from the normativity of empirical statements. In order to find out whether I am using a difficult English expression correctly, I turn to speakers of the English language. And in order to determine whether or not the door is open, I turn to the door. So far, so good.

But what does this triviality show about the link between consensus and objectivity? Does it show that the openness of the door is independent of any consensus? Consider these questions: How far does a door have to be open in order to be properly called 'open'? Is it enough for the door to be unlocked? Is it enough for there to be a considerable gap between the door and the threshold? Is the door open when there is enough of a gap to let an insect pass? Or a child? Or an adult? Or an adult in a wheelchair? Or would we say that in the last-mentioned case the door is not (just) open, but 'wide open?' Surely, in order to answer these questions we must return to community consensus. 'Open' as applied to doors does not have a fixed extension. And since it does not have such extension, there is no sense in which the openness of the door can be determined independently of (tacitly) invoking the community.

The reply will not satisfy an objectivist of Haugeland's ilk. He might come back with a changed example. Suppose our community had agreed that a door is open if a 70 cm-wide table on wheels can be rolled through it.

Imagine further that on a given occasion it turns out that some door does not meet this criterion. And finally, assume that we all insist that the table would pass. Surely, in this case we would all be wrong. Ergo: there is a sense of objectivity that is independent of consensus. In order to evaluate this objection we had better focus on its presuppositions. For us to come out as collectively in error, the objector must make sure that our current collective *judgement* really does contradict our previous practice of judging the openness of doors. The currently considered *judgement*—the *judgement* that the objector wants to come out as in error—must not be allowed to have an effect on what are exemplars, or what are our dispositions for judging similarity. For if it did, it could not be error. In order to get this result, the objector must, as it were, 'freeze' our earlier exemplars and our dispositions. And thereby he gets the result that our *judgement* is wrong.

But this manoeuvre for safeguarding universal error is dubious. The freezing operation is illegitimate since it turns a live linguistic practice into a dead language. Moreover, what exactly does 'wrong' mean in the last sentence of the last paragraph? Wrong in whose opinion? Surely it cannot be in the opinion of our community; for this community regards the *judgement* as correct. Perhaps then we are to think of the community of the objector. Alas, this will not get us away from consensus: it only refers us from one group consensus to the consensus of another group.

To students of the history and philosophy of science much of Haugeland's work on incompatibilities will sound vaguely familiar. Haugeland's incompatibilities remind one of Thomas Kuhn's 'anomalies'. These too depend on skills and standards, and these too are not outside the realm of what is constituted. Haugeland's incompatibilities are a generalization of Kuhn's anomalies in that they are not confined to the sciences. Seeing this parallel is helpful, for it alerts us to an ambiguity that incompatibilities share with anomalies. Kuhn wavers between two readings of 'anomaly'. Sometimes anomalies are 'phenomena judged anomalous by the scientific community'; sometimes anomalies are 'phenomena that are anomalous'. In other words, sometimes 'anomaly' is a social status, sometimes it is non-social fact. Haugeland's generalization of anomalies has not removed this vagueness. On the one hand, Haugeland wants objective phenomena to be what they are, independently of what *anyone* thinks; and independently in particular of what *everyone* thinks. On the other hand, he also insists that incompatibilities only have existence for the committed individual investigator. Something is an incompatibility if an individual investigator feels obliged to treat this something in this way.

Notice that Haugeland's ambiguity is not identical with Kuhn's. Kuhn wavered between fact and *social status*; Haugeland wavers between fact and *individual opinion*. This is disappointing. Haugeland's attempt to make space for a second source of normativity ultimately collapses into talk of the commitments of the individual—commitments that have their exclusive source in the individual herself. It is no coincidence that, when introducing the idea of 'constitutive commitment', Haugeland refers us to existentialism. Most forms of existentialism conceive of commitments in exclusively individualistic terms.

Given the argument of this book as a whole—and given the work of the sociology of knowledge over the past three decades—it should not come as a surprise that I regard the case for 'anomaly as a social status' as overwhelming. All sorts of phenomena could be conceivably counted as smaller or larger incompatibilities; but we only designate some as phenomena to be (eventually) sorted out. And even here we are not as 'committed' as is Haugeland's inquirer. We are happy to populate our 'excluded zone' with anomalies for quite a while. When is an incompatibility substantial enough for it to become a reason for re-evaluating our skills? This is a question like 'when is the door open'.

To sum up, Haugeland has shown that to understand normativity and objectivity is not to understand just one thing. It is to understand very different phenomena. But he has not shown that objectivity is independent of intersubjectivity, or that a whole group could be wrong by its own standards, and in its own (better) *judgement*.

Chapter 19

RELATIVISM

So far in Part III I have explained the reasoning that leads me to combine epistemological relativism with relativism about truth, reality, and objectivity. I have done so through a critical discussion of other—both old and new—theories concerning this triad. It remains for me to take on some of the well-known classical and modern arguments against relativism in general. It is commonly believed among philosophers that these arguments are decisive. Philosophers think that they can discredit an opponent's theory by showing it to have relativistic consequences. They deem a further refutation of relativism unnecessary; allegedly 'we' all know that relativism is a hopeless position. I do not agree. I am unimpressed with the standard arguments against relativism. Let me explain why by dealing with the six arguments that I have encountered most often in academic debates.

'RELATIVELY'

Relativism says that all beliefs or statements are only relatively true. However, before we can even understand what it means to call something 'relatively true' we must already have understood what 'true' means *without* the qualification 'relatively'. Hence relative truth presupposes absolute, unqualified truth. And relativism presupposes its opposite: absolutism.[1]

I did not formulate my position as 'all beliefs or statements are only relatively true'. I prefer putting my own position thus: Which statements are labelled 'true' or 'false' in a given community depends on its prevailing

---

[1] I learned this argument from David Chart in an email discussion.

exemplars, interests, and goals. Changes in any of the latter lead to changes in the former. The sorting of beliefs or statements into 'true' and false statements' is thus done relatively to prevailing exemplars, interests, and goals.

My position is not open to the 'relatively'-objection. The word 'relatively' has two main uses. Sometimes 'relatively' means 'comparatively', 'nearly', or 'partially', as in 'relatively unknown', 'relatively flat', or 'relatively open'. 'Relatively' in this sense usually qualifies an adjective. On other occasions, 'relatively' means 'relationally', or 'in relation to'; as in 'the earth moves relatively to the sun'. In this usage, 'relatively' usually qualifies a verb. 'Relatively X' in the first, adjective-modifying sense presupposes an unqualified sense of X. In order to understand the expressions 'relatively unknown', 'relatively rich', or 'relatively convincing' we first need to grasp the meaning of 'unknown', 'rich', and 'convincing'. But 'relatively' in the second, verb-modifying sense behaves differently. To fully understand what it is for a body to move is to understand what it is for a body to move relatively to a frame of reference.

The relativist is saying that 'sorting of beliefs relatively to given exemplars, interests, and goals' behaves like 'moving relatively to a frame of reference'. Relative sorting is all the sorting there is.

'TRUE OF' AND 'TRUE IN'

A second argument against relativism alleges that relativism is self-refuting in so far as it is obliged to regard absolutism as absolutely false.[2] The starting point of this argument is the relativist position that

(1) No beliefs or statements are absolutely true or false.

According to the objector, (1) is tantamount to (2):

(2) Truth and falsity are relative in all communities.

And from (2) the objector infers both (3) and (4):

(3) Truth and falsity are never absolute in any community.
(4) Absolutism about truth and falsity is absolutely false.

---

[2] I learned this argument from Peter Lipton in a seminar discussion.

It is not difficult to see that (4) contradicts (1), for it makes use of the notion of 'absolutely false'. And hence relativism about truth 'refutes itself'.

The argument rests on equating 'absolutely true' with 'true in all (possible) communities'. If truth-relativity holds in all real and possible communities, so it is thought, then truth-relativity is itself absolute. Surely truth cannot be both relative and absolute at the same time. Here the objector might add a further twist of the argument against finitistic relativism. Imagine that truth-relativism was held true in all possible societies. That would suggest strongly that exemplars, goals, and interests are not, after all, of decisive significance in categorization. Presumably these exemplars, goals, and interests differ from society to society. And yet, on the currently considered assumptions, all societies agree on applying 'true' to relativism. Hence exemplars, goals, and interests do not determine use. And if they do not determine the use of 'true' in this case, why should they do so in other cases?

The way to block this whole line of reasoning is to point out an ambiguity in (2). To say that truth is relative in all communities can mean either that relativism is *true in* all communities, or that it is *true of* all communities. To say that it is *true in* all communities is to say that all communities accept relativism as the correct view. To claim that relativism is *true of* all communities is to claim that all possible communities must sort their beliefs and statements according to contingent and varying exemplars, goals, and interests. Imagine a relativist who accepts, in addition to (1), that the relevant sense of true is 'true in', and that universal adherence makes for absolute truth. This relativist would indeed contradict himself.

No contradiction results if we adopt the 'true of' interpretation. To state relativism as what is 'true of' every culture is not to make a non-relative statement. The statement is relative since its acceptance depends on the exemplars, goals, and interests of the community from within which the global 'true of' statement is made. The 'true of' statement can be judged true by the members of that latter community even if relativism is not regarded *true in* any other community. The relativist urges acceptance of the global 'true of' statement in his community; he is doing his best to make it *true in* his community that relativism is *true of* all communities. If he succeeds, absolutism will be *false in* his community.

RIGHT REASONS

A third objection goes back as far as Plato's *Theaetetus*. It has recently been revitalized by Harvey Siegel (1987). According to this charge, epistemic relativism is incoherent 'because if it is right, the very notion of rightness is undermined, in which case relativism cannot be right' (Siegel 1987: 4). Siegel insists that the absolutist is entitled to demand from the relativist 'right reasons' for his position. And such 'right reasons' had better be non-relative reasons. In particular, they had better be non-relative with respect to the issue between the relativist and the absolutist. But can the relativist deliver the goods without refuting himself? Surely not, if Siegel is to be believed. If the relativist provides the kind of right reasons that the absolutist is after—that is, absolute reasons—then the relativist has refuted himself. If, on the other hand, the relativist provides only relatively right reasons, then the absolutist can stick to his guns, and pronounce that no real reasons have been offered. For, as Siegel stresses, ' "relative rightness" is no rightness at all' (1987: 8).

This is a bad argument. It comes down to insisting that only an absolute reason can be a reason for anything. This is not an argument; it amounts to insisting that absolutism is the correct view. Moreover, the idea is wrong in its general form. Relative rightness often is real rightness. For instance, right moves in chess or checkers are right only relatively—relatively to the rule of the game and the goals of playing—and yet right nevertheless.

The providing of relatively right reasons for relativism is not as 'impotent' as Siegel alleges. Nor is it correct to say that 'the relativist can adopt beliefs (and act) only arbitrarily'. The point to remember here is that the members within a community can disagree, negotiate, and argue over which statements to adopt as true. (And communities can grow and change.) In other words, the relativist can address the absolutist as 'one of his tribe', that is, as one who should find the same sorts of consideration and argument convincing—even if these are not shared by members of other 'tribes'. The argument between relativist and absolutist is, we might say, conducted in a 'quasi-absolutist' form. Both sides argue 'as if' absolutism were right; but whereas the relativist stops at the 'as if', the absolutist seeks to back up the 'as if' with a fact.

THE SELF-VINDICATION OF CULTURES

It is sometimes thought that cultural relativism must think all cultures are self-vindicating. The thought is that the members of any given culture must produce beliefs in accordance with its epistemic standards. Only those beliefs that confirm the standards pass muster. Hence the standards can never come into doubt. By the same token, no culture can ever have a reason to find itself in need of 'epistemic' help from another culture or its standards.

Both worries come out clearly in the writings of Alasdair MacIntyre. MacIntyre formulates relativism in terms of rationality rather than truth or objectivity. Relativism is the doctrine that 'To assert or to conclude this rather than that can be rational relative to the standards of some particular tradition, but not rational as such. There can be no rationality as such. Every set of standards has as much or as little claim to our allegiance as any other' (1988: 352).

MacIntyre contends that, within every tradition, debate on a given issue can reach a point where the members of that very tradition begin to question the success and truth-conduciveness of its standards: 'And this by itself is enough to show that if part of the relativist's thesis is that each tradition, since it provides its own standards of rational justification, must always be vindicated in the light of those standards, then on this at least the relativist is mistaken' (1988: 364).

Moreover, the members of a tradition can come to see that the only way forward is to turn to other, rival traditions and their standards. This undermines the relativist position, MacIntyre alleges, because relativism claims that 'there is no way in which each tradition can enter into rational debate with any other, and no such tradition can therefore vindicate its rational superiority over its rivals' (1988: 366).

If relativism amounts to this, then I am not a relativist. In order to keep relativism in the running as an interesting and important alternative, it should not be saddled with the view that 'every set of standards has as much and as little claim to our allegiance as any other' (1988: 367). Such a claim would make sense only if we could place ourselves outside all standards and choose. In fact we find ourselves embedded in one culture rather than another; and although we are able to recognize the fundamental symmetry between different cultures, we cannot escape our own contingency as members of our own culture and its tradition.

Epistemic standards are not self-vindicating determinants of epistemic practice. Indeed, it is one of the central theses of finitism that standards are social institutions, and as such *products as well as determinants* of action. Standards (like word meanings) only exist as arrays of exemplars. And these exemplars are not 'self-applying': they need to be applied by individuals in communities. Ergo, it is wrong to assume that standards could be beyond change and assessment. Of course, the relativist need not go down the finitistic road to insist on this point. Surely there is nothing contradictory about such a relativist maintaining that one can question some of a given tradition's standards in terms of other standards of that same tradition. All the relativist needs to deny—in order to remain a relativist—is that there is some neutral or privileged ground from which such criticism can be carried out. Exactly the same applies to the encounter between cultures.

CULTURAL RELATIVISM AND METHODOLOGICAL SOLIPSISM

Hilary Putnam does not really believe that it takes another argument to bring down (cultural) relativism: 'we all know that cultural relativism is inconsistent' (1983: 236). But no sooner has he written these words than he presents an argument of his own. So much for consistency.

Putnam's argument is based on an analogy between cultural relativism and methodological solipsism. The *real* solipsist believes that she is the only subject, or, more precisely, that all referents of her thought and talk are nothing but complexes of her very own experiences. The *methodological* solipsist makes a weaker claim. The methodological solipsist says merely that everyone can conceive of themselves as the only subject. Everyone can construct all referents of their thought and talk out of complexes of their very own experiences. Putnam judges methodological solipsism to be inconsistent. This is because it is deeply asymmetrical while insisting on being fully symmetrical. It is asymmetrical in so far as for any given subject, say S, all other subjects are mere constructions out of S's very own experiences. And yet the position claims to be symmetrical since every subject is in the position of S. Put differently, if I am a methodological solipsist, then *you* are

both my construction and my constructor (and not just my construction of
my constructor!). But if you really *are* my construction, then it is unintelli-
gible also to conceive of you as my constructor (1983: 236–7).

Putnam thinks he can identify the same inconsistent structure in cultural
relativism. The asymmetrical part of cultural relativism comes out in the
relativist's claim that

> (*a*) When I say something is *true*, I mean that it is correct according to the norms
> of *my* culture. (1983: 237)

The symmetrical claim is

> (*b*) When a member of a different culture says that something is true, what he
> means (whether he knows it or not) is that it is in conformity with the norms
> of *his* culture. (1983: 237)

Thesis (*a*) commits the cultural relativist to the view that, as far as his own
claims are concerned, truth equals truth-in-his-culture. And here 'his
own claims' include all of his claims about other cultures and claims
made by members of these cultures. Whatever he says about other cultures
is determined by his own culture. For him his own culture has an absolute
privilege vis-à-vis all other cultures. Thesis (*b*) takes this back. (*b*) implies that
all cultures are equal; and that every culture has, for its members, an
epistemic privilege with respect to all other cultures. Putnam concludes
that the 'claim of a *symmetrical* situation cannot be *understood* if the relativist
doctrine is right'. Hence cultural relativism is inconsistent (1983: 238).

What are we to make of this argument? The first thing to note is that it
saddles the relativist with the view that 'true' means 'true for' or 'in
conformity with the norms of my culture'. As I have already mentioned,
this is not a view to which the relativist need commit herself. Moreover, the
relativism defended in this book rejects talk of acting or being 'in conformity
with norms'. Norms are not simple determinants of action.

But maybe Putnam's objection can be given a form that could be directed
against my finitistic relativism. After all, I am committed to saying that the
meaning of 'true' at a given time and for a given community is more or less
fixed by the accepted exemplars, *judgements* of similarity, interests, and goals.
Moreover, when I make claims about another culture, it is the exemplars
(etc.) of my culture that decide which of my claims count as true. All of my

claims about another culture's exemplars (etc.) for truth-talk are judged by our (my culture's) exemplars (etc.) for truth-talk. And in that sense my culture's exemplars (etc.) are for me in a privileged position compared with the exemplars (etc.) of the other culture. At the same time I maintain that my culture has this privileged position only for members of my culture. Members of another culture treat their own culture as their privileged position. Is this not exactly the inconsistent duo of symmetry and asymmetry that Putnam laments?

It is indeed a combination of symmetry and asymmetry, but I am unconvinced that this combination is inconsistent in the way Putnam maintains. Here it is helpful to remember what motivates finitistic relativism in the first place: the observation that our categorizations are determined by contingent constellations of exemplars and interests in our culture. Historical research shows us that our systems of categorization and our theories could have developed very differently if only such contingent constellations had been different. Anthropological research teaches us that other cultures have very different systems of categorization, systems that become accessible only after extended and intensive investigation. Moreover, we find that the systems of categorization of other cultures develop along familiar paths: exemplars, interests, consensus are central elements of these paths. We also notice that often we can convince members of other cultures only by socializing them into our culture. And we recognize the reverse: the process of coming to understand what other cultures hold true is to undergo a (partial) resocialisation. These experiences lead the relativist *both* to maintain that cultures can be understood as standing in a symmetrical relation, *and* to claim that often we cannot—without much work—see another culture from its own point of view. The second is of course tantamount to the idea that our own culture is for us in a privileged position.

What Putnam fails to recognize is that although all other cultures and their truths might be a construction of my culture, the gap between 'being a construction' and 'being a constructor'—between 'being the construction of my culture' and 'being a (possible) constructor of my culture'—is increasingly narrowed on the basis of historical and anthropological research. As we study other cultures, we learn how cultures construct both themselves and other cultures around them. True, we learn all this about cultures-as-constructed-by-us but then again part of what we learn about cultures-as-constructed-by-us is that they all learn about cultures-as-constructed-by-them. Seeing other cultures in this way motivates the thought that our culture is perhaps in a privileged position only for us. The argument is an inductive one: as we construct other cultures, cultures construct one another time and time again, and they do so privileging themselves. We conclude that all cultures do so.

CONCEPTUAL SCHEMES AND TRANSLATION

To round off arguments against relativism I turn to an influential line advanced by Donald Davidson (1984b). The argument depends on Davidson's work on interpretation (discussed earlier in Parts I and II), and it is tailored to attack forms of relativism that rely on a distinction between the 'scheme' and the 'content' of experience. The main targets are Kuhn and Quine. This is not the place to enter the arena of Kuhn and Quine scholarship. I shall therefore try to extract a general argument against all kinds of cognitive relativism.

Take two cultures, C_1 and C_2, that use radically different systems of classification. Think of these radically different systems of classification as radically different languages. Surely, if radical difference is to mean anything here, it must mean partial or complete failure of translatability. In other words, it must be impossible to translate some, or all, of the statements made using the language of C_1 into statements made using the language of C_2.

Davidson denies that we can make sense of such failures of translatability. Take an interpreter of C_1 who confronts a speaker of C_2. How could such an interpreter come to the conclusion that C_2 uses a completely different system of concepts? We know how, according to Davidson, such an interpreter must work. She must assume that the native shares many of her beliefs, and refers to many of the same features in their common physical environment. Unless she works on this assumption, she cannot interpret and translate at all. At this point Davidson identifies a dilemma. On the one hand, if the interpreter is able to work successfully on the assumption that the native shares many of her beliefs, then the native cannot possibly be using a completely different system of categories. On the other hand, consider the possibility that the assumption of shared beliefs proves useless, and all attempts at interpreting the native's utterances fail. Should we now conclude that the interpreter has encountered an alien conceptual world? No, insists Davidson; translatability into a familiar idiom is a *criterion* of something's being a language. Therefore, if all attempts at translation fail, the interpreter should conclude that perhaps she is not dealing with a language at all. And if she is not dealing with a (radically different) language, of course she is not dealing with a radically different system of categorization either.

Davidson has a related argument against mere partial failures of translation. Assume that the interpreter has established a considerable common ground between herself and the native. On the basis of their earlier established common ground, she has successfully ascribed meanings to many words in the native's language and successfully attributed true beliefs to him. But then she encounters utterances that she does not know how to translate. Not knowing how to translate here means this: not knowing how to pair the native's utterance with a true sentence in her own language. Has she now found evidence of radically different categorizations, at least in some domain? According to Davidson, there is no need for a positive reply. The interpreter has, after all, a choice at this point. She can choose to interpret the native as uttering something which is true but not translatable; or she can choose to interpret the native as uttering something which is translatable but false. In so far as the latter is always an option, there is no need to go for the former.

Summa summarum: We can make no sense of either total or partial failure of translatability, and hence no sense of radically different conceptualizations (in different cultures).

Davidson's argument has been widely discussed in the literature and several authors have taken exception to it. For instance, it has been objected that translatability into a familiar idiom is not a criterion of language-hood; or that there might be situations where it is right for the interpreter to opt for true-but-untranslatable rather than for false-but-translatable (Putnam 1989; Lynch 1998: 49–54). I do not want to rehearse these discussions here. Nor do I want to invoke my earlier line of defence according to which languages change and develop in encounters with other cultures. My main objection to Davidson's argument here is more simple.

Davidson construes the whole situation of translation and interpretation as one arising between two cultures where a member of one culture (or linguistic community) tries to understand a member of another culture (or linguistic community). In this scenario Davidson's theses (*a*) that 'translatability into a familiar idiom is a criterion of language-hood' and (*b*) that partial breakdown in translatability can be repaired by attributing false beliefs, are plausible. But the encounter between two members of two cultures is not the place where failures of translatability are established. Such claims are typically made by historians or anthropologists *talking about* two cultures, neither one of which is their own. Take a historian (as a member of culture C_3) who claims that C_1 and C_2 have radically different conceptual systems. In doing so, the historian translates statements of both C_1 and C_2 into his home language, and then points out that such translation was impossible for members of C_1 and C_2. To get an intuitive grasp of this situation, think of the home language as our ordinary language, and the languages of C_1 and C_2 as the languages of quantum physics and chess respectively. There seems nothing wrong with claiming that these languages are radically different and perhaps 'incommensurable' while maintaining at the same time that we can make sense of both languages in terms of ordinary language. Or think of the two descriptions of the mini-world in Chapter 17. The two descriptions of the two worlds might well be radically different even though, in this case, we happen to have resources to make both of them intelligible to us. This is not to say, of course, that ordinary language is always the common ground in which all differences are mediated. The point is rather that we can establish radical failure of translation between two cultures—using the resources of a third culture. And thus Davidson's celebrated argument fails.

Chapter 20

SUMMARY

In Part III I have complemented the communitarian epistemology of testimony of Part I, and the communitarian epistemology of empirical belief of Part II, with a communitarian finitistic form of relativism concerning truth, reality, and objectivity.

Finitism is a communitarian theory of what it is to master a language. It makes community consensus central in the constitution of normativity. (I argued for this thesis in Chapter 14.) Finitism says that terms have no fixed extensions. The only extensions there are the 'pseudo-extensions' of arrays of exemplars concerning correct use. The categorization of newly encountered entities is guided by these exemplars, as well as by interests. This was the topic of Chapter 15.

In Chapter 16 I applied finitism to 'true' and 'false'. Obviously, if finitism applies to all terms, it must also apply to the two classical truth-values. Applying finitism to truth leads to radical and surprising consequences. If 'true' does not have a fixed extension, then it is simply incoherent to speak of, or tacitly rely on, the idea of 'all true statements' (or 'all true propositions', or 'all true beliefs', or 'all true sentences'). And if this idea is illegitimate, then so are traditional ways of thinking about scientific progress ('we are getting ever closer to the truth'). Truth finitism does not answer the same question as do better-known pragmatist or correspondence theories. Finitism has no answer that would compete with formulas like 'truth is expediency', 'truth is consensus', or 'truth is correspondence'. But the finitistic theory of meaning constitutes an important constraint on all theories of truth. The finitistic constraint rules out theories of truth that make use of fixed extensions. As we saw above, none of the well-known theories was able to escape unscathed.

In Chapter 17 I turned from truth to reality, and reviewed the contemporary debate between realists ('innocent', 'external', 'absolute', 'metaphysical') and anti-realists ('irrealism', 'internal realism', 'pluralism', 'relativistic Kantianism'). I criticized ideas and arguments of both sides of the debate where they were based on mistaken semantic assumptions (of fixed extensions). In particular I rejected the notion of 'one true description of the world', talk of 'determinate meanings and truth-values within a conceptual scheme', and the idea of once-and-for-all incompatibilities between conceptual schemes. I also pointed out that (global) realism and (global) anti-realism both fall foul of finitistic constraints.

Chapter 18 discussed Brandom's and Haugeland's proposals on how to make space for the possibility of objectivity, that is, for the possibility of community-wide error and ignorance. Brandom believes that attitude-attribution itself provides us with a realm of non-perspectival objects; Haugeland suggests that incompatibilities among our skills and their objects are objective, and independent of community consensus. I argued that both proposals fail. Brandom overlooks that the 'non-perspectival-ness' of objects is itself a relative and perspectival matter. Objects are treated as non-perspectival by the attributer of attitudes. But any attributer of attitudes can herself become an 'attributee' for *another* attributer of attitudes. And this further attributer will treat her objects as merely perspectival. Haugeland's suggestion failed because his notion of incompatibility is ambiguous and individualistic.

Finally, in Chapter 19 I took up six arguments against relativism in general. The most famous among them were Plato's self-refutation charge (updated by Siegel), Putnam's argument based on the parallel between methodological solipsism and cultural relativism, and Davidson's criticism of the very idea of conceptual schemes. I showed that none of these arguments is decisive.

EPILOGUE

In this essay I have sought to give a general characterization and defence of 'communitarian epistemology'. I have attempted to motivate this position by critically contrasting its accounts of testimony and empirical belief with more traditional proposals concerning the same phenomena. I have also outlined a theory of meaning and truth that naturally goes hand in hand with communitarianism. Since I have already summarized the argument at the end of each part, I shall confine myself here to clarifying a number of general issues regarding the project as a whole.

I regard the development and defence of communitarian epistemology as very much an ongoing project, towards which the present study is no more than an initial and modest contribution. But if this book is at least roughly on the right track, then the general project sketched here should be central to the epistemological agenda. In any case, my primary goal has not been to present a communitarian alternative to all traditional positions but rather to bring that alternative to the attention of other philosophers.

One way of providing a road map for further research is to return to an idea frequently mentioned in Part I. This is the traditional idea of the four 'sources of knowledge', perception, memory, reasoning, and testimony. While I have provided the general outline of a communitarian account of testimony, I have not worked out communitarian epistemologies for the three other sources—albeit that Part II at least gestures towards the general form such epistemologies would take in the case of perception and reasoning.[1] This challenge clearly needs to be met at some point if communitarian epistemology is to be permanently established as a serious contender in epistemology at large. Moreover, the very title of Part II ('Empirical

[1] The writings of David Bloor (e.g. 1997) too contain many suggestions for such project.

Belief') signals that I still have to deliver an account of 'non-empirical belief'. Again, given what is said in Parts II and III, the careful reader will not find it difficult to imagine the general shape of such a position, but clearly the topic deserves much more extensive attention.

It also needs to be acknowledged that I have critically engaged with only some alternative positions. Thus I have discussed neither key figures in the history of philosophy, such as Locke or Kant, nor important contemporary positions like the neo-pragmatism of Richard Rorty, or the feminist epistemology of Sandra Harding or Helen Longino. Mining the history of philosophy either for important communitarian insights or else for striking individualistic oversights is undoubtedly a fruitful exercise, as many insightful studies by feminist historians of philosophy have demonstrated (e.g. Lloyd 1984). In the future, I hope to pursue such studies myself, focusing in particular on communitarian themes in German Idealism and the phenomenological tradition.[2]

It will also be important, at some point, to work out in detail how communitarian epistemology relates to Rorty's 'end of epistemology' thesis. In lieu of such more extensive treatment, suffice it here to say only that communitarian epistemology does not share Rorty's equation 'foundationalism = epistemology'. Hence the failure of foundationalism is no reason for giving up on epistemology altogether. Moreover, I have already emphasized the common ground that exists between communitarian epistemology and feminism. Clearly, any epistemology that focuses on the ways in which knowledge and politics are intertwined is close to the project pursued here. This is so in particular since most feminist epistemologists have not confined themselves to investigating the links between knowledge and gender relations. It thus will not do to think of feminist epistemology as merely a part of the broader communitarian project. At the same time, it must be remembered that not all feminist epistemologists see themselves as epistemological communitarians—indeed, feminist epistemologists are at present debating the relative strengths and weaknesses of communitarian and individualist positions (Antony 1996; Longino 1999). Rorty's and feminists' work might also provide a useful foil for further developing the relativistic position advocated in Part III.

---

[2] For my earlier work on these traditions, see Kusch (1984, 1989, 1995).

Throughout this book I have emphasized my indebtedness to the sociology of knowledge in general, and the work of Barnes, Bloor, Collins, and Shapin in particular. This might lead some readers to worry whether communitarian epistemology is a label for the endeavour of handing epistemology over to the sociologists. Undoubtedly, the relationship between this book and theoretical writings in the sociology of knowledge is close. And having situated myself for some time now on the very boundary between philosophy and sociology, I have myself lost any clear intuition I might once have had on how to tell the two fields apart. Moreover, work on the history of philosophy has taught me that many philosophers are prone to deal with uncomfortable and provocative philosophical ideas by declaring them out of (the) bounds (of philosophy proper) (Kusch 1995). In any case, I would insist that the ideas of this book are philosophical at least in so far as they relate to—overlap with, complement, cohere with, contradict, and support—things other philosophers have said. In other words, the position outlined here seems to me to belong within the same argumentative space as do better-known epistemological positions.

Finally, adopting the communitarian epistemology proposed here does not commit one to rejecting all, or even most of, other work in epistemology. Communitarian epistemology is first and foremost a set of answers to 'second-order questions about the rationality of belief'. Thus it leaves much of the work on 'first-order epistemological questions' untouched. Put differently, there is a place for normative–prescriptive epistemology—even for normative–prescriptive epistemology that addresses itself to the individual in (physical) isolation. The communitarian epistemologist insists that all such normative–prescriptive endeavours have their roots in local contexts and contingencies. But that is not to question their usefulness and importance. Nor does the insight that knowledge is a social status, and usually imposed on groups rather than isolated individuals, provide an argument against writing manuals on epistemic self-improvement. After all, 'married couple' is a social status, too; and yet we value manuals on how to be good husbands or wives, written for individual men and women.

References

ADLER, J. E. (1994), 'Testimony, Trust, Knowing', *Journal of Philosophy*, 92: 264–75.

AIRAKSINEN, T. (1982), 'Contextualism, a New Theory of Epistemic Justification?', *Philosophia*, 12: 37–50.

ALANEN, L., S. HEINÄMAA, and T. WALLGREN (eds.) (1997), *Commonality and Particularity in Ethics* (Basingstoke: Macmillan).

ALCOFF, L., and E. POTTER (eds.) (1993), *Feminist Epistemologies* (London: Routledge).

ALSTON, W. P. (1993), 'Epistemic Desiderata', *Philosophy and Phenomenological Research*, 53: 527–51.

——(1996), *A Realist Conception of Truth* (Ithaca, NY: Cornell University Press).

ANNIS, D. B. (1978), 'A Contextualist Theory of Epistemic Justification', *American Philosophical Quarterly*, 15: 213–19.

——(1982), 'The Social and Cultural Component of Epistemic Justification: A Reply', *Philosophia*, 12: 51–5.

ANTONY, L. (1996), 'Sisters, Please, I'd Rather do it Myself: A Defense of Individualism in Feminist Epistemology', *Philosophical Topics*, 23: 59–94.

——and C. WITT (eds.) (1993), *A Mind of One's Own: Feminist Essays on Reason and Objectivity* (Boulder, Colo.: Westview Press).

ARMSTRONG, D. M. (1973), *Belief, Truth and Knowledge* (Cambridge: Cambridge University Press).

ARMSTRONG, B. F. (1984), 'Wittgenstein on Private Languages: It Takes Two to Talk', *Philosophical Investigations*, 7: 46–62.

AUDI, R. (1988), 'Foundationalism, Coherentism, and Epistemological Dogmatism', *Philosophical Perspectives*, 2: 407–42.

——(1997), 'The Place of Testimony in the Fabric of Knowledge and Justification', *American Philosophical Quarterly*, 34: 405–22.

——(1998), *Epistemology: A Contemporary Introduction to the Theory of Knowledge* (London: Routledge).

AUSTIN, J. L. (1962), *How to do Things with Words* (Oxford: Clarendon Press).

——(1964), *Sense and Sensibilia* (Oxford: Oxford University Press).

——(1979), 'Other Minds', in J. L. Austin, *Philosophical Papers*, ed. J. O. Urmson and G. J. Warnock, 3rd edn. (Oxford: Oxford University Press), 76–116.

——(1999), 'Truth', in Blackburn and Simmons (1999: 149–61).

AXTELL, G. (1997), 'Recent Work on Virtue Epistemology', *American Philosophical Quarterly*, 34: 1–24.

BACH, K. (1975), 'Performatives are Statements Too', *Philosophical Studies*, 28: 229–36.

BAIER, A. (1986), 'Trust and Antitrust', *Ethics*, 96: 231–60.

—— (1997), 'Doing Things with Others: The Mental Commons', in Lili Alanen *et al.* (1997: 15–44).

BAKER, G. P., and P. M. S. HACKER (1984), 'Critical Study: On Misunderstanding Wittgenstein: Kripke's Private Language Argument', *Synthese*, 58: 407–50.

BARNES, B. (1983a), 'On the Conventional Character of Knowledge and Cognition', in K. D. Knorr-Cetina and M. Mulkay (eds.), *Science Observed: Perspectives on the Social Study of Science* (London: Sage), 19–52.

—— (1983b), 'Social Life as Bootstrapped Induction', *Sociology*, 17: 524–45.

—— (1988), *The Nature of Power* (Cambridge: Polity Press).

—— (1992), 'Realism, Relativism and Finitism', in D. Raven, L. van Vucht Tijssen, and Jan de Wolf (eds.), *Cognitive Relativism and Social Science* (New Brunswick, NJ: Transaction Publishers), 131–47.

—— (1995), *The Elements of Social Theory* (London: UCL Press).

—— D. BLOOR, and J. HENRY (1996), *Scientific Knowledge: A Sociological Analysis*, (London: Athlone Press).

BARNES, J. (1980), 'Socrates and the Jury', *Proceedings of the Aristotelian Society*, suppl. vol. 54: 193–206.

BENDER, J. W. (ed.) (1989), *The Current State of the Coherence Theory* (Dordrecht: Kluwer).

BEZUIDENHOUT, A. (1998), 'Is Verbal Communication a Purely Preservative Process?', *Philosophical Review*, 107: 261–88.

BHATTACHARYYA, S. (1994), 'Epistemology of Testimony and Authority: Some Indian Themes and Theories', in Matilal and Chakrabarti (1994: 69–97).

BLACKBURN, S. (1984a), *Spreading the Word: Groundings in the Philosophy of Language* (Oxford: Clarendon Press).

—— (1984b), 'The Individual Strikes Back', *Synthese*, 58: 281–301.

—— and K. SIMMONS (1999), *Truth* (Oxford: Oxford University Press).

BLAIS, M. J. (1985), 'Epistemic Tit for Tat', *Journal of Philosophy*, 82: 363–75.

—— (1990), 'Misunderstandings of Epistemic Tit for Tat: Reply to John Woods', *Journal of Philosophy*, 87: 369–74.

BLOOM, P. (2000), *How Children Learn the Meanings of Words* (Cambridge, Mass.: MIT Press).

BLOOR, D. (1974), 'Popper's Mystification of Objective Knowledge', *Science Studies*, 4: 65–76.

—— (1982), 'Durkheim and Mauss Revisited: Classification and the Sociology of Knowledge', *Studies in History and Philosophy of Science*, 13: 267–97.

—— (1983), *Wittgenstein: A Social Theory of Knowledge* (New York: Columbia University Press).

—— (1991), *Knowledge and Social Imagery*, 2nd edn. (Chicago: Chicago University Press).

—— (1996), 'Idealism and the Sociology of Knowledge'.

—— (1997), *Wittgenstein, Rules and Institutions* (London: Routledge).

BONJOUR, L. (1985), *The Structure of Empirical Knowledge* (Cambridge, Mass.: Harvard University Press).

—— (1999), 'The Dialectic of Foundationalism and Coherentism', in Greco and Sosa (1999: 117–42).

BRANDOM, R. (1994), *Making it Explicit: Reasoning, Representing, and Discursive Commitment* (Cambridge, Mass.: Harvard University Press).

—— (2000), *Articulating Reasons: An Introduction to Inferentialism* (Cambridge, Mass.: Harvard University Press).

BREWER, B. (1999), *Perception and Reason* (Oxford: Clarendon Press).

BUDD, M. (1984), 'Wittgenstein on Meaning, Interpretation and Rules', *Synthese*, 58: 303–23.

BURGE, T. (1993), 'Content Preservation', *Philosophical Review*, 102: 457–88.

—— (1997), 'Interlocution, Perception, and Memory', *Philosophical Studies*, 86: 21–47.

—— (1998), 'Computer Proof, Apriori Knowledge, and Other Minds', *Philosophical Perspectives*, 12: 1–37.

CANFIELD, J. V. (ed.) (1986), *The Private Language Argument, The Philosophy of Wittgenstein*, vol. ix (New York: Garland).

—— (1996), 'The Community View', *Philosophical Review*, 105: 469–88.

CHAKRABARTI, A. (1994), 'Telling as Letting Know', in Matilal and Chakrabarti (1994: 99–124).

CHAMPLIN, T. S. (1992), 'Solitary Rule-Following', *Philosophy*, 67: 285–306.

CHISHOLM, R. M. (1989), *Theory of Knowledge*, 3rd edn. (Englewood Cliffs, NJ: Prentice-Hall).

CHRISTENSEN, D., and H. KORNBLITH (1997), 'Testimony, Memory, and the Limits of the A Priori', *Philosophical Studies*, 86: 1–20.

COADY, C. A. J. (1992), *Testimony: A Philosophical Study* (Oxford: Clarendon Press).

CODE, L. (1987), *Epistemic Responsibility* (Hanover: University Press of New England).

—— (1991), *What can she Know?* (Ithaca, NY: Cornell University Press).

COHEN, S. (1986), 'Knowledge and Context', *Journal of Philosophy*, 83: 574–83.

—— (1987), 'Knowledge, Context, and Social Standards', *Synthese*, 73: 3–26.

COLLINS, H. M. (1985), *Changing Order: Replication and Induction in Scientific Practice* (London: Sage).

—— (1990), *Artificial Experts* (Cambridge, Mass.: MIT Press).

—— and M. KUSCH (1998), *The Shape of Action: What Humans and Machines can Do* (Cambridge, Mass.: MIT Press).

CORSARO, W. A. (1997), *The Sociology of Childhood* (Thousand Oaks, Calif.: Pine Forge Press).

CRAIG, E. (1982), 'Meaning, Use and Privacy', *Mind*, 91: 541–64.

——(1990), *Knowledge and the State of Nature* (Oxford: Clarendon Press).

——(1997), 'Meaning and Privacy', in B. Hale and C. Wright (eds.), *A Companion to the Philosophy of Language* (Oxford: Blackwell), 127–45.

DANCY, J., and E. SOSA (eds.) (1992), *A Companion to Epistemology* (Oxford: Blackwell).

DAVIDSON, D. (1980), *Essays on Actions and Events* (Oxford: Oxford University Press).

——(1984a), *Inquiries into Truth and Interpretation* (Oxford: Oxford University Press).

——(1984b), 'On the Very Idea of a Conceptual Scheme', in Davidson (1984a: 183–98).

——(1989a), 'A Coherence Theory of Truth and Knowledge', in LePore (1986: 307–19).

——(1989b), 'The Myth of the Subjective', in Krausz (1989: 159–72).

——(1990), 'Afterthoughts, 1987', in A. Lalachowski (ed.), *Reading Rorty* (Oxford: Blackwell), 134–8.

——(1991), 'Three Varieties of Knowledge', in A. Phillips Griffiths (ed.), *A. J. Ayer: Memorial Essays*, Royal Institute of Philosophy suppl. 30 (Cambridge: Cambridge University Press), 153–66.

——(1999a), 'Reply to A. C. Genova', in Hahn (1999: 192–4).

——(1999b), 'Reply to Roger F. Gibson', in Zeglen (1999: 134–5).

DAVIES, S. (1988), 'Kripke, Crusoe and Wittgenstein', *Australasian Journal of Philosophy*, 66: 52–66.

DeROSE, K. (1992), 'Contextualism and Knowledge Attribution', *Philosophy and Phenomenological Research*, 52: 913–31.

——(1995), 'Solving the Skeptical Problem', *Philosophical Review*, 104: 1–52.

——(1999), 'Contextualism: An Explanation and Defense', in Greco and Sosa (1999: 187–205).

DRETSKE, F. (1981), 'The Pragmatic Dimension of Knowledge', *Philosophical Studies*, 40: 363–78.

DUMMETT, M. (1994), 'Testimony and Memory', in Matilal and Chakrabarti (1994: 251–72).

DURKHEIM, É. (1983), *Pragmatism and Sociology*, trans. J. C. Whitehouse, ed. J. B. Allcock, with Preface by A. Cuvillier (Cambridge: Cambridge University Press).

ESFELD, M. (2001), *Holism in Philosophy of Mind and Philosophy of Physics* (Dordrecht: Kluwer).

EVANS, G. (1982), *The Varieties of Reference*, ed. J. McDowell (Oxford: Clarendon Press).

FAULKNER, P. (1998), 'David Hume's Reductionist Epistemology of Testimony', *Pacific Philosophical Quarterly*, 79: 302–13.

——(2000), 'The Social Character of Testimonial Knowledge', *Journal of Philosophy*, 97: 581–601.

FODOR, J. A. (1997), 'The Dogma that didn't Bark: A Fragment of a Naturalized Epistemology', in Kornblith (1997b: 191–216).

FORRESTER, J. (1997), *Truth Games: Lies, Money, and Psychoanalysis* (Cambridge, Mass.: Harvard University Press).

FOUCAULT, M. (1974), *The Archaeology of Knowledge* (London: Tavistock).

FRICKER, E. (1987), 'The Epistemology of Testimony', *Proceedings of the Aristotelian Society*, suppl. vol. 61: 57–83.

——(1994), 'Against Gullibility', in Matilal and Chakrabarti (1994: 125–61).

——(1995), 'Telling and Trusting: Reductionism and Anti-Reductionism in the Epistemology of Testimony', *Mind*, 104: 392–411.

FRICKER, M. (1998), 'Rational Authority and Social Power: Towards a Truly Social Epistemology', *Proceedings of the Aristotelian Society*, NS 98: 159–77.

FRIEDMAN, M. (1996), 'Exorcising the Philosophical Tradition: Comments on John McDowell's *Mind and World*', *Philosophical Review*, 105: 427–67.

FULLER, S. (1988), *Social Epistemology* (Bloomington: Indiana University Press).

FUMERTON, R. (1988), 'The Internalism/Externalism Controversy', *Philosophical Perspectives*, 2: 443–59.

GADAMER, H.-G. (1960), *Wahrheit und Methode* (Tübingen: Mohr).

GALISON, P. (1997), *Image and Logic: A Material Culture of Microphysics* (Chicago: University of Chicago Press).

GENOVA, A. C. (1999), 'The Very Idea of Massive Truth', in Hahn (1999: 167–91).

GERRANS, P. (1998), 'How to be a Conformist, Part II: Simulation and Rule Following', *Australian Journal of Philosophy*, 76: 566–86.

GIBBARD, A. (1990), *Wise Choices, Apt Feelings* (Oxford: Oxford University Press).

GIBSON, R. F. (1999), 'McDowell on Quine, Davidson and Epistemology', in Zeglen (1999: 123–34).

GILBERT, M. (1989), *Social Facts* (London: Routledge).

——(1996), *Living Together: Rationality, Sociality, and Obligation* (Lanham, Md.: Rowman & Littlefield).

——(2000), *Sociality and Responsibility: New Essays in Plural Subject Theory* (Lanham, Md.: Rowman & Littlefield).

GILLETT, G. (1995), '*Humpty Dumpty and the Night of the Triffids*: Individualism and Rule-Following', *Synthese*, 105: 191–206.

GOLDMAN, A. I. (1985), *Epistemology and Cognition* (Cambridge, Mass.: Harvard University Press).

——(1992), *Liaisons: Philosophy Meets the Cognitive and Social Sciences* (Cambridge, Mass.: MIT Press).

——(1993), 'Epistemic Folkways and Scientific Epistemology', *Philosophical Issues*, 3: 271–84.

——(1999), *Knowledge in a Social World* (Oxford: Oxford University Press).

GOODMAN, N. (1978), *Ways of Worldmaking* (Indianapolis: Hackett).

——(1989), 'Just the Facts, Ma'am!', in Krausz (1989: 80–5).

GRECO, J. (1993), 'Virtues and Vices of Virtue Epistemology', *Canadian Journal of Philosophy*, 23: 413–32.

—— and E. SOSA (eds.) (1999), *The Blackwell Guide to Epistemology* (Oxford: Blackwell).

GROVER, D. (1992), *A Prosentential Theory of Truth* (Princeton: Princeton University Press).

HAACK, S. (1993), *Evidence and Inquiry: Towards Reconstruction in Epistemology* (Oxford: Blackwell).

—— (1998), 'Reflections on Relativism: From Momentous Tautology to Seductive Contradiction', in S. Haack, *Manifesto of a Passionate Moderate* (Chicago, Ill.: University of Chicago Press), 149–66.

HABERMAS, J. (1981), *Theorie des kommunikativen Handelns* (Frankfurt am Main: Suhrkamp).

HACKING, I. (1989), 'The Parody of Conversation', in LePore (1989: 447–58).

HAHN, L. E. (ed.) (1998), *The Philosophy of P. F. Strawson* (Chicago: Open Court).

—— (ed.) (1999), *The Philosophy of Donald Davidson*, Library of Living Philosophers, vol. xxvii (Chicago: Open Court).

HANKINSON NELSON, L. (1990), *Who Knows? From Quine to Feminist Empiricism* (Philadelphia: Temple University Press).

HARDING, S. (1991), *Whose Science? Whose Knowledge? Thinking from Women's Lives* (Milton Keynes: Open University Press).

HARDWIG, J. (1985), 'Epistemic Dependence', *Journal of Philosophy*, 82: 335–49.

—— (1991), 'The Role of Trust in Knowledge', *Journal of Philosophy*, 88: 693–704.

HART, H. L. A. (1961), *The Concept of Law* (Oxford: Clarendon Press).

HAUGELAND, J. (1998), 'Truth and Rule-Following', in J. Haugeland, *Having Thought: Essays in the Metaphysics of Mind* (Cambridge, Mass.: Harvard University Press), 305–61.

HOLTON, R. (1994), 'Deciding to Trust, Coming to Believe', *Australasian Journal of Philosophy*, 72: 63–76.

HORWICH, P. (1990), *Truth* (Oxford: Blackwell).

HUME, D. (1966), *An Enquiry concerning Human Understanding*, ed. A. Selby-Bigge, 2nd edn. (Oxford: Clarendon Press).

HUNTER, J. S. (1980), 'The National System of Scientific Measurement', *Science*, 210: 867–75.

ITKONEN, E. (1978), *Grammatical Theory and Metascience: A Critical Investigation into the Methodological and Philosophical Foundations of 'Autonomous' Linguistics* (Amsterdam: Benjamins).

JAMES, W. (1975), *Pragmatism and the Meaning of Truth* (Cambridge, Mass.: Harvard University Press).

KIM, J. (1997), 'What is "Naturalized Epistemology"?', in Kornblith (1997b: 33–56).

KIRKHAM, R. L. (1992), *Theories of Truth: A Critical Introduction* (Cambridge, Mass.: MIT Press).

KITCHER, P. (1993), *The Advancement of Science: Science without Legend, Objectivity without Illusions* (Oxford: Oxford University Press).

KNORR CETINA, K. (1995), 'How Superorganisms Change: Consensus Formation and the Social Ontology of High-Energy Physics Experiments', *Social Studies of Science*, 25: 119–47.

——(1999), *Epistemic Cultures: How the Sciences Make Knowledge* (Cambridge, Mass.: Harvard University Press).

KORNBLITH, H. (1987), 'Some Social Features of Cognition', *Synthese*, 73: 27–41.

——(1994), 'A Conservative Approach to Social Epistemology', in Schmitt (1994: 93–110).

——(1997a), 'Beyond Foundationalism and the Coherence Theory', in Kornblith (1997b: 131–46).

——(1997b), *Naturalizing Epistemology*, 3rd edn. (Cambridge, Mass.: MIT Press), 131–46.

——(1999), 'In Defense of a Naturalized Epistemology', in Greco and Sosa (1999: 158–69).

KRAUSZ, M. (ed.) (1989), *Relativism: Interpretation and Confrontation* (Notre Dame, Ind.: University of Notre Dame Press).

KRIPKE, S. (1982), *Wittgenstein on Rules and Private Language* (Cambridge, Mass.: Harvard University Press).

KUHN, T. (1996), *The Structure of Scientific Revolutions*, 3rd edn. (Chicago: Chicago University Press).

KUSCH, M. (1984), *Einzelheit und Allgemeinheit. Einführung in die Philosophie G. W. F. Hegels*, Publications of the Department of Philosophy, University of Jyväkylä, vol. xxi.

——(1989), *Language as Calculus vs. Language as Universal Medium: A Study in Husserl, Heidegger and Gadamer* (Dordrecht: Kluwer, Synthese Library).

——(1991), *Foucault's Strata and Fields: An Investigation into Archaeological and Genealogical Science Studies* (Dordrecht: Kluwer).

——(1995), *Psychologism: A Case Study in the Sociology of Philosophical Knowledge* (London: Routledge).

——(1999), *Psychological Knowledge: A Social History and Philosophy* (London: Routledge).

KVANVIG, J. L. (1992), *The Intellectual Virtues and the Life of the Mind: On the Place of the Virtues in Epistemology* (Savage, Md.: Rowman & Littlefield).

LAGERSPETZ, E. (1995), *The Opposite Mirrors: An Essay on the Conventionalist Theory of Institutions* (Dordrecht: Kluwer).

LATOUR, B. (1999), 'Circulating Reference', in B. Latour, *Pandora's Hope: Essays on the Reality of Science Studies* (Cambridge, Mass.: Harvard University Press), 24–79.

LEHRER, K. (1986), 'The Coherence Theory of Knowledge', *Philosophical Topics*, 14: 5–25.

——(1987), 'Personal and Social Knowledge', *Synthese*, 73: 87–107.

LEHRER, K. (1990a), *Metamind* (Oxford: Clarendon Press).

—— (1990b), *Theory of Knowledge* (London: Routledge).

—— (1997), *Self-Trust: A Study of Reason, Knowledge, and Autonomy* (Oxford Clarendon Press).

—— and C. WAGNER (1981), *Rational Consensus in Science and Society* (Dordrecht: Reidel).

LENNON, K., and M. WHITFORD (eds.) (1994), *Knowing the Difference: Feminist Perspectives in Epistemology* (London: Routledge).

LePORE, E. (ed.) (1989), *Truth and Interpretation: Perspectives on the Philosophy of Donald Davidson* (Oxford: Blackwell).

LEWIS, C. I. (1946), *An Analysis of Knowledge and Valuation* (LaSalle, Ill.: Open Court).

LEWIS, D. (1969), *Convention: A Philosophical Study* (Cambridge, Mass.: Harvard University Press).

—— (1996), 'Elusive Knowledge', *Australasian Journal of Philosophy*, 74: 549–67.

LILLEGARD, N. (1998), 'How Private must an Objectionably Private Language Be?', *Paideia: Philosophy of Language*, www.bu.edu/wcp/Papers/Lang/LangLill.htm

LIPTON, P. (1998), 'The Epistemology of Testimony', *Studies in History and Philosophy of Science*, 29: 1–33.

LLOYD, G. (1984), *The Man of Reason: 'Male' and 'Female' in Western Philosophy* (Minneapolis: University of Minneapolis Press).

LOCKE, J. (1975), *An Essay concerning Human Understanding*, ed. P. H. Nidditch (Oxford: Oxford University Press).

LONGINO, H. E. (1990), *Science as Social Knowledge* (Princeton: Princeton University Press).

—— (1999), 'Feminist Epistemology', in Greco and Sosa (1999: 327–53).

LYNCH M., and R. McNALLY (forthcoming), 'DNA Evidence and Probability: A Situated Controversy', in K. Ammann (ed.), *Nature and Culture: Genetic Engineering and the Inexorable Dissolution of a Modern Distinction* (Bielefeld: Deutsches Hygiene Museum and University of Bielefeld).

LYNCH, M. P. (1998), *Truth in Context: An Essay on Pluralism and Objectivity* (Cambridge, Mass.: MIT Press).

McDOWELL, J. (1993), 'Wittgenstein on Following a Rule', in A. W. Moore (ed), *Meaning and Reference* (Oxford: Oxford University Press), 255–93.

—— (1994), *Mind and World* (Cambridge, Mass.: Harvard University Press).

—— (1998), *Meaning, Knowledge, and Reality* (Cambridge, Mass.: Harvard University Press).

McGINN, C. (1984), *Wittgenstein on Meaning: An Interpretation and Evaluation* (Oxford: Blackwell).

MacINTYRE, A. (1988), *Whose Justice? Which Rationality?* (London: Duckworth).

MacKENZIE, D. (1999), 'Slaying the Kraken: The Sociohistory of a Mathematical Proof', *Social Studies of Science*, 29: 7–60.

MALCOLM, N. (1995), *Wittgensteinian Themes: Essays 1978–1989*, ed. G. H. von Wright (Ithaca, NY: Cornell University Press).

MATILAL, B. K., and A. CHAKRABARTI (eds.) (1994), *Knowing from Words* (Dordrecht: Kluwer).

MILLIKAN, R. (1990), 'Truth Rules, Hoverflies, and the Kripke–Wittgenstein Paradox', *Philosophical Review*, 94: 323–53.

MOORE, J. A. (1991), 'Knowledge, Society, Power, and the Promise of Epistemological Externalism', *Synthese*, 88: 379–98.

MOSER, P. K. (1989), *Knowledge and Evidence* (Cambridge: Cambridge University Press).

PEACOCKE, C. (1981), 'Reply: Rule-Following: The Nature of Wittgenstein's Arguments', in S. Holtzmann and C. M. Leich (eds.), *Wittgenstein: To Follow a Rule* (London: Routledge & Kegan Paul), 72–95.

PEIRCE, C. S. (1931–58), *Collected Papers of Charles Sanders Peirce*, ed. C. Hawthorne, P. Weiss, and A. W. Burks (Cambridge, Mass.: Harvard University Press).

PETTIT, P. (1993), *The Common Mind: An Essay on Psychology, Society, and Politics* (Oxford: Oxford University Press).

PITCHER, G. (1964), 'Introduction', in G. Pitcher (ed.), *Truth* (Englewood Cliffs, NJ: Prentice-Hall), 1–15.

PLANTINGA, A. (1993a), *Warrant: The Current Debate* (Oxford: Oxford University Press).

—— (1993b), *Warrant and Proper Function* (New York: Oxford University Press).

POPPER, K. (1972), *Objective Knowledge: An Evolutionary Approach* (Oxford: Clarendon Press).

PUTNAM, H. (1981), *Reason, Truth and History* (Cambridge: Cambridge University Press).

—— (1983), 'Why Reason can't be Naturalized', in Putnam, *Realism and Reason, Philosophical Papers* vol. iii (Cambridge: Cambridge University Press), 229–47.

—— (1989), 'Truth and Convention: On Davidson's Refutation of Conceptual Relativism', in Krausz (1989: 173–81).

—— (1990), *Realism with a Human Face* (Cambridge, Mass.: Harvard University Press).

—— (1992), *Renewing Philosophy* (Cambridge, Mass.: Harvard University Press).

—— (1994), *Words and Life*, ed. J. Conant (Cambridge, Mass.: Harvard University Press).

QUINE, W. V. O. (1999), 'Philosophy of Logic', in Blackburn and Simmons (1999: 144–6).

QUINTON, A. (1982), 'Certainty and Authority', in A. Quinton, *Thoughts and Thinkers* (London: Duckworth), 65–74.

RADFORD, C. (1970), 'Knowledge—By Examples', in M. D. Roth and L. Galis (eds.), *Knowing: Essays in the Analysis of Knowledge* (New York: Random House), 155–70.

REID, T. (1966), *Inquiry into the Human Mind*, ed. A. Selby-Bigge, 2nd edn. (Oxford: Clarendon Press).

RESCHER, N. (1973), *The Coherence Theory of Truth* (Oxford: Clarendon Press).

RESCHER, N. (1974), 'Foundationalism, Coherentism, and the Idea of Cognitive Systematization', *Journal of Philosophy*, 19: 695–708.

ROBINSON, G. (1992), 'Language and the Society of Others', *Philosophy*, 67: 329–41.

RORTY, R. (1980), *Philosophy and the Mirror of Nature* (Oxford: Blackwell).

——(1982), *Consequences of Pragmatism: Essays, 1972–1980* (Brighton: Harvester Press).

——(1991), *Objectivity, Relativism, and Truth, Philosophical Papers*, vol. i (Cambridge: Cambridge University Press).

——(1998a), 'Antiskeptical Weapons: Michael Williams versus Donald Davidson', in Rorty (1998c: 153–65).

——(1998b), 'The Very Idea of Human Answerability to the World: John McDowell's Version of Empiricism', in Rorty (1998c: 138–52).

——(1998c), *Truth and Progress, Philosophical Papers*, vol. iii (Cambridge: Cambridge University Press).

ROTH, M. D. (1991), 'Knowledge and Evidence', *Dialogue*, 30: 591–602.

RUSSELL, B. (1912), *Problems of Philosophy* (Oxford: Oxford University Press).

——(1999), 'William James's Conception of Truth', in Blackburn and Simmons (1999: 69–92).

SAINSBURY, M. (1998), 'Philosophical Logic', in A. Grayling (ed.), *Philosophy 1: A Guide through the Subject* (Oxford: Oxford University Press), 61–122.

SANDEL, M. J. (1982), *Liberalism and the Limits of Justice* (Cambridge: Cambridge University Press).

SCHMITT, F. F. (ed.) (1994), *Socializing Epistemology: The Social Dimensions of Knowledge* (Lanham, Md.: Rowman & Littlefield).

——(forthcoming), 'Testimonial Justification: The Parity Argument', *Studies in History and Philosophy of Science*.

SEARLE, J. R. (1995), *The Construction of Social Reality* (London: Allen Lane).

——(1998), 'Truth: A Reconsideration of Strawson's Views', in Hahn (1998: 384–401).

SELLARS, W. (1997), *Empiricism and the Philosophy of Mind* (first pub. 1956; Cambridge, Mass.: Harvard University Press).

SHAPIN, S. (1994), *A Social History of Truth* (Chicago: University of Chicago Press).

—— and S. SCHAFFER (1985), *Leviathan and the Air-Pump* (Cambridge, Mass.: Harvard University Press).

SIEGEL, H. (1987), *Relativism Refuted: A Critique of Contemporary Epistemological Relativism* (Dordrecht: Reidel).

SOSA, E. (1991a), *Knowledge in Perspective: Selected Essays in Epistemology* (Cambridge: Cambridge University Press).

——(1991b), 'The Raft and the Pyramid: Coherence versus Foundations in the Theory of Knowledge', in Sosa (1991a: 165–91).

STEVENSON, L. (1993), 'Why Believe what People Say?', *Synthese*, 94: 429–51.

STOUTLAND, F. (1997), 'Why are Philosophers of Action so Anti-Social?', in Lili Alanen *et al.* (1997: 45–74).

STRAWSON, P. F. (1949), 'Truth', *Analysis*, 9: 83–97.

—— (1974), 'Freedom and Resentment', in P. F. Strawson, *Freedom and Resentment* (London: Methuen), 1–25.

—— (1994), 'Knowing from Words', in Matilal and Chakrabarti (1994: 23–7).

—— (1998), 'Reply to John Searle', in Hahn (1998: 402–4).

—— (1999), 'Truth', in Blackburn and Simmons (1999: 162–82).

STROLL, A. (1994), *Moore and Wittgenstein on Certainty* (New York: Oxford University Press).

SUMMERFIELD, D. (1990), '*Philosophical Investigations* 201: A Wittgensteinian Reply to Kripke', *Journal of the History of Philosophy*, 28: 417–38.

TANENISI, A. (1999), *An Introduction to Feminist Epistemologies* (Oxford: Blackwell).

TAYLOR, C. (1989), *Sources of the Self: The Making of Modern Identity* (Cambridge, Mass.: Harvard University Press).

TRIPLETT, T. (1990), 'Recent Work on Foundationalism', *American Philosophical Quarterly*, 27: 93–116.

TUOMELA, R. (1995), *The Importance of Us: A Philosophical Study of Basic Social Notions* (Stanford, Calif.: Stanford University Press).

UNGER, P. (1986), 'The Cone Model of Knowledge', *Philosophical Topics*, 14: 125–78.

VENDLER, Z. (1972), *Res Cogitans: An Essay in Rational Psychology* (Ithaca, NY: Cornell University Press).

WELBOURNE, M. (1993), *The Community of Knowledge* (Aldershot: Gregg Revivals).

—— (1994), 'Testimony, Knowledge and Belief', in Matilal and Chakrabarti (1994: 297–313).

—— (forthcoming), 'Is Hume Really a Reductivist?', *Studies in History and Philosophy of Science*.

WILLIAMS, B. (1972), 'Knowledge and Reasons', in G. H. von Wright (ed.), *Problems in the Theory of Knowledge* (The Hague: Kluwer), 1–11.

—— (1985), *Ethics and the Limits of Philosophy* (Cambridge, Mass.: Harvard University Press).

WILLIAMS, MEREDITH (1991), 'Blind Obedience: Rules, Community and the Individual', in K. Puhl (ed.), *Meaning Scepticism* (Berlin: de Gruyter), 93–125.

WILLIAMS, MICHAEL (1986), 'Do we (Epistemologists) Need a Theory of Truth?', *Philosophical Topics*, 14: 223–42.

—— (1991), *Unnatural Doubts* (Oxford: Blackwell).

—— (1999*a*), *Groundless Belief: An Essay on the Possibility of Epistemology*, 2nd edn. (Princeton: Princeton University Press).

—— (1999*b*), 'Skepticism', in Greco and Sosa (1999: 35–69).

WILLIAMSON, T. (1995), 'Is Knowing a State of Mind?', *Mind*, 104: 533–65.

WILLIAMSON, T. (2000), *Knowledge and its Limits* (Oxford: Oxford University Press).

WITTGENSTEIN, L. (1968), *Philosophical Investigations*, 3rd edn. (Oxford: Blackwell).

—— (1969), *On Certainty* (London: Blackwell).

WOODS, J. (1989), 'The Maladroitness of Epistemic Tit for Tat', *Journal of Philosophy*, 86: 324–31.

WRIGHT, C. (1986), 'Does *Philosophical Investigations* I. 258–60 Suggest a Cogent Argument against Private Language?', in P. Pettit and J. McDowell (eds.), *Subject, Thought, and Context* (Oxford: Clarendon Press), 209–66.

ZAGZEBSKI, L. (1996), *Virtues of the Mind: An Inquiry into the Nature of Virtue and the Ethical Foundations of Knowledge* (Cambridge: Cambridge University Press).

—— (1999), 'What is Knowledge?', in Greco and Sosa (1999: 92–116).

ZEGLEN, U. (ed.) (1999), *Donald Davidson: Truth, Meaning and Knowledge* (London: Routledge).

Index